'Yet';

A Story of Triumph Over Childhood Separation,
Trauma, and Disability

Who Do I Think You Were?®

'Yet':
A Story of Triumph Over Childhood Separation, Trauma, and Disability

Helen Parker-Drabble

Published by Animi Press 2025

Copyright © Helen Parker-Drabble

All rights reserved. No part of this book may be reproduced or used in any manner without written permission of the copyright owner except for using quotations in a book review; the use of quotations in articles, books, theses, dissertations or similar. For more information, visit: helen@helenparkerdrabble.com.

978-1-9162466-7-6 eBook　　978-1-9162466-8-3 Paperback
978-1-9162466-9-0 Hardback　　978-1-0684013-0-5 Large print paperback

The author and publisher gratefully acknowledge permissions granted to reproduce the copyrighted material included in this book. We have tried to trace all copyright holders and get their permission for the use of copyrighted material. The publisher apologises for any errors or omissions which can be amended in any future edition.

This book has been deposited with the British Library in accordance with The Legal Deposit Libraries Act 2003.

Cover by Miblart | Typesetting by C'est Beau Designs
Proofreading by Sarah Cook and Helen Baggott

Cover photographs:

Fresh air treatment at King Edward VII Memorial Hospital for Crippled Children, c. 1920–1939. Licensed from ©Picture Sheffield (Image s07418).

A staged photo showing some boys in bed on the veranda and other boys standing in a plaster Thomas splint. Licensed from ©Picture Sheffield (Image w00567).

Harry Drabble, 1935.

Harry Drabble aged 20, 1955.

Helen Parker-Drabble is a proud author member of the Alliance of Independent Authors. ALLi is an ethical non-profit membership organisation for those who want to control their intellectual property and publish independently. ALLi provides trusted advice, supportive guidance, and a range of resources within a welcoming and dynamic community of independent authors and advisors.

If you would like to know more about the Alliance of Independent Authors, please follow my affiliate link: https://allianceindependentauthors.org/?affid=7961 or visit www.allianceindependentauthors.org/.

This book is dedicated to
Harry Drabble, 1934–2022,
son, brother, husband, father, friend, uncle, grandfather,
teacher and mentor.

In memory of Michael Grimsley (1944–2023) who spent his childhood similarly, but who would rarely speak about it.

Joseph (Joe) Mulryan (1912–1999) was diagnosed with a TB hip and went to King Edward's isolation hospital aged 6. He was an inpatient for one year and treated with traction and crutches with calipers. His mum walked two-and-a-half hours each way once a month to visit him. Joe returned home only to relapse and then spent further time in Loxley House.

Brian John Tringham, (1910–1998). Spent several months in 1924 at the Orthopaedic Hospital, Oswestry (partly in traction) following a hip reconstruction performed by Mr (later Sir) Robert Jones. Brian had no family nearby. He was taught to knit – but there was not much alternative therapy. He retained a life-long gratitude to Sir Robert and contributed to his memorial fund when Sir Robert died.

Neil Anderson – baptised the day war broke out at Sheffield Cathedral (3 September 1939), died 25 April 1941 at City General Hospital, in isolation with chronic pneumonia.

Haydn Anderson – in isolation at Lodge Moor with suspected pneumonia. Survived. Now 89 years old.

Derek Godbehere
Brian Oxley
Dorothy Stocks
Brian Tringham
Laura Newson
Margaret Watson
Barbara Smith
Peter Ashmore
Joyce Moore
Jean Lawrence
John William Harrington
Audrey Newheiser
Grace Rachel Bird
Winifred Holling 1931–2021
Eileen Margaret Richards 1935–2020
Ernest Green (1935–2020)

Florence Cadman
Doreen Cadman
Grace Rachel Bird
Maura Armitage
Marcia Clark
Margaret Kelly
John Lindley
Valerie Hanwell
Sheila Newheiser
Bob Shaw
Betty Wylie
Margaret Ena Curbishley
Mark Gatenby
Ernest Green
Robert (Bob) Goodison
Terence (Terry) Fowler

and to the countless children and their families who didn't have a voice during this traumatic period of English history.

Do not weep for me, for I have lived.
Harry Drabble 2022

Contents

Why Share Dad's Story? ... 1
The Drabble/Parker Family Tree ... 6

PART ONE ... 7
Timeline ... 7
Chapter 1. A Life-changing Diagnosis ... 9
Chapter 2. Medical Treatment ... 28
Chapter 3. Psychological Harm ... 40
Chapter 4. Daily Life in the Hospital ... 49

PART TWO ... 69
Timeline ... 69
Chapter 5. Discharge on the Outbreak of War ... 71
Chapter 6. Back to Rivelin ... 102
Chapter 7. Life Begins ... 114

PART THREE ... 135
Timeline ... 135
Chapter 8. Can't Do to Can Do ... 138
Chapter 9. Emerging from Education and Battling Disability ... 176
Chapter 10. A Love Story Defies Expectations ... 202

APPENDICES ... 235
Appendix A: Bovine Tuberculosis – A Crime Against Society ... 236
    Symptoms of bovine tuberculosis ... 236

Conflicting advice	237
Pasteurising milk: A simple solution?	242
Milk legislation	244
Appendix B: About the King Edward VII Memorial Hospital	248
Appendix C: 'On Ilkla Mooar Baht 'at' (On Ilkley Moor Without a Hat, c. 1850)	249
Appendix D: Leonard Turner's Tragic Discovery	250
Appendix E: Harry's Termly Reports and Diploma from the Central Technical School (CTS)	252
18 Book Club Suggestions for Discussion	261
From the Author	264
Acknowledgements	265
Endnotes	267
Index	295

Why Share Dad's Story?

Author's note: Please be aware that I use outdated, but once commonly used language, such as 'cripple', 'disabled', and 'patient', in relation to people with a disability in this book. While the former has particularly derogatory connotations, they were all of their time and my father used them to describe himself. Using these terms does not reflect my views.

No one believed me.
'Children couldn't have been treated like that.' But we were.

When I was around seven years old, I was fascinated by my father's early experiences and naively tried to talk him into writing a book. I did not understand why he flinched at my suggestion. As I grew older, Dad told me, 'When I was two, society wrote me off as a "cripple" incapable of learning. One who should be kept away from "normal" people.'

It was important to Dad to share his life lessons with people. One trick, in particular, helped him move forward when everything looked impossible. He found that if he added the word 'yet', when he started berating himself about something he couldn't do, it reminded him that change and learning is a process. He said this took the pressure off him so that he could work out the steps he needed to take to get from 'can't do' to 'can do'. It saddened him to realise how many limitations we place on ourselves, and he was frustrated he could not help more people to overcome obstacles and achieve their definition of success. However, he took many of the skills he learnt as a child into his adult life as a manager and as a music teacher working from home for 35 years. After he died, people who knew him sought me out to tell me he had helped them to think differently about whatever had challenged them, and how this had changed their lives for the better. One student, James, said that Dad's 'endless patience and enthusiasm was infectious. I was pushed where needed and supported when I was struggling. They say a good teacher stays with you for life and I am pleased to say that Mr Drabble proves this rule.' Another, Vicky, described him as 'a truly amazing man [who] had a significant impact on my life and direction of travel'.

With Dad's knowledge, over the last 20 years of his life, I jotted down the snippets he told me. As an adult, I tried not to prod his 'demons' to satisfy my curiosity, but I listened to him when they prodded him. In his last years, I gently quizzed him more about the family. He generously dug deep to answer as clearly as he could. We discussed my article 'How Key Psychological Theories Can Enrich Our Understanding of Our Ancestors', which covered three generations of our family, including my mother.[1] He read it carefully and approved it before I submitted it for peer review. I was deeply moved when he told me the psychological aspects that I bring to my writing are 'perhaps, the most important perspective of all'. He said he was sorry he'd stopped following developments in psychology to concentrate on his role as a provider. I told him that it was in his bookcases that I discovered psychology. I still have the books he loaned to me when I started studying psychology A level.

As Dad's kidneys slowly failed, I watched helplessly as he cut the tethers that bound him to events, activities, people and living. Dad believed 'the unexamined life is not worth living', but his conclusions had often been private ones that fed into personal biannual and annual plans. Towards the end of his life, particularly during the nearly two years he lived through the COVID-19 pandemic, he shared a lot, restating and reflecting on the experiences that shaped him. He said he was deeply grateful for contracting bovine tuberculosis (bTB), recognising that if he hadn't had the experiences that followed, his life would have been impoverished. He thanked me for the research findings that put his experiences into perspective and for giving him the opportunity to finally bury his demons. I explained, 'Very few accounts of survivors of bovine tuberculosis exist. That makes yours an important story.'[2] Years ago, I'd said that if he didn't write his story I would, but I later checked with him, 'Would you rather I didn't write about your life?' He replied, 'No, experiences are an important part of history, but that doesn't mean I want to be the one to write about mine.'

After a consultant gave him three months to live in February 2022, Dad decided he wanted to collaborate on the project. We talked about its format, whether it should perhaps be a fictionalised tale, or an anonymised biography. He suggested that, as a collaboration, its effectiveness would lie in combining his words and experience with historical and current psychological theory. Given his need to conserve his energy, I left it to him to drive the pace and to choose what he wanted to talk about. A favourite saying of Dad's was, 'Life can only be understood backwards; but it must be lived forward' (Soren Aabye Kierkegaard, 1813–55). This book is the culmination of the experiences, memories, feelings and thoughts he shared. It is my attempt to share his life as he lived it.

He came to realise his story could represent the hidden, unbelievable truth of hundreds of thousands of British children who had been disabled by bovine TB and that it could raise awareness of the psychological price paid by these children (and their descendants) when their psychological needs were not recognised, or were misunderstood.

Dad knew that tuberculosis is not only increasing worldwide but also becoming drug resistant, and he thought that mistakes in the way children were treated may be repeated. He said, 'Maybe my story will help someone.' After Dad read some early chapters and extracts, just before he died, I checked in with him again, 'I don't have to share what I have written with the family, or publish it. It's been enough for me to share this experience with you.' He replied, 'Publish.'

As Tara Westover, the author of the exceptional and astute memoir *Educated*, reminds us, 'We are all of us more complicated than the roles we are assigned in the stories other people tell.'[3] I can't tell you of all Dad's many layers in this book, but I can say I saw him as a remarkable, gentle, loving and non-judgemental man. It grieves me enormously he did not live to comment on this final version. I take comfort in one of the last things he said to me, 'You have an exceptional understanding and I trust you with my life.' I am tremendously proud of him.

Helen
2025

PS Around four million new book titles are published each year, and reviews (especially on Amazon) are one of the few ways independent authors can be discovered. If you read *Who Do I Think You Were?* *'Yet': A Story of Triumph Over Childhood Separation, Trauma, and Disability*, I would be grateful if you left a review on Amazon, GoodReads or at your favourite store.

The Drabble/Parker Family Tree

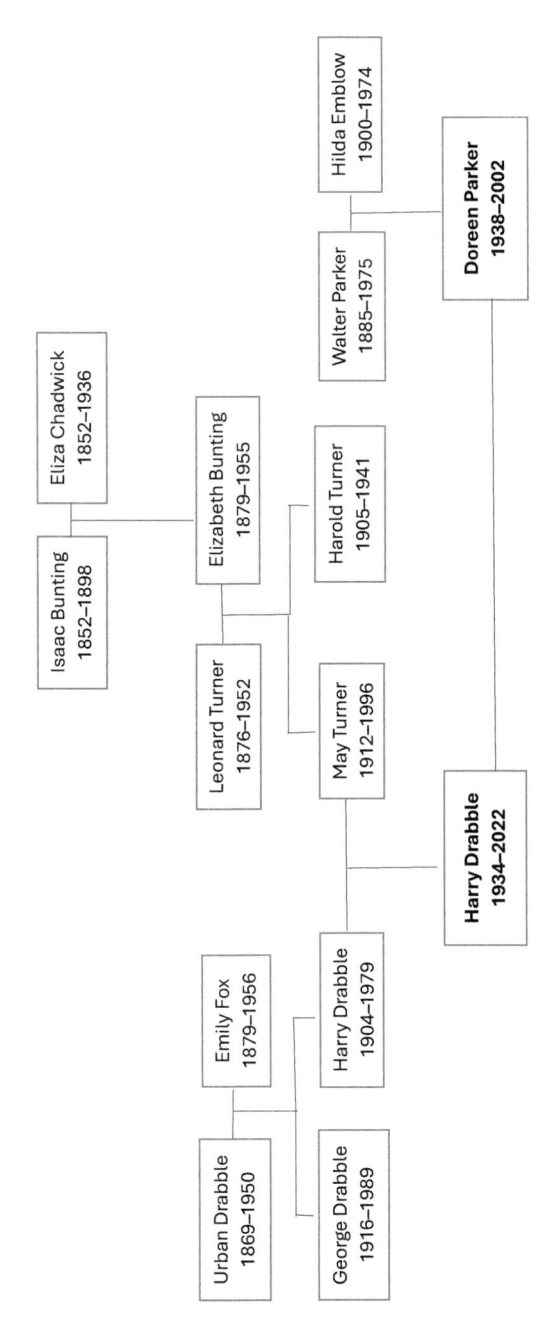

- Hilda Emblow 1900–1974
- Walter Parker 1885–1975
- Doreen Parker 1938–2002

- Eliza Chadwick 1852–1936
- Isaac Bunting 1852–1898
- Elizabeth Bunting 1879–1955
- Harold Turner 1905–1941
- Leonard Turner 1876–1952
- May Turner 1912–1996
- Harry Drabble 1934–2022

- Emily Fox 1879–1956
- Harry Drabble 1904–1979
- Urban Drabble 1869–1950
- George Drabble 1916–1989

PART ONE

Timeline

DATE	AGE	EVENT
4 Dec. 1934		Born at the Jessop Hospital for Women, Sheffield
23 Dec. 1934	3 weeks	Baptised Heeley Parish Church, Heeley, Sheffield
24 Dec. 1934	3 weeks	Moved to 44 Butterthwaite Road, Shiregreen Estate, Sheffield
22 June 1935	6 mths	Harry wins Heeley Parish Church baby competition
Summer 1935	6 mths	Holiday in a sidecar on the tandem to Betws-y-Coed, Wales
c. July 1937	2.5	Outpatient appointment Westfield Terrace, Royal Hospital, Sheffield
c. July 1937	2.5	Admitted to the nursery ward, Royal Hospital, Sheffield
19 July 1937	2.5	Admitted to King Edward VII Memorial Hospital for Crippled Children, Rivelin

1

A Life-changing Diagnosis

Harry was born in the Jessop Hospital for Women on the corner of Gell Street and Leavygreave Road, near Sheffield City Centre, on 4 December 1934. The hospital was two miles from the room his parents shared in his maternal great-grandmother's house in the suburb of Heeley.

His mother, May, had been keen to start a family as soon as she married. However, she knew nothing about contraception, and Harry Senior did not want to become a father quickly. He later admitted to her he had used condoms bought from the barbers to stop her from conceiving. Reminiscing with me in the late 1970s, May reflected that her ignorance as a young woman, which included basic information about men's and women's bodies, was not unusual. She told me she did not see a completely nude male until her son was born.

Studio photo of May Turner and Harry Drabble on their wedding day 15 April 1933.

A Life-changing Diagnosis

Childbirth was still risky, but despite 45 out of 1,000 women dying in childbirth, and Harry's initial reluctance, a year after their marriage, the couple were eagerly anticipating the birth of their first child.[4] It is unlikely May attended antenatal appointments. Nationwide, half of women expecting babies did not, although 4,264 did so in Sheffield in 1934.[5] Unlike many of her friends, family and neighbours, May continued in domestic service after she married, and worked until just before Harry was due.[6]

May thought herself fortunate to occupy one of the 165 maternity beds in 'the Jessop', as it could only accommodate a quarter of Sheffield's expectant mothers.[7] She said she did not know how Harry would be born until she was in the delivery room and a midwife told her, 'The baby comes out the same way they got in.' May added, 'I thought they would unzip my tummy.'[8] She also told me a story of how the delivery nurse had labelled Harry wrongly when he had been taken from her after birth so he could be checked over. Apparently, when May was handed an infant to feed, despite her usual deference, she insisted the baby handed to her was not hers. The nurse tried to reassure her that this was her child, but May would not take the baby. The ward sister heard what May had to say, and bustled off. After a hasty investigation, a swap took place.

According to a midwife's account, the swaddled babies slept in a metal cot hung on the rail at the bottom of their mother's bed.[9] The mothers were confined to bed during their two-week stay. When a baby cried, a midwife 'tore down the ward, comforted the child, reassured the mother and put the baby back down ... It was detached in a way ... the baby became the nurse's concern rather than the mother's.'[10] The mothers were given their babies to breast-feed as close to 6 am, 10 am, 2 pm, 6 pm and 10 pm as possible.

While May was in hospital, Osborn Steelworks gave Harry Senior the rise in responsibility and pay that was traditional at the time for men entering fatherhood. His new wage gave him the opportunity to apply for one of the many new council houses built by Sheffield Corporation. So, clutching his payslips to prove he was a reliable worker in steady, respectable employment and could afford the rent, Harry spent a night queuing outside Sheffield Town Hall in the hope of a new home for his new family.[11]

As they were still living in Heeley, Harry was baptised at the parish church on 23 December 1934.

Heeley Parish Church, Gleadless Road, Heeley, Sheffield.
Photograph by Terry Robinson. This file is licensed under the Creative Commons Attribution-Share Alike 2.0 Generic licence.

The council granted Harry Senior a new three-bedroom council house on the Shiregreen estate on the north-east fringe of Sheffield, close to open fields, Butterthwaite Farm, Blackburn Brook and Hartley Brook Dike. The house was one of 4,472 built on this estate alone. Harry said:

Shiregreen was a desirable estate. When we moved in, it was a model estate and the people in it had to have a minimum standard of earnings and education to be allowed to live there.

44 Butterthwaite Road is the house on the left.
2024 ©Google

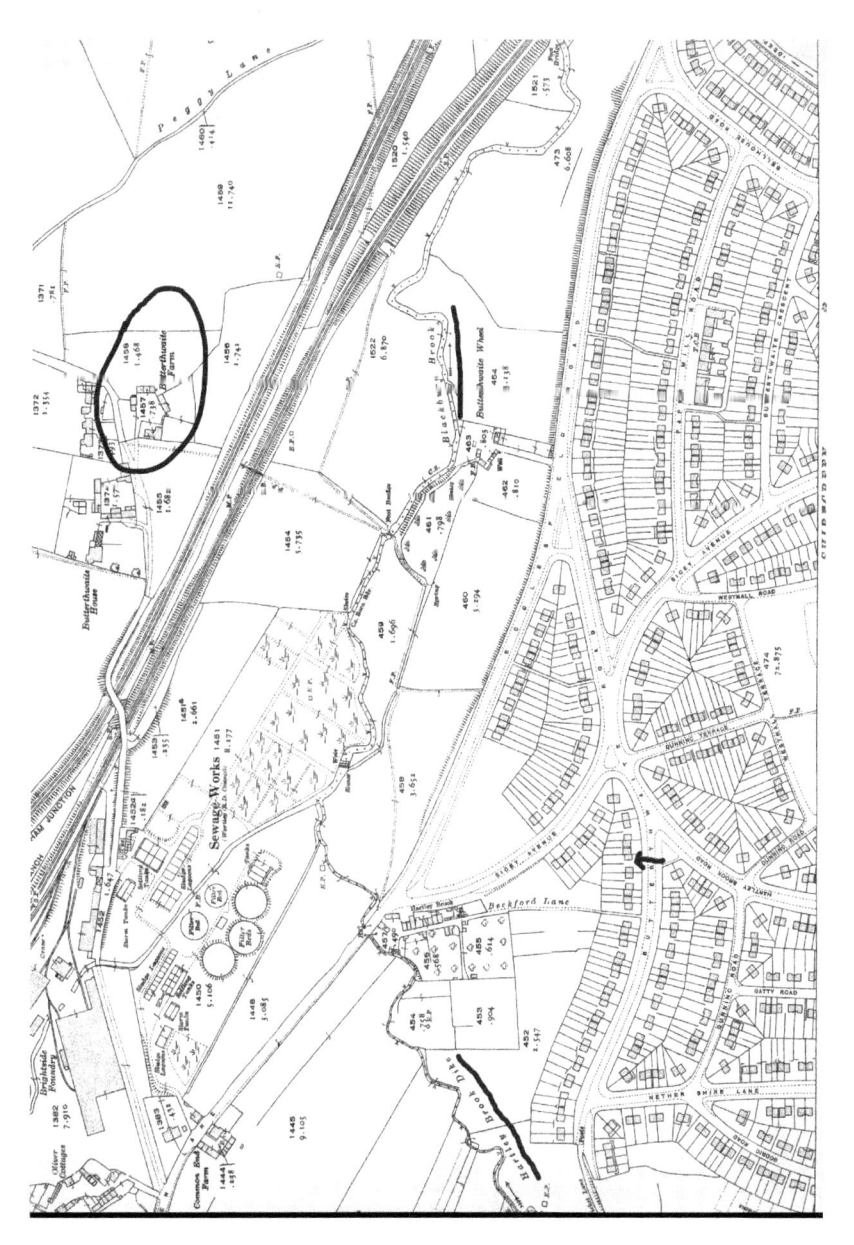

'Yet': A Story of Triumph Over Childhood Separation, Trauma, and Disability

Map of Shiregreen estate showing Harry's house, the nearby brook, dike and Butterthwaite Farm.[12]

A Life-changing Diagnosis

On Christmas Eve 1934, May and Harry were thrilled to move with their three-week-old son to their new house at 44 Butterthwaite Road. It had an upstairs bathroom, a downstairs toilet and a garden to soothe Harry after his gruelling shifts in the steelworks. Their new home was quite a step up. Harry Senior had lived with four siblings in a two-up two-down with an outside toilet at 71 Wallace Road, Neepsend. Here he had slept alongside his two brothers on the front-room floor, where, due to lack of space, he lay with his head under the sideboard. May's wedding certificate noted she lived at 155 Wallace Road when they married, presumably with her parents.

In 1936, referring to Sheffield, author George Orwell wrote in his diary: 'It seems to me, by daylight, one of the most appalling places I have ever seen.' He went on: 'In whichever direction you look you see the same landscape of monstrous chimneys pouring forth smoke which is sometimes black and sometimes of a rosy tint said to be due to sulphur.'[13]

Orwell stayed with Kate and Gilbert Searle at 154 Wallace Road, on the hill opposite the gasworks, from 2–4 March 1936. He described Wallace Road and Neepsend in his book *The Road to Wigan Pier*.[14] It shocked the nation.

> One particular picture of Sheffield stays by me. A frightful piece of waste ground … trampled quite bare of grass and littered with newspaper, old saucepans etc. To the right, an isolated row of gaunt four-room houses, dark red, blackened by smoke. To the left an interminable vista of factory chimneys, chimney behind chimney, fading away into a dim blackish haze.[15]

'Where The Shells Came From' (Sheffield), c. 1927.
By artist Reginald Belfield.
In the public domain.

Born later, into a different class, May might have taken the 11-plus exam, and gone to grammar school, even university. However, her father Leonard held a common view at the time, 'It's not worth

A Life-changing Diagnosis

educating girls.' (More about Leonard can be found at Appendix D.) Instead, like so many of her peers, she went into domestic service when she left school at the age of 14. Her time as a general live-in servant included washing and ironing for a Jewish family with at least two daughters. May said it was hard work, but her employers encouraged her curiosity about food and household management, and allowed her to take time off for singing and elocution lessons. May told me she was happy in the detached house in Fulwood with its large garden.

Harry's parents met on a steam train when May was travelling with her father to fish at Bardney. Harry Senior loved steam engines. He noted when they sped up and slowed down and took every opportunity to ask the driver questions. At the end of the journey, May noticed how easily he struck up a conversation and watched him thank the train driver. She later told me: 'Everyone talked to him. I think it's because he always looked them in the eye.' The couple married in 1933 just before May's 21st birthday.

Since her marriage, life had improved enormously for May, Harry's slim, blonde and petite mother. She had been a malnourished, underweight child who, while at the beck and call of her demanding alcoholic parents, dreamed of bread dipped into a can of condensed milk. Growing up, May had the tricky job of extracting her father, Leonard, from the pub.[16] When she could, she escaped to her grandmother Eliza's house. Harry described May's grandmother as 'a religious woman, and deeply superstitious'.

May told me she rejected her own chaotic parenting and kept to the steady routine from the maternity ward, putting Harry to sleep, feeding him and bathing him by the clock. She added that

Eliza became her role model for motherhood. But May was also an avid reader with a hunger for knowledge, so she may have collected the coupons and sent away for *The Motherhood Book* offered by the *Daily Independent*. This also recommended feeding by the clock, but said three hourly during the day was best, 'with babies over 5lb in weight being given only boiled water during the hours of true darkness'.[17] *The Motherhood Book* also told mothers 'too much handling stimulates the nerves and leads to wakefulness'.[18] It further advised that 'mothering time should be the most delightful hour of the day' and is 'the most permissible time for the mother ... to take her little one gently in her arms and indulge in simple mother-play'.[19] Did May take such prescriptive advice to heart, or did she trust her instincts?

If May had read further, she might have discovered that bovine tuberculosis can result from drinking infected milk. Unfortunately, it said nothing about boiling the milk before giving it to babies and toddlers.[20]

Osborn Steelworks employed Harry Senior as an assistant roller.[21] Affectionately nicknamed 'Bud' by his colleagues because of his short stature, Harry Senior had an easy manner that people from all walks of life

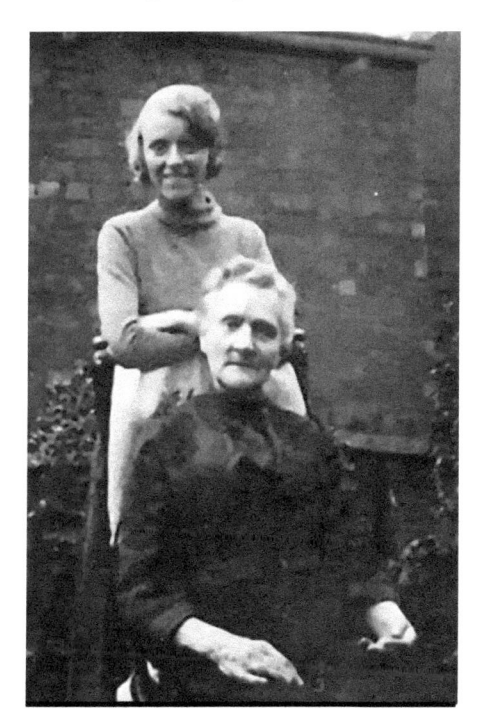

May Turner with her grandmother Eliza Bunting, née Chadwick.

warmed to. In contrast, May did not feel she should go into department stores because, 'they weren't for the likes of me'.[22]

At six months old, Harry was a bubbling, blond, blue-eyed infant. He was quick to chuckle and curious about his surroundings. In the summer of 1935, his proud mother entered him into the Heeley Parish Church Baby Competition in Sheffield, where the doctor acting as judge awarded him 98 points out of a possible 100. May was elated. He won the first prize of a studio photograph which she hung in their living room.

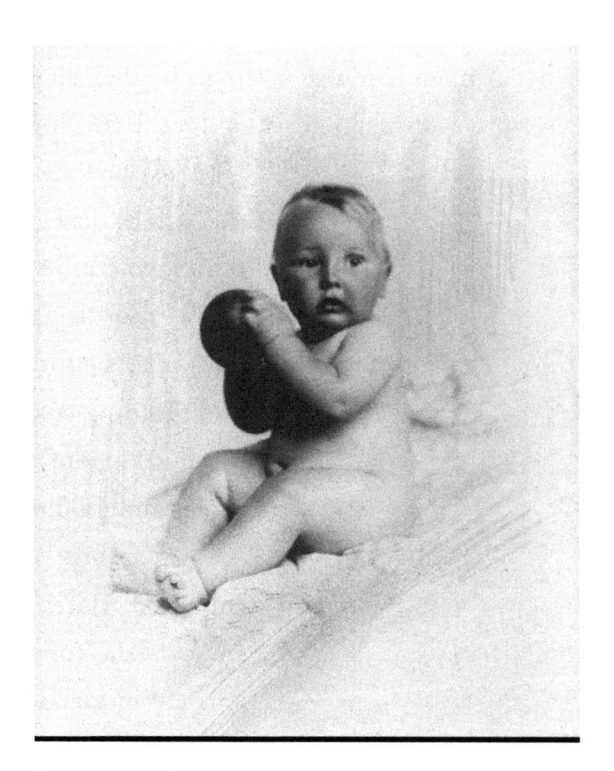

Studio portrait of Harry Drabble, aged seven months, 1935.
The photograph was part of the first prize in Heeley Parish Church Baby Competition, and was taken by Yates & Henderson, 35 Fargate, Sheffield.
In the author's collection.

Heeley Parish Church Baby Competition score sheet, 22 June 1935.
In the author's collection.

A Life-changing Diagnosis

Harry and May had bought a tandem before they married and they would often cycle 100 miles or more at the weekend. Harry Senior had a good working knowledge of England and Wales gleaned from a cycling map.

ABOVE: May Drabble, née Turner, with the couple's tandem, c. 1933.

Images in the author's collection.

LEFT: Front cover of the reduced survey British Isles coloured Tourists and Cyclists 1921 map.[23]

Harry was also good at map reading, but more importantly, as his son said later in life, 'Dad had an instinctive sense of space. He always knew where he was.'

As a baby, Harry travelled with his parents in an adapted sidecar attached to the tandem, so they could continue exploring the countryside. Shortly after the baby competition, Harry and

May slung on their knapsacks, and cycled 150 miles to Betws-y-Coed, near Snowdon in North Wales. They took in Chester Castle, cycled along the River Dee and visited Swallow and Conwy Falls. Numerous day trips followed, when her husband came home from a long shift and would say to May, 'Let's get lost tomorrow.'

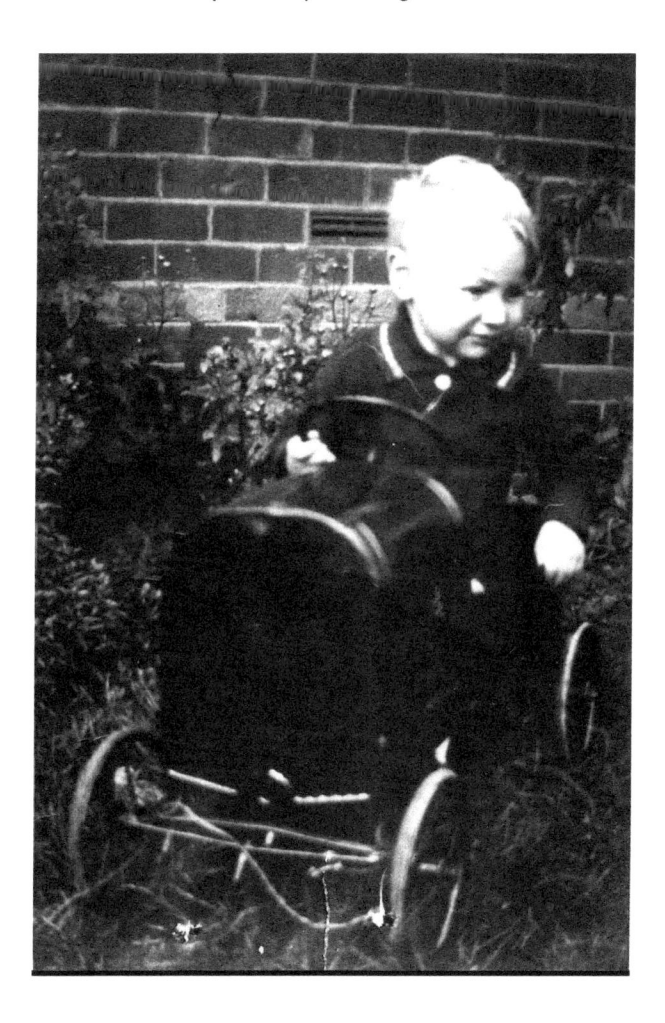

Harry Drabble, aged about 18 months old, in a bright red metal car. The photo is believed to have been taken in the back garden of 44 Butterthwaite Road. *In the author's collection.*

May loved life with her family and was reluctant to disturb it when her son started limping. She hoped it would right itself, but May's father, Leonard, who had a 'gammy' leg, told her, 'That limp needs looking at.' Harry Senior gave her the money to take their infant to a doctor, who referred him to an orthopaedic surgeon, and the surgical tuberculosis officer for Sheffield, Dr Creswell Lee Pattison. Paediatric consultants were not introduced until the National Health Service began in 1948.[24]

May was worried when she took Harry to the outpatient appointment clinic at the Royal Hospital, Sheffield in July 1937. After Dr Pattison examined him, the close relationship Harry enjoyed with his parents was shattered when a nurse pulled young Harry from his mother's arms. In an interview, a nurse who, as a patient in another hospital, had been separated from her parents when she was six years old in 1948 considered that 'children were forcibly removed from the parents in a manner which was not necessary and which was designed to distress both parties'.[24] And later, as a nurse in 1960, she recalled: 'So this toddler that by now was distraught, sobbing, I went to pick him up, because he was just, he was just left on the cot to break his heart and sob, so I went to pick him up and just as I did, he was like a little monkey, his arms around me … I'm going to get upset again hanging to me. It was awful. And so the good children's nurse came and put a harness on him and fastened him down … it was awful. I think, one of the worst things and he was just left to get on with it. And I don't know why …'[25] When she was interviewed, she said she 'felt that the children's nurses wanted to exert power over children, parents and other nurses and that this partially explained their lack of "human" care'.[26]

Harry was admitted to the Royal Hospital's nursery ward for tests. He was just two-and-a-half years old. May was distraught. Powerless, she was forced to return home and explain to her husband that she had left their child at the hospital. Harry later described the 'white-hot fury' when he was taken from his mother as 'someone is going to pay'.

Facade of 20 Westfield Terrace, which served as the outpatients' department for the Royal Hospital. *By Warofdreams – Own work, CC BY-SA 3.0, licensed under the Creative Commons Attribution-Share Alike 3.0 Unported licence.*

Image of the outpatients' area, taken from the film *Centenary of the Royal Hospital Sheffield, 1932*, Wellcome Collection.[27] *In the public domain.*

A Life-changing Diagnosis

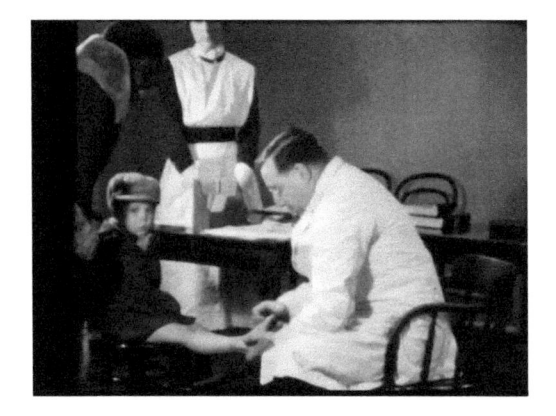

Child orthopaedic appointment with a surgeon and a mother anxiously looking on. *The images on this page were taken from a 1932 film about the Royal Hospital, Sheffield.*

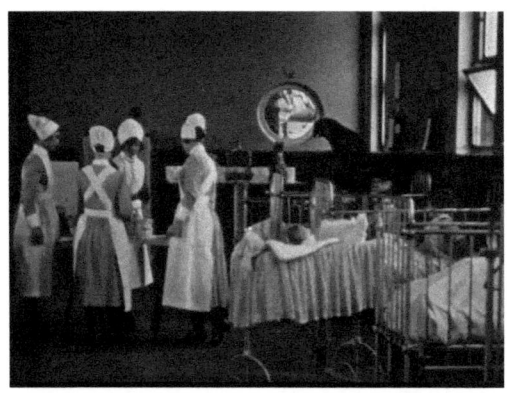

Nursery ward. Image taken from a 1932 film about the Royal Hospital, Sheffield. The Royal Hospital, which sourced their milk from a single Derbyshire farm. The milk was regularly tested for organisms that caused disease.

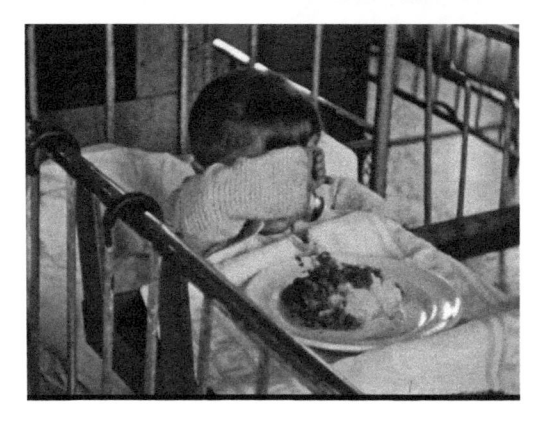

A child eating in their cot on the nursery ward.

Dr Pattison was also the medical superintendent of the King Edward VII Hospital for Crippled Children. (More about the hospital can be found at Appendix B.) He gave May the shattering diagnosis that Harry had been infected with *Mycobacterium bovis* (*M. Bovis*), commonly known as bovine TB, bTB or non-pulmonary tuberculosis. It is a chronic disease of mammals, particularly cattle, but can be transmitted to people. It was identified in 1898 after Robert Koch discovered the tubercle bacillus caused tuberculosis in 1881. Bovine TB can affect the lungs, lymph nodes and other parts of the body, particularly the joints. People are usually infected by eating or drinking contaminated, unpasteurised dairy products, as was infant Harry, or, more rarely, by eating infected meat.

The bacteria *Mycobacterium bovis* can lie dormant or take months or years to develop. However, within eight weeks after infection, some bovine TB symptoms include 'fever, sore throat, swelling of the tonsils and cervical lymph nodes, and vague stomach symptoms'.[28] The most important indicators in children were stiffness and, initally, an intermittent limp, particularly in the morning or after resting. The limp was caused by restricted movement and, later, by pain around the hip region. (You can read more about bovine TB in Appendix A.)

In 1934, the year Harry was born, the *Sheffield Independent* reported: 'There were not fewer than 4,000 fresh cases of tuberculosis bovine origin occurring every year in England and Wales, and about 2,000 deaths.'[29]

Dr Pattison informed May that he would admit Harry for treatment, provided she and Harry Senior signed him over for the necessary time. Devastated, May and Harry agreed their son should be transferred to the King Edward VII Memorial Hopsital for Crippled Children by ambulance. It was seven miles from home, and the first time the toddler had been in such a small motor vehicle or travelled without a parent. His mother was not allowed to follow on. May could only wait helplessly until her husband received a postcard giving one parent permission to visit. The separation was agonising. For months after Harry's admission, May would wake believing she heard him crying.

Society permitted professionals significant control over children's care and told parents that doctors and nurses 'knew best'. May and Harry were powerless. Their young son had entered a system where emotional support for children and parents was not available. Parents were excluded from hospitals and their child's care. The couple had to trust that doctors and nurses possessed the medical knowledge required to treat and care for Harry, and accept their clinical objectivity and detachment. In the absence of information from the medical staff, did May turn to *The Motherhood Book* and discover that bovine tuberculosis was as serious as consumption (pulmonary tuberculosis), and 'a complete recovery of movement in the joint [was] not likely to occur. In any case, treatment [would] last for two years and often considerably more'?[30]

Harry's six-month-old self had been prizeworthy. Two years later, he was a child with a disability, being hidden out of sight.

The middle ambulance is the type Harry remembered as a child.
Image taken from a 1932 film about the Royal Hospital, Sheffield.

In Sheffield, the Hospital Council brokered an amalgamation of the ambulance services of the voluntary hospitals, the municipal hospitals (mainly isolation institutions) and the City Watch Committee, whose vehicles were used for street accidents.

This joint working was underpinned by the provision of St John's first-aid volunteers, who managed patients during their transport, with women providing the bulk of the support.[31]

King Edward VII Memorial Hospital for Crippled Children, Rivelin, c. 1921, postcard.
In the author's collection.

2

Medical Treatment

Being admitted to the babies' quarantine ward at the King Edward VII Memorial Hospital for Crippled Children, in the Rivelin Valley, Sheffield in July 1937 was likely a bewildering and terrifying experience for two-and-a-half-year-old Harry.[32] At home, he had loved kicking a ball in the garden. In the hospital, he was strapped down in one of the two steel cots in the observation ward, without even a soft toy or familiar blanket. Both of these were deemed to be an infection risk, which could close a ward or even the entire hospital.[33] Harry was still in pain, but had no one to soothe him. He would come to refer to the hospital as 'Rivelin'.

Aerial photograph of the King Edward VII Orthopaedic Hospital in the Rivelin Valley.[34] *Photograph from an archive compiled by Jean Bruce, 'King Edwards collected 2008–2018'.*

The hospital was one of 40 orthopaedic hospitals in Britain.[35] It was largely funded by the 'Penny in the Pound' scheme, a city-wide

'Yet': A Story of Triumph Over Childhood Separation, Trauma, and Disability

contributory scheme, which involved workmen like Harry Senior pledging 1 penny out of every pound earned to the hospital fund.[36]

Harry vividly recalled the traumatic memory of being separated from his mother. In his mind's eye, he could see a 'child-friendly' clock on the children's ward as he lay in his iron-barred cot. He focused intently on the black metal silhouette of a girl and boy dancing either side of its face, because a nurse had pointed to it and said, '"When that figure gets round to there, your mother will come." Of course, she never did.' The betrayal Harry experienced when the hands lined up and his mother did not appear was acute. He said it taught him that people are unreliable, but added, 'Everyone has experiences like that.'

Once Harry's quarantine was over, he was moved to the babies' ward. The wards were all-white. There were no pictures on the wall, no books, no toys, no lessons and no radio. Besides bovine tuberculosis, the hospital treated congenital deformities, rickets and paralysis from polio. With patients taken outside for open-air treatment, the establishment acted as a sanatorium as well as an orthopaedic hospital.

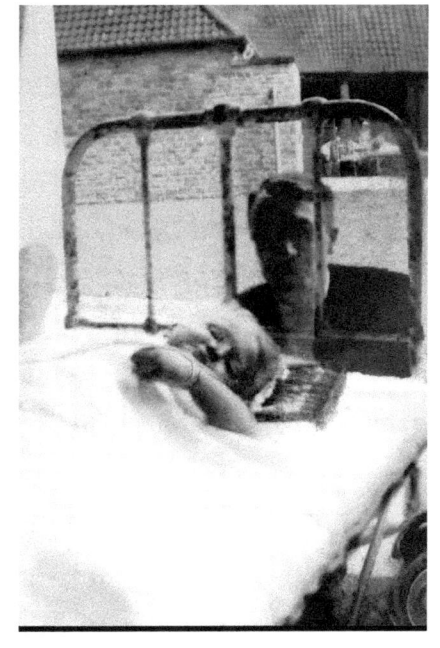

Harry with his father Harry Senior in the fresh air at the King Edward VII Memorial Hospital for Crippled Children, c. 1937.
In the author's collection.

Dr Pattison ruled out Perthes' disease (a childhood hip disorder initiated by a disruption of blood flow to the head of the femur that causes the bone to die, stopping growth), and then confirmed Harry's diagnosis of bovine TB after taking a history, viewing his X-rays, examining his swollen and stiff joints, and carrying out a painful bone biopsy and a lumbar puncture to see if the disease had spread to his spine. However, orthopaedic surgeon Maud Forrester-Brown wrote that a definitive diagnosis could only be made when it was known how long the joint should be kept still before the symptoms started again. She added that even when treatment started early, there were no guarantees that the child could use their joint in the future.[37]

Maud Frances Forrester-Brown (1885–1970) was an author and the first woman orthopaedic surgeon in Britain. She was a visiting surgeon to children's clinics across the South-West of England, performing hundreds of operations. In 1921, she became the first female member of the British Orthopaedic Association. She rose to vice-president of the Orthopaedics section of the British Medical Association in 1938.[38] Maud was not the only female orthopaedic surgeon. In 1937, the Rivelin's house surgeon was Kathleen Shannon.[39]

The diagnosis of bovine TB was devastating for Harry's parents. They are unlikely to have known that 23 children aged 10 years or younger died in Sheffield of bone and joint tuberculosis that year.[40] What they did know was that society would largely write off their little boy once he was admitted to the hospital, because work opportunities mostly depended on working-class men being strong and physically able. They were helpless to protect Harry once he had been admitted.[41] May and Harry also knew that those with physical disabilities were strongly discouraged from marrying or having children of their own. Despite bovine tuberculosis not being infectious in the same way as pulmonary tuberculosis, 'the stigma attached to the disease itself meant sanitorium staff were regarded with caution outside the hospital gates'.[42]

Treating tuberculosis of the spine, hip and other joints was difficult and painstakingly slow, involving immobilisation for many months, or even years of hospitalisation. The inflammatory process of bovine TB rapidly destroyed large areas of children's soft bone.[43] It would destroy Harry's left hip socket, the neck of the femur, and his right elbow. The articular cartilage that covered the ends of the joint in his left hip and his right elbow would also be demolished. New bone is not created in tuberculosis as it can be with fractures, arthritis, or other conditions. Over time, the shaft of the femur was forced into the space where the socket had been, which shortened his left leg. Some of the hip damage and dislocation could have been caused by infant Harry putting weight on the inflamed joint before the condition was diagnosed.[44]

As the disease attacked the tissue and bone of Harry's joints, pus-filled abscesses frequently formed. These were often located deep in the hip joint or pelvis, which made them hard to identify and access. Abscesses could also surface beneath the skin. The pressure they created often caused pain, and they were frequently accompanied by a high temperature. A localised abscess could lead to general sepsis if left undrained and, prior to the widespread use of antibiotics, could be fatal.[45] However, abscesses were rarely aspirated unless they came to bursting point, because of the risk of secondary infection. As Dr Pattison said, 'He who opens a tuberculosis focus opens a door for death to enter.'[46]

The abscesses that burst naturally or were drained were packed with sphagnum moss. Local women and children collected the packing material for the hospital from the boggy moors above Sheffield.[47] Sphagnum bandages inhibit the growth of bacteria and produce a sterile environment by keeping the pH level around the wound low.[48] The moss had been used medicinally for centuries, including during the First World War. It was an ideal dressing because it absorbed up to 20 times its volume in liquid.[49]

Before antibiotics, TB of the hip was treated with skilful splinting, traction, rest, sunlight, fresh air and good nutrition. The general aim was to reduce, as much as possible, the deformity caused by the infection. Although the understanding of vitamins and minerals was not greatly developed until the 1930s–1940s, cod liver oil had been given to TB patients in the 19th century.[50] The oil was also prescribed to Harry and the other patients at Rivelin, partly because Mrs May Mellanby, a medical researcher, and Dr Pattison were conducting studies to build evidence that cod liver oil reduced tooth decay in children.[51] It is rich in vitamins A and D and has added calcium and potassium salts, all needed for bone health.[52]

To relieve Harry's pain, maintain joint stability, and possibly improve future mobility, his hip joint had to be immobilised. He was first strapped to a Jones double hip-abduction frame (see figure 2). This fixed his legs in a triangular position for months.

After about nine months on the Jones frame, if X-rays suggested that movement in the hip might still return, then the patient was allowed either to move around in bed or to try sitting up in the ambulatory splint. However, the frame did not work for Harry.

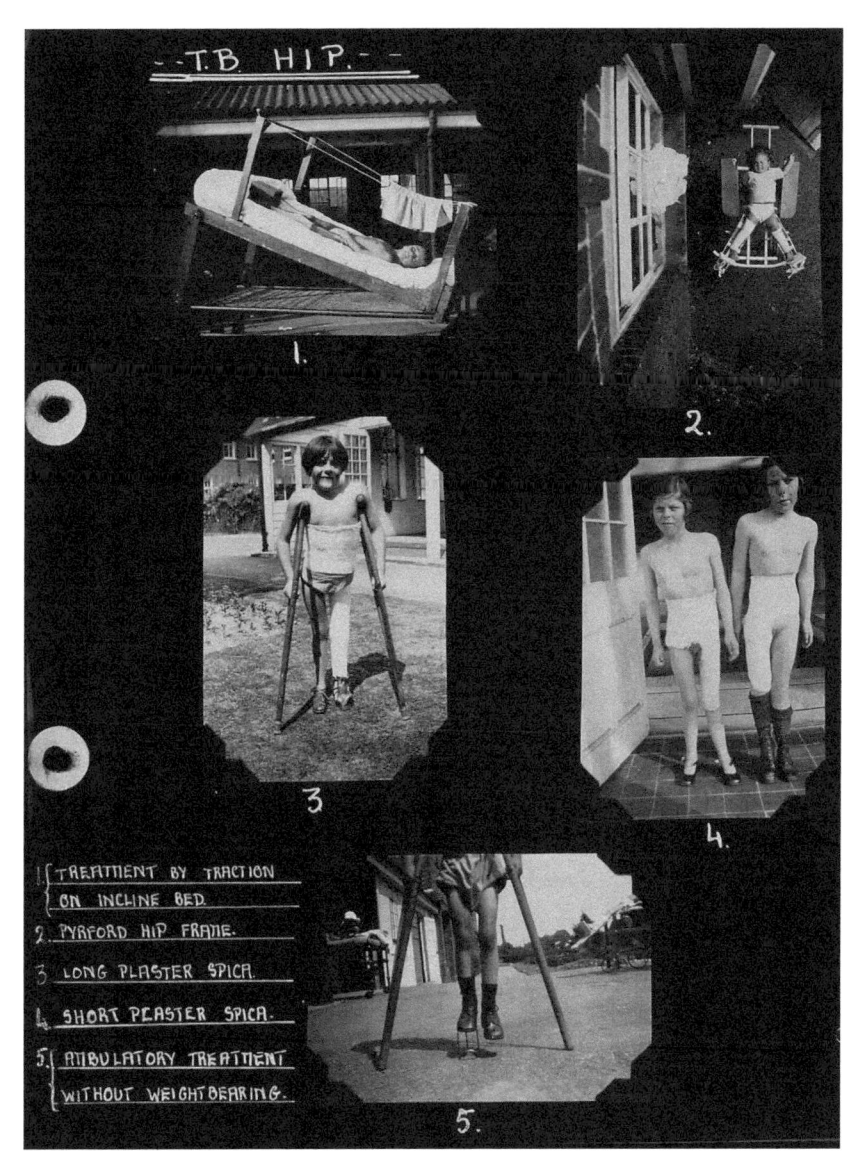

'Yet': A Story of Triumph Over Childhood Separation, Trauma, and Disability

TB hip. Short plaster spica. Wellcome Reference 29326i.[53]
The author has obscured the girls' genitalia in figure 4 as they had cut-outs in their plaster casts, leaving them exposed in the original photo.

33

Medical Treatment

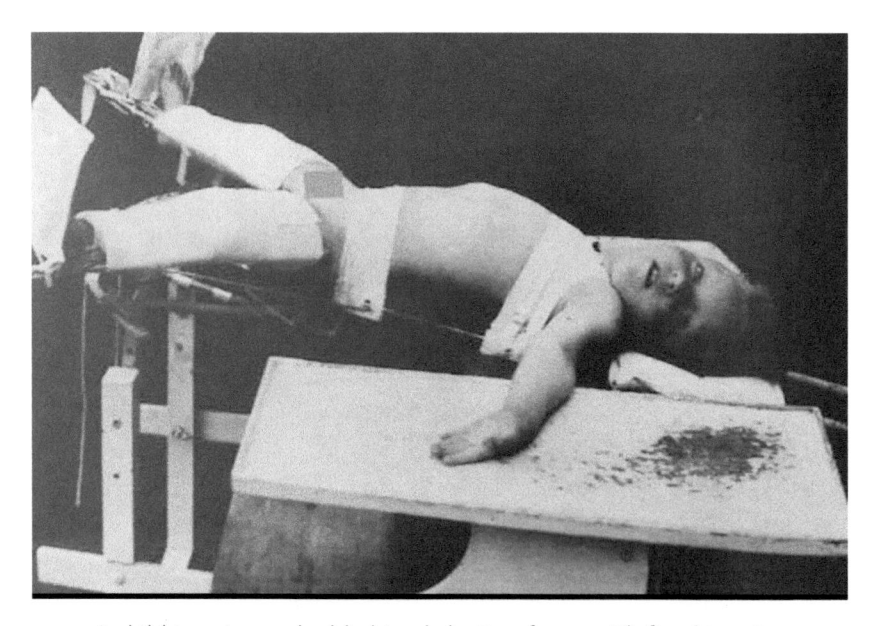

A child in a Jones double hip-abduction frame with fixed traction to both lower limbs. Adhesive strapping kept it in place. When this apparatus is properly applied, it stops the hip joint from moving. *From* A History of King Edward VII Orthopaedic Hospital Sheffield *by E.G. Herzog, Orthopaedic Surgeon Emeritus, 1986, page 22 unpublished.*

Next, Dr Pattison ordered Pugh's method of slinging.[54] Harry's left thigh was put in traction and fixed to a bar at the foot of a tilted bed. 'The adhesive strapping must be very strong because the object of the method is to allow the child to wriggle constantly, like a fish on a hook; this keeps up the circulation in the muscles and their tone, and keeps the hip joint mobile in all the cases where this is possible; some have so much cartilage destruction before they come under treatment that it is impossible.'[55]

The rotation of Harry's hip was controlled by putting a light shoe or boot on the foot and nailing the heel to a wooden crossbar. This prevented the foot from twisting, or the hip from rotating. Harry's right leg was free, so that it did not atrophy, as it did when bandaged on a frame. Hip traction helped to relieve hip pain and muscle spasm, to keep the joint as mobile as possible.[56]

It was imperative that Harry did not try to sit up, so the nurses tied him to his bed. 'A firm canvas restrainer across the upper part of the sternum and round the shoulders [was used]; this does not hinder respiration in any way.'[57] A contemporary of Harry's, Derek Godbehere, born in Sheffield in 1930, was admitted to the boys' ward of the King Edward VII Memorial Hospital for Crippled Children in 1936. He also experienced being strapped down and said *'I hadn't been in long, I'd got out of bed and couldn't get back in, my legs had gone. They put me back in bed and tied bandages around my chest and the bed frame. I was tied down, but I could move a little from side to side, but I didn't let on.'* [58]

After five months, Harry had a dislocated hip, so it had to be fixed in place. He was therefore encased in plaster of Paris from under his armpit down the full length of his body with holes to allow him to urinate and defecate. A bar between his legs kept the structure rigid.[59] It took more than a week to build up the cast.

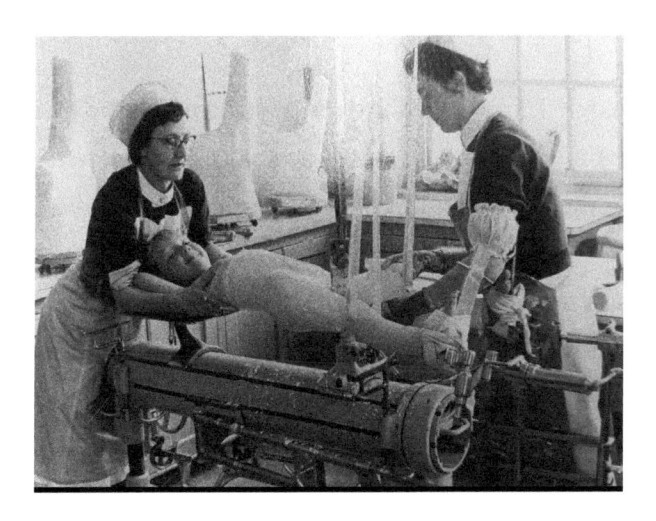

Application of a plaster spica at King Edward VII Hospital – *Nursing Mirror* 1956 to commemorate the opening of new facilities. *From Jean Bruce's* King Edward VII 2008–2018. *Sheffield, 2018.*

Medical Treatment

Harry talked of his extreme vulnerability in this position. The smiling child in this photograph is likely displaying a trauma response to the situation. If you were suspended in mid-air being plastered and you knew you would remain immobile for months and were asked to smile for the camera, would you do so, regardless of how you felt? The feeling of betrayal by nurses and doctors Harry had been encouraged to trust was a lasting memory. He said:

> *They were doing their job, but there are ways of doing it.*
> *They weren't doing it as one should with a sick child.*
> *I didn't trust them anymore because I never knew what they were going to do to me.*

There were difficulties with body casts. An orthopaedic surgeon wrote: 'Plaster has the drawback of keeping light and air from the skin and inducing more muscle atrophy than a simple splint, which permits movement for a few degrees in any direction, sufficient to keep up some muscle tone. It is also heavy, and therefore less good for the general health of a patient who has been so long in bed.'[60]

Once in plaster, Harry was sometimes suspended above a hospital bed. The young trainee nurses (known as probationers) inserted bed pans in the gap between him and the mattress routinely after meals. Instead of toilet paper, his exposed bottom was wiped with tow linen fibre waste.

Early each morning, whatever the weather, a probationer pushed Harry's bed onto the purpose-built covered colonnade outside his ward for his fresh air treatment. Each bed was covered with a tarpaulin when it rained or snowed. Sometimes the snow was a foot deep before it was removed.

A staged photograph of girls taking fresh air treatment at the King Edward VII Memorial Hospital for Crippled Children, c. 1920–39. Licensed from ©Picture Sheffield (Image s07418).

Derek commented: *'I was often on the veranda and even had snow on the bed. It was a different snow to nowadays, it wasn't wet. The nurses just shook it off from time to time. Once I complained of the cold. They put me on the ground and rolled me up like lino. I couldn't get my arms out. I didn't complain any more after that.'*[61]

Harry found it a joy to be outside surrounded by a myriad of trees: lime, larch, birch and Scotch fir, and oak, elm and sycamore.[62] Flat on his back, he could not see much of them, but he loved to listen to their 'rustling as they talked to each other'. Occasionally, a squirrel scampered over his bed.

Rest was believed to be a vital treatment, if it was 'enforced, uninterrupted and prolonged'.[63] The medical view was that 'just lying in bed is not resting ... Resting is done with the mind as well as the body'.[64] Therefore, Harry and the other children were told not to talk to each other. Nor from the moment Harry was admitted to Rivelin was he allowed to feed himself. While he quickly learnt to swallow while flat on his back, he loathed being fed and the aversion stayed with him for life.

Once the TB infection appeared dormant, and the clinical and X-ray signs suggested steady progress of healing, Harry was taken out of the plaster cast.

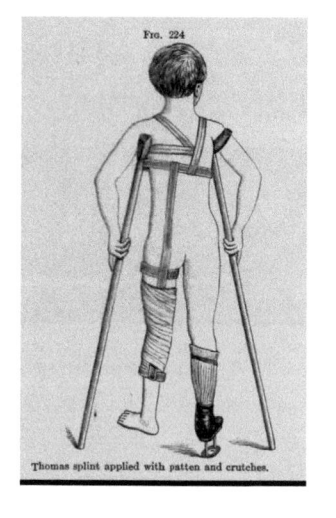

Thomas splint applied with patten and crutches.[65]
From A Treatise on Orthopaedic Surgery by Royal Whitman. Out of copyright.

Children were believed to have recovered when they could fully move their hip (which was rare) or when the remaining bones fused. Staff carefully monitored them to be sure healing had taken place rather than a child being in a temporary dormant stage.[66] It was common for children to suffer multiple relapses.

Treatment was not Harry's parents' only concern. If the hip – or elbow – contained living tubercle bacilli, Harry could die suddenly from tubercular meningitis, a known complication of the infection.[67] Harry remembered with horror the sound of children's screams being smothered when they were given a lumbar puncture without anaesthetic. It was done on the ward, without privacy screens. The procedure was used to diagnose and treat meningitis, but he did not know that at the time and he worried it would be done to him, too.[68] It can only be hoped that May and Harry Senior did not read the newspaper report of an inquest into the death of a boy not quite three years old, who had died of meningitis earlier at Rivelin.[69] Between visits, all they could do was to hope they would not receive a postcard that said Harry was 'seriously ill'.

King Edward VII Hospital. A staged photo showing some boys in bed on the veranda and other boys standing in a plaster Thomas splint, mainly using crutches. The child's unaffected leg was fitted with a patten to stop the child from inadvertently putting weight on the tuberculous joint. One boy has his arm in plaster.
Licensed from ©Picture Sheffield (Image w00567).

3

Psychological Harm

Two-year-old Harry was subject to the will of professionals who, presumably, had his physical welfare at heart, but with whom no emotional bond was tolerated. It was around six weeks before he was allowed a visitor. Most nurses and doctors believed that a quiet child was a happy one, and that parents upset their children by visiting them. Consequently, children were often left to 'settle' before a visit. Reduced visiting also limited the chance that children picked up another infection. Although the hospital gave parents cheap bus tickets, some children still did not see their parents for years at a time due to poverty, work, parental responsibilities, or the inability to travel to the hospital.[70] Harry was fortunate that his family never missed an opportunity to visit.

May and Harry Senior had to accept the hospital's visiting rules: only one close adult relative was allowed to visit for one hour once a month on a Sunday, although this was often cancelled at short notice by post, usually without explanation. No visit could be shared. It is possible May and Harry were grateful to visit at all, as some hospitals, such as the Westminster Infants Hospital, did not allow parental visits at all, and, from 1939, The Hospital for Sick Children, Great Ormond Street, stopped visits from the beginning of January to the end of March.[71] Because Harry was strapped to a tilted frame or in a chest-to-ankle body plaster, his parents could not cuddle him. Gifts of toys, books and comforters were an infection risk, and therefore confiscated. They were not returned, although, years later, when exploring on crutches, Harry recalled seeing such items in a large walk-in cupboard and wondered what happened to them.

It is unlikely May felt welcomed by the senior nursing staff. It was common for working-class parents, particularly mothers, to be blamed for their child's illness, particularly if the disease was stigmatised (as was tuberculosis), linked to poverty or poor nutrition or because of ignorance especially if the parent was working class.[72] Harry's parents may also have believed that their son's inability to see off the tuberculosis infection was inherited.[73] For Harry, losing his mother's care might have felt brutal. But the junior nurses were also traumatised by being forced to ignore their patients' emotional needs.

Pioneering psychiatric social worker and psychoanalyst James Robertson started studying children's separation from their mothers alongside psychiatrist Dr John Bowlby at the Tavistock Clinic in London in 1948. It came too late to benefit Harry, but it can help us understand something of what Harry and others in his situation suffered. Robertson explained infants like Harry cried, rattled the side of their cot, thrashed around, and looked towards any noise which suggested their mother's return. Finally, they just sat desolate, tearful, or deeply silent, but rather than having settled in, they were emotionally overwhelmed and traumatised and did not know why their parents had apparently abandoned them. As Robertson, author of *Separation and the Very Young*, pointed out, 'If a nurse stopped beside a silent toddler, he would usually burst into tears at the human contact and the nurse would be rebuked for "making him unhappy".[74] However, it was the possibility of interaction with someone that cracked the facade and allowed the pent-up longing to break through.[75]

STAGES OF MOTHER–CHILD SEPARATION

Children separated from their mother behaved predictably. Robinson described three stages.

Protest	The child expected a response to their cries. When their mother did not come, the child was visibly upset and would look out for her. According to Robertson, who also visited children at home, if a doctor discharged a child at this stage, he invariably found the 'settled' state in the hospital ward had given way to clinging to the mother, temper tantrums, disturbed sleep, bedwetting, regression and aggression, particularly against the mother as if blaming her.
Despair	When a mother remained absent, the child gave up hope, cried intermittently, without energy, and sounded monotonous. They become withdrawn and quiet and were seen as having 'settled-in'.
Denial and detachment	The child showed more interest in their surroundings and seemed happy, which Robertson named a danger sign. He wrote 'The child cannot tolerate the intensity of distress, he begins to make the best of his situation by repressing his longing for the mother who has failed to meet his needs, particularly his need of her as a person to love and be loved by.'[76]

Denial and detachment (continued)	The child stopped crying or seeking attention. If someone came to their bed, they often lacked the normal reserve around strangers, but this was a sign of desperation. When the mother visited, the child hardly responded, and no longer cried when she left.
Once the child returned home, it could seem as if the child did not want any mothering at all.

Outside of visiting times, two-year-old Harry was 'alone and unsupported to face the fears, frights and hurts of the hospital ward'.[77] He watched the changing faces of the 16- to 18-year-old probationer orthopaedic nurses for clues about this new world. Even when a child was so ill that they needed to be closely monitored, the nurse sat quietly out of sight behind the head of the immobile child, so that they would not make demands. Harry was not part of a group, nor did he make friends in Rivelin. He said, 'I didn't have time for the other boys. They appeared as ignorant and as damaged as I was.'

It was tough for May and dad Harry to find their loving son apparently indifferent. If either parent brought something with them, he did what he could to destroy it before the staff took it away.

Until we collaborated on this book at the end of his life, Harry spoke of the shame he felt about his childhood tantrums, his feelings of aggression, and the overwhelming anger he had felt against his mother. He was relieved to learn these were normal reactions to his trauma.

Robertson explained that the unconscious psychological defences experienced by those who looked after the children were 'so powerful that the kindest of staff could be wholly unaware of the emotional abuse they were practising and colluding in'.[78] Before we condemn, we need to consider that the staff may also have had a very different experience from the supportive and nurturing parenting that we aspire to.

The teenage probationers and student nurses were mainly drawn from working-class and lower-middle-class families and completed their training isolated and far away from home. They were expected to look to the ward sister for the way to behave in this new environment. They were not allowed to comfort or play with the children, not that they had the time to do so. Senior nurses were not usually deliberately unkind. But child development, the understanding of how trauma affects children, and the need of their patients to have strong attachment figures was not understood by hospital staff. Therefore, the opportunity to help Harry cope and mitigate the emotional damage inherent in medical treatment and being taken away from his family was lost. The probationers and senior staff were not aware that these desperate children had serious, unmet emotional needs that could deeply affect their current and future relationships.

Even if May had told her family doctor about Harry's changed personality and challenging behaviour, when Harry had been discharged from hospital, the number of children the local child guidance clinic could treat was limited.

Originating in the USA, child psychology was introduced into the new child guidance clinic, which opened in London in 1927. It was funded by the Commonwealth Fund of New York. Sheffield's child guidance clinic started in 1937, probably supported by the Board of Education.[79] At the clinic, depending on their perceived need, the child met with a psychiatrist, a psychologist, or a psychiatric social worker. One of the clinic's basic ideas was that during each child's emotional and psychological development, any child might experience a period of maladjustment. The fear was that these children would destabilise the family and the wider society so they hardly seem child-focused. While child guidance sought to be a form of preventive medicine promoting children's mental well-being, the clinic in Sheffield focused on children who were 'nervous, insubordinate', had 'intellectual disorders' or were resistant to treatment or cure.[80]

As nurses before them had done, the probationers soon learned they had to dissociate from the extreme distress and the normal attachment-seeking behaviour of their patients. The students' natural empathy became blunted. They became deaf and blinkered so that they could emotionally protect themselves and complete their work. They came to believe that this process was commonplace, necessary and inevitable. Robertson noted they became task-driven and did not treat their patients with the tenderness or empathy they would probably have shown to their child relatives. The nurses' defence against the pain they were surrounded by became stronger over time, and they repressed the feelings that could have enabled them to change how they interacted with their vulnerable patients.

Besides not responding to the children, Robertson noted that the probationers' tasks were broken up so that even at meal-times no one nurse regularly gave a child their food. Nor were children assigned to named nurses. Ward rotation was part of nurse training; there were also staff shortages and always more tasks to be done. The nurses simply did not have the opportunity to build relationships with their patients, even if this was allowed by their superiors.

In Robertson's view, staff ignorance of the emotional development of children, and their fierce psychological defences, protected the experienced staff from their suppressed anxiety about the distress displayed by the children in their care. Because of the nurses' inability to empathise with their suffering, the children were profoundly more affected than they might have been. Even though the later Platt Report of 1959 'advised that parents should have greater access to wards and be allowed to help with the care of their child, institutional resistance and inertia meant that the pace of change was glacial'.[81]

It would be comforting to believe that when Dr Herzog became the medical superintendent at the King Edward VII Hospital in 1952, training and awareness had moved forward so much that Herzog could recognise the suffering of children on the wards, but this was not Harry's experience of constant changes of staff and neighbouring patients in the nearest beds.

Surgeons, too, could be convinced that the children in their care were happy. Dr E.G. Herzog (and his wife) were well liked by Harry. Herzog wrote in 1986: 'In spite of what has been said in recent years, I am convinced that the children at King Edward VII Hospital were very cheerful and happy. This opinion was not based on any preconceived ideas but on the simple observation of what actually went on, on the wards.'[82] It is difficult to believe Dr Herzog spent much time on the wards observing the children's day-to-day life in hospital or understood how different this was from their home life. His probable ignorance also informed the change to visiting hours in 1952:

> I would to this day argue that daily and constant visiting is quite unnecessary in cases of this type. The children are staying long enough to make an adjustment; they get friendly with particular nurses; they form little groups among themselves ... An important factor in maintaining morale was that we had few children under the age of three. Those aged four and five were old enough to realise that there was something wrong with their knee or their hip and the 'nurse and the doctor would make them better'. They did not show any signs of feeling that their parents had abandoned them.[83] (Dr Herzog, 1986)

It is worth considering that many doctors came from middle- and upper-class families and were often educated at boarding school from a young age, and then attended university. It is likely they too experienced attachment injuries when their education separated them from their parents. If so, it would appear they may not have been best placed to understand and advocate for children separated from their parents.

Life was difficult for the nurses, too. They lived in fear of the senior nurses, the matron and the doctors. Although the students had high levels of responsibilities, particularly on night duty, the repressive nurses' homes treated them as if they were children. They had one afternoon off a week, and went to the post office at the end of Rivelin Valley Road where it joins the Manchester Road to post their letters, buy bottles of pop and sweets.[84] The Lancet Commission on Nursing in 1932 concluded that trained nurses should be given substantial pay rises and the probationers should have their hours reviewed.[85] It was also recommended they be given reasonable freedom and privacy befitting adult women. The report commented that all nurses should be relieved of domestic duties, such as keeping the nurses' home clean.[86] By 1937, working hours were limited to 44 per week for those under the age of 16, and 48 for those aged 16 and over, but little else changed.[87]

Throughout the 1950s, James Robertson and his wife Joyce (a psychiatric social worker) continued to advocate for the humane treatment of children in hospitals and institutions in the face of worldwide denial from the professionals.[88]

4

Daily Life in the Hospital

In Rivelin, you were a patient among many.
You were anonymous.

Harry took a while to tune in to what many of the nurses and doctors were saying. He understood the probationers better, as they often came from the working class, even if they were not from his area of Sheffield. Harry and his father spoke in a broad Yorkshire accent, which Harry told me was little changed from Emily Brontë's use of Yorkshire dialect in *Wuthering Heights*.

What was clear to him was that his day started when the night nurse shoved a thermometer into his armpit at 6 am. Silent probationers then brought warm water in a white enamel bowl to each bedside. Each child was thoroughly but quickly washed by a different nurse. Any conversation Harry started was cut short or ignored. Cold water arrived in an enamel mug, along with a wooden toothbrush. The children were always visible. There were no curtains around their beds; there was no privacy whatsoever. Their genitalia were not covered.

When breakfast came with another enamel mug of drinking water, there was no time to linger.

> *We were given three meals a day, as well as elevenses and threes, but I was always hungry. Elevenses was bread and dripping and a mug of hot bitter cocoa. If you were lucky, you got some brown meat jelly, an occasional bit of bacon or crackling in the dripping.*

Harry went on, 'We would see our treatment as third world now, but the hospital had very little money. It was one up from a workhouse and run on a shoestring – and that had been donated.'

The main meal was 'dinner', served at lunchtime. Harry stayed awake after a meal so he could look out for the 'kitchen people', who sometimes came in with leftover food. The cook only came on the ward about once a year. Harry ate everything with relish, including the least favourite dish on the weekly menu – the mildly liver-tasting, chewy tripe and onions, boiled in milk.[89]

While his treatment could be seen as inhumane, Harry's youth was lived in parallel to the growing understanding of child psychology and development. Unfortunately, Harry and his companions would not benefit from the slow recognition of children's emotional needs.

Harry said:

> *Hospital life was organised, but crude. There was nothing to soften it. It was lonely, but I couldn't name the feeling then. You weren't happy. No one would tell you what you were suffering from, or what treatment you could expect. We were institutionalised. The staff ignored the boys, unless they*

misbehaved. The boys weren't very nice to the nurses, either. There were more nurses in the girls' ward. They did more for girls.

Occasionally, without warning, someone new arrived and someone left. You had to do what you were told. In later years, I never did, as a matter of principle, but it was probably a fault.

He added that life was not much better for the medical staff:

Doctors and nurses just had to get on with what they had to do. They had no time for the patient's well-being. It was the routines and practical tasks that mattered. It made their job more difficult if you were obviously homesick.

The routine was mainly to keep infection at bay, 'everything had to be scrubbed constantly', including Harry. Otherwise, the ward was orientated more to the needs of nurses, doctors' rounds and the hospital institution. He said:

Often, on a ward round, Matron had two nurses walking behind her, including the sister for that ward, who would be answering quick-fired questions, which included how the beds were made. The ward sister routinely got quite a lot of stick and were told they hadn't trained the probationers properly, but plaster beds [one where the occupant was in plaster] couldn't be kept up to the usual standard, as the plaster flaked on to the sheets.

> *The sisters kept everything as tight as a drum. But for Matron, it was a case of 'speak when you're spoken to' for the sisters as well. Matron exercised her status and routinely turned on her underlings, who were told how disappointing they were.*

The nursing staff were not allowed to marry. They were isolated in nursing accommodation on site, where they were forced to live according to Matron's rules and timetable. This included when to get up, where and what they ate, and when they went to bed. Their sleeping space and belongings were regularly inspected by more senior staff.

Usually, the children had little direct contact with the sisters. Harry saw them as 'automatons who always walked quickly on silent, rubber-soled shoes'. Eating one's food was strictly enforced. One day, Sister Jones was brought in to force a young Harry to eat his rice pudding. Harry explained, 'I poured it over her head. If I made a fuss, it was always for a purpose. I loved the daily rice pudding, but I couldn't bear being fed and couldn't see why I couldn't feed myself. I could balance my plate or bowl on my chest and use my left hand to feed myself. I got my way in the end.'

The sisters also ruled over the ward-maids. Harry said:

> *Maintenance people were about the place. Every day ward-maids cleaned the corridors, halls, and the wards. All the floors had to be swept, washed with a mop and bucket, dried and polished. The maids wouldn't dream of talking to a patient. While the children had no status, the ward-maids had even less. They were usually*

> *recruited from the workhouse and lived in. Some of them seemed low in intelligence; another might have a harelip or be volatile. Like the nursing staff, they were overworked. There was a lot to do and never enough people to do it.*

Derek, who was on the boys' ward while Harry was with the younger ones, received a little attention from a ward-maid. In an interview, he said, *'There was not much love there. One of the cleaners used to give me a kiss occasionally.'* [90]

Being a hospital for children with tuberculosis meant the windows and doors were always open, whatever the season or the weather. There was no heating in any of the buildings on site.

The young nurses in charge of the ward at night had their main meal in the middle of their shift. Harry learned that if he slept during the day, and was awake at night, the homesick young women would often bring him a meal and stay and talk for a few minutes. He said that 'during the day they had no time for you, at night you were an individual. Those conversations saved my sanity. They were bright, curious, can-do people. They weren't interested in gossip or rumour, only in concrete things. I couldn't get enough of their company.'

Harry depended on the young women responsible for his physical well-being, but from an early age he refused to accept he had no autonomy. Contrary to some others on his ward, who appeared to believe they could do nothing to improve their circumstances, Harry reacted differently to his medically sanctioned removal from his family. Maybe this was because he started with a strong, healthy attachment to his mother and so he was more able to cope with adversity.[91] Whatever protected him, rather than stay mired in the shame and pessimism common to traumatised children, he became acutely observant and learned to (mostly) step back from the overwhelming feelings of aggression and anger which, if he expressed them, did not elicit the love, care and attention he craved. Without an emotional connection to those around him, Harry felt separate from everyone. 'I was against the rest of the world and fought to make sense of it.'

As Harry grew older, he worked out the best way to get what he needed. For example, he studied which bed position brought a child the most attention and often found a way to be the one occupying it. However, the advantage did not always last long as the beds were moved around regularly. On his return to the hospital as an adult, he was told this was so that the children did not get too attached to their neighbour, or to hide that someone was 'going downhill', or to make it easier for the staff to stop someone moving around in their bed.

> *I questioned everything. I needed to understand. We weren't told anything. Everything seemed random. There was no content to conversation, including what was said on the doctor's rounds. I thought it was just children the staff didn't talk to, but later, my parents told me they were told nothing meaningful either. I had to make sense of every damned thing. Last time that was done, so this time it might be like that? Why are you doing that? I must have been a pain, unless I was on one-to-one.*

Despite being unable to sit up, and with one arm in plaster, Harry sought ways to be something other than a helpless child in bed with a powerless and bleak existence. He continually looked for ways to get around the strict dos and don'ts of institutional life, where questions such as 'Please, can I …?' were always met with 'No'. Finding ways to loosen the restraints of ward life enabled him to do things that would not normally be sanctioned. For example, each week, hundreds of bandages were boiled to be reused. Once washed, they were twisted together and left to dry. It was the 16- to 18-year-old probationers' responsibility during their off-duty time to unravel and roll them, ready to be used again. Harry asked if he could do it. He was no longer invisible; he became the one that could roll bandages faster and neater than anyone else. Each time he returned to the hospital after a spell at home, Harry took on the job.

Once you know the rules, you can try to find a way around them or use them to your advantage.

Harry never knew if an attempt to change something would have a pay-off or what information might come out of it, but he deliberately used everything he could to 'build on his possibilities and widen his horizons'. He said, 'It was a lesson for life.'

Provoked by the deprivation and the extreme social isolation, he formed a deep connection to the natural world as he lay sheltered by the trees that surrounded him. Whatever the season or the weather, Harry always volunteered to be out on the veranda. Outside, Harry saw the ever-changing colour of the sky and the dense deciduous trees and felt the air move across his face. He listened to the birds and watched them swoop overhead. He heard the off-duty nurses laughing on the tennis court and the thwack of a ball against a racket, and listened out for the young foxes' 'ack-ack' sound as they played. At night, there were the owls and the bats to listen out for. When he spent the nights outside, he was often the only child out there, especially when it got colder, but away from the ward and the sisters, the probationers seemed more human.

A nurse shivering in her uniform and woollen cape would repeatedly come out to my bed, her arms wrapped around a couple of earthenware hot water bottles, to take away a couple of cold ones. I would ask her questions. Why she'd left home or how difficult her brothers were. I got to know all the probationers well.

Outside the boys' ward, King Edward VII Hospital, 1942.
Licensed from ©Picture Sheffield (Image w00567).

The boys might be flat on their backs, but they were still boys. Harry talked of 'chuckers' – rolls of paper or a magazine tied in the middle and swung like a lasso.

I used them to threaten boys who were annoying me on the ward. To tie up the magazines, I got hold of very good garden fibre used to tie up plants. Expensive glossy magazines were as effective as a steel tube. You then needed a strong rope to tie on to the magazine strong enough to pull a bed.

I would throw a rope with a rolled mag at the end of it and threaten to pull his bed towards me. He was helpless then. We were all helpless, really. I was taking him from his safe place, and he didn't know what would happen, so he would decide to 'shut up' after all. I never lost. I'm not proud. I was not a nice child.

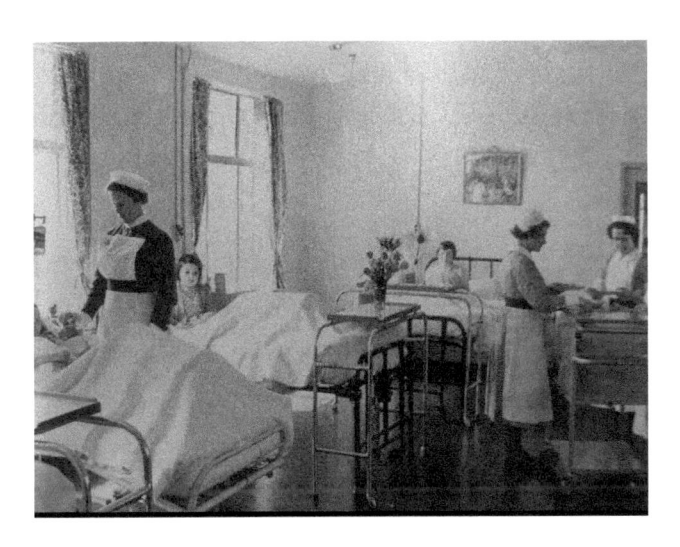

'Dinner Time in Ward D', King Edward VII Hospital. Although this is a girls' ward, it shows how a rolled magazine could hook around the bars of a bed to move it.[92]

Daily Life in the Hospital

My playground was in my head. Thinking was my freedom. In my head, there were no limitations. The other boys only wanted a laugh. Silly talk, nothing of substance. There was no information. I couldn't bear it. Thank God for my mother, I couldn't have a conversation with her without thinking.

Some of his peers were taken for operations in the on-site theatre. Although doctors thought Harry should not be treated surgically as a child, they did not tell him, so he lived in fear that it would be his turn next.

Harry had vivid memories of being put in the full body plaster. Apart from when he was cleaned, it was the only time he was touched. He talked of being suspended from a metal frame at the mercy of a senior nurse who seemed to enjoy her power over her charges. He spoke of feeling vulnerable, but explained why this feeling became so much more acute when it came time to take the plaster off. Replastering had to be done every two to four months as he grew, but its removal meant suspension again, this time with the 'sadist' nurse sawing the plaster off with a rotating saw. There was nothing to stop the blade from slicing into Harry's flesh, and the plaster coming off always meant long, painful wounds. These were an infection risk, and the cuts itched unmercifully once the new plaster was back on and the skin started to heal. When he could, Harry hid a knitting needle, so when no one was watching he would slide it into the cast and try to relieve some of the itching.

> *The removal of the plaster casts was horrendous. First, six-foot shears were pushed down between my flesh and the full cast. I'd grown, so they had little room to work in, but it had to come off. So, they usually had to use the circular saw. It was not until after the war that the hospital began using something that had protected soldiers' flesh.*

Derek told me he vividly recalled his fear of the staff removing his first plaster cast, *'I saw these bloody great croppers coming toward me ... Christ, what's going on here?'* [93] Sadly for Harry and fellow patients, plastic surgeon Homer Hartman Stryker would not invent the plaster cast cutter until 1947. This sawblade vibrated rather than rotated, so the skin could withstand contact, usually without cuts to the flesh.

Although Harry looked forward to moving his body again, he said:

> *Exposure was awful. I didn't have any protection anymore. The air felt odd on my newly exposed skin. I had no muscles to speak of. My legs were as thin as sticks. I couldn't move a foot or a toe to stop someone from rolling me on to the board, which fitted on to the top of the bath. But the dead skin had to be scrubbed off. Every touch and movement felt violent. If the plaster had been taken off because of a sore, it was treated with mentholated spirit. It felt as if it was burning into my soul.* [94]

Derek told me, 'When I put my hand down the plaster, there were so much dead skin it were like snow.'[95]

If the plaster had been removed to treat a sore, Harry would be put back into plaster straight away. At other times:

> *A nurse would arrive and tell me I was getting up, but first I had to learn to walk. As I had been lying horizontally for so long, I had to get accustomed to being upright. Each morning, for a little longer each day, I was put in a wooden frame, which was then fastened to the foot of the bed to hold it, and me, upright. It didn't feel good. When I was young, after a few days of this treatment, one probationer stood me on her feet, held my hands and walked me around. I couldn't straighten my right arm, so we were off-balance to start with. It felt awful. I felt I was going to fall. After I had been fitted with a made-to-measure brace by Old Tom, I was given my crutches and left to work out how to balance by myself.*

Aluminium splints, the walking caliper, the spine and hip frames, and the posterior spinal supports were essential in orthopaedic practice to treat and correct physical injuries and deformities in children.

After Harry's cast was taken off, he was fitted with an ambulatory splint, and allowed to stand on his healthy right leg. The splint kept the hip joint immobile.

Derek said, 'When I came out of plaster, Old Tom made me splints made with a steel strut and straps like a cowboy, fastened on the thigh. I had another two around the waist.'[96] Occasionally, when Harry was mobile, he sneaked off to see Tom in the splint-maker's workshop. It was a small wooden construction in Coppice Wood, behind the main buildings.[97] He said:

> *It wasn't easy to keep my balance and get up the steep steps on crutches, but I refused to be beaten. I knew I would learn something if I made the effort.*

The splint-maker's workshop in Coppice Wood behind the King Edward VII Orthopaedic Hospital, formerly the King Edward VII Memorial Hospital for Crippled Children.[98]

'Old Tom' (Tom Bradley) was 'skilful, conscientious and devoted to the hospital'.[99] He worked in wood, metal and leather, and made Jones abduction frames and crutches, mounted plaster beds, surgical corsets, and bespoke shoe alterations.[100] Dr Herzog wrote about how Tom went with him to other orthopaedic hospitals, financed by the hospital management committee, and was always on the lookout for new ideas he could incorporate into his designs. Tom's seemingly minor changes made an enormous difference to the user. Harry said Tom never let on to the staff that he 'was somewhere where he had no business to be'.

On three days a week, if Harry and his fellow (primarily working-class) patients were considered well enough, occupational therapists would encourage them to take up basic embroidery, needlework and artificial flower-making. This activity gave the children, who, apart from the TB in their bones, were often otherwise well, an outlet that also raised much-needed funds for the hospital. Most of the boys refused to take part in such female-orientated occupations. For Harry, 'anything was better than nothing', although the 'woeful' standard of what was produced upset him.

By the time Harry was 11 years old, he had become a smoker. He was not the only child who smoked, and most of the adults around him did, too. Harry collected as many cigarette packets as he could get hold of and cut them into four strips to make origami dogs to sell. Artificial flowers made with elaborate copper wiring were also popular. The occupational therapists gave out ladies' cotton or woollen stockings, which had been dyed different colours, and he turned them into dog shapes with embroidered faces. Cardboard cases were given to the children, too. These Harry embroidered with a different motif on the front, creating collectable sets.

For many years, Harry dreamed of escaping from the hospital. He built up a map of the site in his head and noted what each building was used for. He asked questions about how people got to the hospital, and what time the buses arrived and left the bus stop, and listened out for visitors sharing their experiences of travelling there. Snippets about anything were filed away.

One might think that the limited visiting meant Harry's parents spent the whole time they were at the hospital at their son's bedside. However, as well as visiting Harry, they both befriended children who had no visitors, either because their parents could not get away or they did not live near enough to visit. Harry told me he understood, and explained there was nothing to be said anyway, beyond: 'How are you?', 'Same as last time?', 'What are they doing with you?', 'Have you seen the doctor?', 'When are you coming home?' The unvarying script bored all of them. They could change nothing and little happened out of the usual routine in the hospital. On Harry's part he might have agreed with Betty MacDonald, an American tuberculosis patient, who observed, 'When the family told me tales of happenings at home, I found them interesting but without strength, like talk about people long dead.'[101]

Even Christmas brought little that Harry wanted to talk about.

Some years there would be Christmas carols if there was a musical nurse who liked to show off, but it was not celebratory. It was something done to you, rather than for you.

Harry Senior and May missed very few visits over the years, but Harry was delighted to see his paternal Uncle George when he took their place. George was 12 years younger than his father.

He was rare in the family. Perhaps because his own son had life-affecting osteomyelitis after falling down the stairs at 18 months old, kindly George had time for Harry, listened to him and spoke to him of things that 'mattered'.[102] It was a lifelong regret that Harry did not see him often and get to know his youngest uncle better, but George's positive outlook left a deep impression.

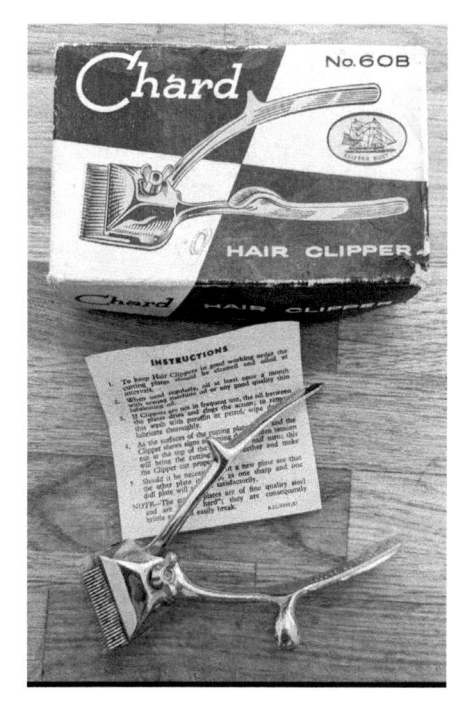

While occasional hairdressers visited the women and girls, the boys' hair was often left uncut.[103] The boys found their longer hair shameful. Parents were not allowed to cut it but, in his late teens, Harry convinced his mother to bring in hand clippers for him.

An example of hair clippers, Chard No. 608.
In the author's collection.

The clippers had two rows of sharp teeth. At rest, those teeth were stationary, and you could move it up the scalp and, as you went forward, your hair went between the teeth. You could alter the length. By cutting very close at a tilt you could get a smooth short back and sides. They were hard to use, but I got a stronger left hand from using them.

However, personal items were against the rules, and the clippers were not easily hidden. Harry found the best way was to keep them moving around the ward. In return for their use, he negotiated for non-sugar treats and contraband that other children's parents smuggled in. Eventually, the clippers were found and confiscated, but it was a small triumph.

General visitors included an incongruous church group who turned up, sang for a little while and left without talking to any of the children. Another group 'sang folk songs at us'. Harry was frustrated he could not get a copy of the book they were singing from as he wanted to match the words he heard with what appeared on the page. Sea shanties, and, strangely, drinking songs, were included in their repertoire.

Words and their meaning were important to Harry, so it is unsurprising he remembered one song all his life: the 18th-century satirical song 'The Vicar of Bray'. It told the story of a vicar appointed during Henry VIII's reign who changed his faith to Catholic when Mary I was on the throne and back to Protestant when Elizabeth I succeeded. It would be the first piece he learnt on the violin aged around 14 years old.

The Vicar of Bray
In good King Charles's golden days,
When loyalty no harm meant,
A zealous High Churchman was I,
And so I got preferment;
To teach my flock I never miss'd,
Kings were by God appointed,

And damn'd are those that do resist,
Or touch the Lord's anointed.

As he grew older, the children were sometimes allowed to sing. The songs went from ward to ward with the patients. Others were introduced by newly admitted patients and were added to the general repertoire. One of the many songs Harry sang to his own children in the 1970s when driving on family motor-caravanning holidays was this one:

Mother, mother, fetch me home,
From this convalescence home.
I've been here a year or two,
Now I want to come to you.
Here comes the doctor every morning,
Takes your hand and says 'good morning'
'Are you better, are you worse?
Please, can you tell me where's your nurse?'
Here comes a nurse with a red-hot poultice,
Slaps it on and takes no notice.
'Agh!' says the patient, 'that's too hot.'
'Ah' says the nurse, 'I'm sure it's not.'
Goodbye to Dr Pattison,
and all the patients, too.
Goodbye to dear old Rivelin and
Jolly old matron, too.

This song, with lyrics tweaked to fit, was sung by children in institutions all around the country from at least the early 1900s.

Harry said the children were often told 'Soon you'll be back home.' He commented:

I think it was meant to give us hope, but it was another lie. I didn't want to go home. I didn't have friends to return to. At least in the hospital, I knew the rules.

PART TWO

Timeline

DATE	AGE	EVENT
3 Sept. 1939	4	Britain declares War on Germany
3 Sept. 1939	4	Harry discharged from King Edward VII Memorial Hospital for Crippled Children
29 Sept. 1939	4	National Register data collection – Harry recorded at 44 Butterthwaite Road
1 Oct. 1939	4	Started at Beck Road Council School, Beck Road, Shiregreen
1 July 1940	5	Occupation of Guernsey and Jersey
6 July 1940	5	Admitted to King Edward VII Memorial Hospital for Crippled Children
16 July 1940	5	Hitler warns of preparation to invade Great Britain
12–13 Dec. 1940	6	First night of Sheffield Blitz
15–16 Dec. 1940	6	Second night of Sheffield Blitz
16 Aug. 1941	6	Discharged from King Edward VII Memorial Hospital for Crippled Children
Oct. 1941	6	Admission to the Home for Idiots and Imbeciles
2 Feb. 1942	7	Enrolled Hartley Brook School Junior department

DATE	AGE	EVENT
Nov. 1943	8	Sister born
8 Sept. 1944	9	Removed from the register of Hartley Brook School Junior department
16 Sept. 1944	9	Admitted to King Edward VII Memorial Hospital for Crippled Children
20 Nov. 1944	9	Antibiotic streptomycin first administered to critically ill TB patient, USA
9 Dec. 1944	10	Discharged from King Edward VII Memorial Hospital for Crippled Children
8 May 1945	10	Victory in Europe Day
9 May 1945	10	Street Party Butterthwaite Road

5

Discharge on the Outbreak of War

In the lead-up to the Second World War, there was an enormous government campaign to recruit volunteers and 'to cement in Britain the notion that any future conflict would represent a "people's war" in which each citizen would contribute an equal share towards victory'.[104] Appeals appeared in newspapers, posters, leaflets, films, newsreels and radio broadcasts, so there is no doubt volunteering would have been on Harry Senior's mind. It is likely that Harry and May had tuned in to the Prime Minister's broadcast on national service at 9.25 pm on Monday 23 January 1939.[105] Neville Chamberlain told listeners, 'It is for you to show the world what a free people is prepared to do in defence of their liberties and the ideals in which they believe.'[106] Newspapers also encouraged their readers to undertake national service. 'It was the duty of every man and woman who was capable of undertaking some national service to rally to the appeal which Sheffield was now making.'[107] Men were told to join up to defend their family and protect their home. Those out of work because of the economic depression were expected to sign up for full-time employment, although less than a third of recruits were anticipated to be paid full-timers.[108] In January, Chamberlain also wrote a letter to the nation published in a 48-page guide titled *National Service*,[109] which was delivered to every household in

Britain.[110] Chamberlain's main message was on page 1: 'The desire of all of us is to live at peace with our neighbours. But to ensure peace, we must be strong. The country needs your service and you are anxious to play your part. This guide will point the way. I ask you to read it carefully and to decide how you can help.' May would have presumably understood she was contributing by looking after Harry.

A foreword by Sir John Anderson, MP, laid out the government's needs and invited people to judge what service they could give. It stressed, 'You may already be engaged in work vital to the country's security which is itself national service,' but pointed out, 'there may be cases where part-time duties, for example in air raid precautions, would not interfere with a man's usual occupation.' The booklet explained training for new duties was necessary in case of emergency and listed the civilian services needed. Stapled into the middle of the booklet were two postage-paid application forms.

In May 1939, Sheffield's mayor broadcasted an appeal seen in cinemas. By the end of July, 60 million leaflets were also delivered to households.[111] Harry Senior volunteered part-time with the Auxiliary Fire Service, later the National Fire Service (AFS/NFS).

The National Service Guide booklet carried this appeal for AFS recruits: Large numbers of recruits are wanted for the Auxiliary Fire Service. The functions of this service are:

- To augment the public fire brigade in an emergency by completing the crews for additional firefighting appliances.

- To man the appliances brought into use in an emergency at the auxiliary fire stations.
- To provide crews for the patrol units equipped with trailer pumps.
- To provide drivers of lorries, vans and cars, watch room attendants, telephonists, and staff for various fire stations and miscellaneous duties.

Melton Tunic. The tunic is double-breasted and made of wool with brass buttons. The patch denotes that this example is from the Brighton area.
With the kind permission of the National Emergency Services Museum.

National Fire Service patent great coat. It was never used, but was created as an example. It is made of wool with chrome buttons with the patent tag still attached.
With the kind permission of the National Emergency Services Museum.

Discharge on the Outbreak of War

A Brodie helmet, also called a Tommy helmet. It is khaki with a wide red band, which indicates the rank of Company Officer. You may be able to see that there were once two thin bands, for a section officer. The number 7 denotes that the division was Derby.
With the kind permission of the National Emergency Services Museum.

National Fire Service peak cap. It has a red crown band with the NFS badge at the front. The cap is wool with a wool visor.
With the kind permission of the National Emergency Services Museum.

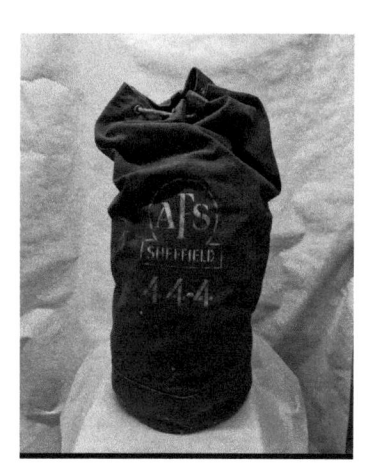

Auxiliary Fire Service kit bag. The AFS was a civilian volunteer service that was later merged with the local authority fire service to become the National Fire Service. The 444 is likely a Sheffield fire station. The owner of this kit bag went on to join the NFS. The bag is grey with a cord tie.
With the kind permission of the National Emergency Services Museum.

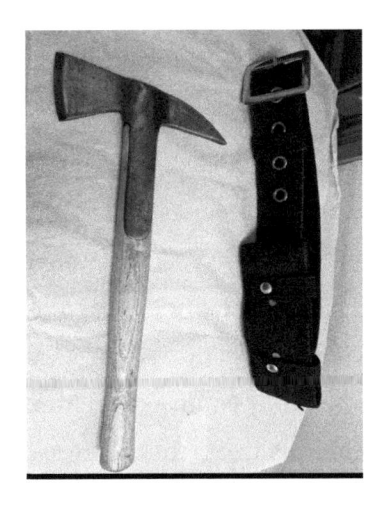

An Auxiliary Fire Service axe and belt. The axe and belt belonged to the same owner as the AFS kit bag. The belt is canvas with stud buttons; the axe has a wooden handle. The belt would also have had a thin coil of rope. These were likely issued to this person when they joined the AFS and would have continued in use after the merger with the NFS. The NFS also had leather belts with black-handled axes.
With the kind permission of the National Emergency Services Museum.

Harry's first visit home, at the outbreak of the Second World War, was probably his most difficult.[112] While the staff had occasionally referred to his leaving, the actual decision to send him back to his family was a shock. He did not know what to expect of life outside the hospital. The still images in his head belonged to his two-and-a-half-year-old self, rather than the nearly five-year-old he was now.

> *I had a picture of each room and the garden, but it was a physical shock when I arrived. It was not as I had thought it would be. I was a stranger in a strange place. Every time I was let out of Rivelin, I had to relearn and manage different circumstances that I didn't understand.*

There was no family suggestion of Harry being evacuated when he was discharged, possibly because he needed to be near the King Edward VII Hospital when his hip pain started bothering him again, or maybe his parents refused to let him go. Whatever the

Discharge on the Outbreak of War

reason Harry stayed, Sheffield saw only 15 per cent of its children evacuated.[113]

Clutching his gas mask that smelt of rubber, Harry was taken to Butterthwaite Road by ambulance with a volunteer escort on the day Britain and France declared war on Germany: 3 September 1939.[114] It would appear the doctors released as many children as they could before wounded soldiers arrived in England. A postcard was sent to Harry's parents to tell them when they could expect him.

Each time he went home, he found his image of the house was out of date. Rooms had been redecorated, new linoleum or carpet put down. Plants had grown, moved or been changed. On the hospital veranda, Harry had been surrounded by nature. Now, from a bedroom window, he watched the industrial chimneys billowing metallic-tasting smoke and struggled to breathe in the thick yellow smog. For a while, Harry had to go to bed and was not to bear weight. Like Derek, he remembered his splints ruining his bed sheets.

Harry was allowed to play with toys again, but his blocks, ride-on car and favourite stuffed toys had vanished. Later, his Dinky cars, Meccano set, the aeroplane and hangar, and his 'fabulous' heavy train set, which he could hardly pick up or wind because it was so stiff, would also disappear. He explained:

> *In working-class homes nothing unused was kept if it could be sold on, but I didn't know that. My parents tried to make up for my losing my toys, but I didn't want to know. They took me to a toy shop, but I wasn't interested in new ones. Thoughts were my toys.*

According to the detailed studies recounted in *Separation and the Very Young*, it was common for youngsters released from hospital to go through a period of 'marked anxiety and irritability' when they got home.[115] Temper tantrums, bedwetting, incontinence and a fear of further abandonment were the norm. Children home from the hospital often slept badly. Some sought cuddles from their mothers, their main carers, but the contact often ended in the children biting, hitting or scratching them.

In his book, Robertson described a three-and-a-half-year-old child who was discharged. Typically, the youngster was no longer cuddly and squirmed out of her mother's arms. 'She did not fit into the reciprocity of family life. She was self-centred, not selfish but intent on looking after herself; ... her needs had not been met by others, and now she had no expectation of being looked after by her parents.'[116] This description tallies with Harry's experience. When I interviewed Derek, he told me that when he came out after 18 months in Rivelin, *'People always said I was different to anyone else. Hospital changed my character. I couldn't show my feelings. I don't get flustered, don't panic. I seem calm. Some people saw me as cold. It's not that I don't feel. I feel it inside, but I can't show it. I'm not good at showing my feelings.'*[117]

Like Derek, Harry was irrevocably changed. To his lifelong regret, Harry struggled at first to return any family feelings. He did not know this was a normal reaction to his hospitalisation. He said:

Minimising contact between parents and child left us a brick wall to get over each time I came out. Home also felt small and claustrophobic. I wanted none of it. It's not that they were anything but kind and supportive, but they didn't know what to do with me, nor I them.

Many children became fearful of reminders of the hospital such as white overalls. Throughout his life, Harry detested all-white rooms, or having someone put something in his mouth (a shuddering reminder of being fed in the hospital). As if the overwhelming kaleidoscope of emotions was not enough for a five-year-old to handle, Harry came out of Rivelin when the country was at war. He said he knew his parents could not keep him safe.

While he was out and about with his mother, Harry discovered that trenches had been dug in the parks, and anti-aircraft guns and searchlights had been set up around the city.[118] Fifty Anderson shelters were set up on recreation grounds and in parks as demonstration models for the public.[119] Despite the shelter being delivered free to families with an income of less than £250 a year in the run-up to, and at the beginning of, the war the Drabbles' shared a neighbour's shelter. (Did May believe her son would be in hospital, and decide she did not want to be alone when Harry Senior was at work?)

Harry Senior may have helped dig in the neighbours shelter, which was 6 feet tall, 6.5 feet long, and 4.5 feet wide, and positioned 4 feet underground. Sandbags surrounded the entrance. It was recommended the arched roofs be covered with a layer of soil, and many people later planted their shelter with shallow-rooted vegetables such as cabbages, marrows, spinach, leeks and shallots.

Instead of an Anderson shelter, the local authority delivered a table shelter (later renamed a Morrison shelter) to 44 Butterthwaite

Road. The government envisaged that people would sleep inside the reinforced cage, which had been designed to withstand a house collapsing on it. May was relieved that Harry Senior was in a reserved occupation as an assistant steel roller.[120] It did not take him long to use the three tools that were supplied with the pack to put together the 359 parts in the sitting room. Once constructed, it measured 6.5 feet long, 4 feet wide and 2.5 feet high, with welded wire mesh sides and a metal floor. Harry Senior tucked it into the corner of the sitting room by the window furthest from the front door. Harry Junior escaped into it when he 'wanted to think'. Workmen painted a white 'T' on the house wall next to the front door, to alert rescue crews to its presence.

A couple sleeping in a Morrison shelter during the Second World War.
The Ministry of Information Photo Division Photographer, public domain.

Before the war, Britain imported two-thirds of its food – including half of the country's meat and most of its onions, cheese, sugar, fruit (including tomatoes) and wheat. German U-boats tried to sink as many of Britain's supply ships as possible. As a result, fewer supplies were delivered. The government was worried that there would be serious shortages, so rationing was introduced in the hope that everyone would have access to their fair share of essential foods. By November 1939, the government had organised the postal delivery of the first of half a million ration books.[121] The rationing of meat, cheese, tea and butter started on 8 January 1940.

That month Prime Minister Winston Churchill said of rationing:

> We are embarking upon a widespread system of rationing. That is not because there is a danger of famine or because the Navy has not done its part in keeping open the oceans, the seas and the harbours. We are rationing ourselves because we wish to save every ton of imports, to increase our output of munitions, and to maintain and extend our export trade, thus gaining the foreign credits wherewith to buy more munitions and more materials of war, in order that the whole life-energy of the British nation and of the British Empire, and of our Allies, may be directed to the last ounce, to the last inch, to the task we have in hand. This is no time for ease and comfort. It is the time to dare and endure. That is why we are rationing ourselves, even while our resources are expanding. That is why we mean to regulate every ton that is carried across the sea and make sure that it is carried solely for the purpose of victory.[122]

Food rations

Item	Maximum level	Minimum level	April 1945
Bacon and ham	8 oz (227 g)	4 oz (113 g)	4 oz (113 g)
Sugar	16 oz (454 g)	8 oz (227 g)	8 oz (227 g)
Loose tea	4 oz (113 g)	2 oz (57 g)	2 oz (57 g)
Meat	1 s. 2d.	1 s	1s. 2c. (equivalent to £3.18 in 2023[35])
Cheese	8 oz (227 g)	1 oz (28 g)	2 oz (57 g) Vegetarians were allowed an extra 3 oz (85 g) cheese[36]
Preserves	1 lb (0.45 kg) per month 2 lb (0.91 kg) marmalade	8 oz (227 g) per month	2 lb (C.91 kg) marmalade or 1 lb (0.45 kg) preserve or 1 lb (0.45 kg) sugar
Butter	8 oz (227 g)	2 oz (57 g)	2 oz (57 g)
Margarine	12 oz (340 g)	4 oz (113 g)	4 oz (113 g)
Lard	3 oz (85 g)	2 oz (57 g)	2 oz (57 g)
Sweets	16 oz (454 g) per month	8 oz (227 g) per month	12 oz (340 g) per month

Weekly adult food rations during the war.[123]

Food rationing in the United Kingdom began in January, 1940 with butter, bacon and sugar. Meat was first rationed in March, 1940; margarine, cooking fat and tea in July, 1940 and cheese in May, 1941. Preserves were rationed from March, 1941 to December, 1948. A special distribution scheme for eggs was started in June, 1941 and a similar one for milk in October, 1941. The distribution of a wide variety of other important foods is controlled through the points rationing scheme which was introduced in December, 1941. The personal points scheme covering chocolate and sweets started in July, 1942 and ended in April, 1949. Bread, which was first rationed in July, 1946 was de-rationed in July, 1948, but the offtake of flour from the mills is still restricted. The special distribution scheme for potatoes which was introduced in November, 1947 was disbanded in April, 1948. Soap rationing, which is also undertaken by the Ministry, started in February, 1942.

Extract from 'Our Food Today', No. 1 Ministry of Food Rationing in the United Kingdom, page 1.

By August 1942, all food was being rationed apart from vegetables and bread, which were in short supply. Ration amounts fluctuated throughout the war as supply levels rose and fell according to shipping losses from U-boat action, domestic agricultural output and the needs of the military.[124] People bought tinned food, rice and cereal through a points system, using their allowance of 16, and later 20, points per month, depending on the availability of supplies.

FOOD RATIONS, JANUARY 1940

Shoppers were given 16 coupons per month, which would allow them to buy:

- Rice: 8 coupons
- Sardines: 2 coupons
- Sultanas: 8 coupons
- Skimmed milk: 5 coupons
- Currants: 16 coupons
- Baked beans: 2 coupons
- Biscuits (dry): 2 coupons
- Biscuits (sweet): 4 coupons
- Herrings: 2 coupons
- Stewed steak: 20 coupons
- Rolled oats: 2 coupons
- Sausage-meat: 12 coupons
- Best red salmon: 32 coupons per small tin[125]

Harry said:

One good thing about being home was I could eat as much as I wanted, but I never put on much weight.

Meanwhile, Harry's mother continued to dose Harry with vitamins and cod liver oil at home. He said he did not mind the oily substance, but mentioned that the concentrated orange was an acquired taste. Under rationing, a four-year-old was entitled to three pints of milk a week (with an additional half pint when the child turned five years old). I expect May now knew to boil the milk before giving it to Harry. Was it difficult to get him to drink it? She might have hid it in porridge, thick vegetable soups or, when she had eggs, presented it as a treat in Yorkshire pudding, custard or rice pudding.

Sheffield was a mass producer of weapons and ammunition, so it was expected to be targeted by bombers, particularly as, at the beginning of the war, Hadfields Steelworks was the only place in Britain capable of producing 18-inch armour-piercing shells.[126] The city's English Steel Corporation Vickers was also vulnerable, as it started out with the only 15-ton drop hammer in the country and churned out the Rolls-Royce Merlin engines used to power Spitfire aircraft. Vickers operated seven days a week, in 16-hour shifts, and made 168 crankshafts every day for Spitfire and Hurricane aircraft and the Lancaster bomber.[127] Sheffield's steelworks produced 872 Matilda tanks, 515 Churchill tanks and over 116,000 tank components.[128]

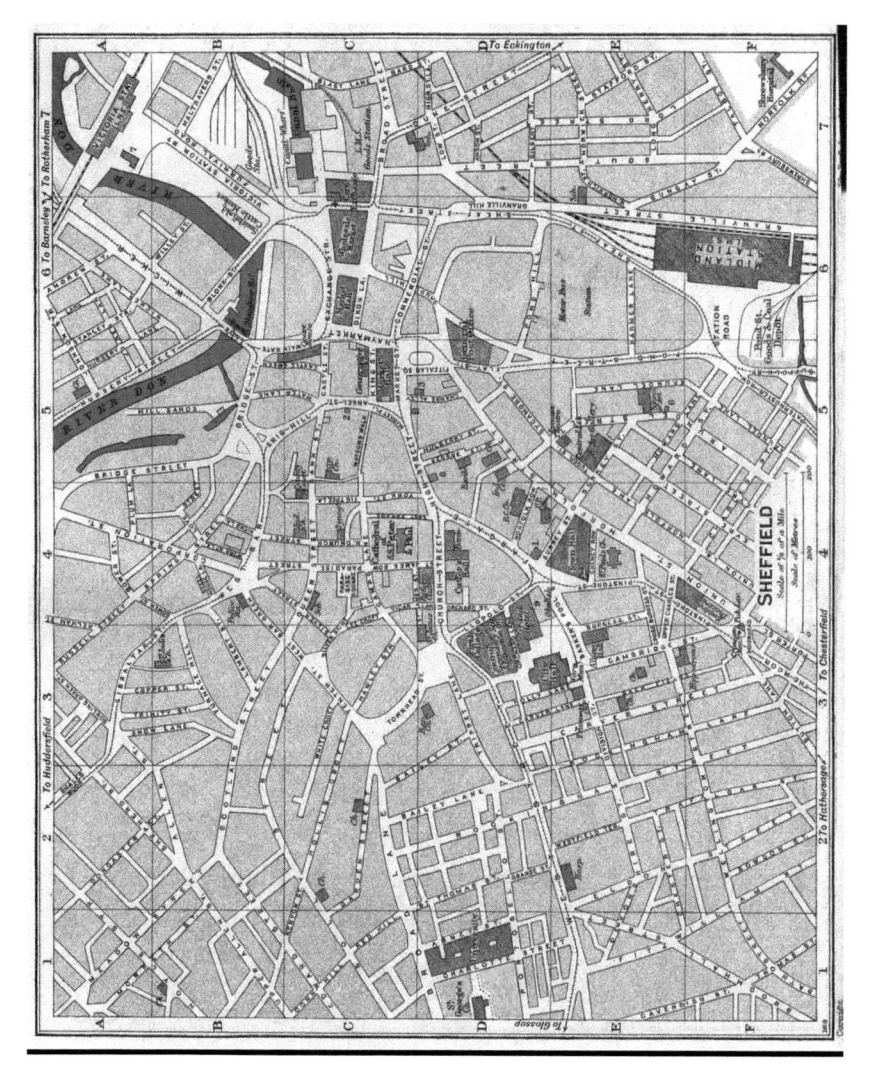

Sheffield Town Plan 1939, Licensed Image Alamy GK3WA7.

Harry knew his father was employed in the steelworks, Samuel Osborn & Co., at the Clyde Steelworks site, 44–46 the Wicker, and had been since leaving school aged 12. Listening to so much talk around him, was he aware that his father's workplace was a likely target for the German Air Force (the **Luftwaffe**)?

On 20 November 1939 Harry heard the first air raid wail its warning, and on 10 December Sheffield's 36 air raid sirens were tested.[129] When the siren sounded, did May pick up a prepacked bag and head to her near neighbour's shelter? She probably took an old metal biscuit tin holding important certificates, the rent book, insurance documents, photographs and other precious documents. If she had hot water, she could have made a flask of tea and grabbed any homemade biscuits or plain cake. She might have hung her knitting and crochet bag around Harry's neck, along with his gas mask, as on crutches, he could carry nothing. May passed everything she'd packed to her neighbour and then entered the Anderson shelter backwards, feeling for the small wooden steps.[130] Did Harry slither backwards on his stomach to be guided by his mum? The shelter was cold, damp and earthy. It could feel claustrophobic, but now her son was home, May felt sure it was the best place he could be when the bombing started.

From the spring of 1940, Harry Senior increased his usual fruit and vegetable production. That year he planted edible French marigolds near the beans, marrows and tomatoes, sunflowers with the potatoes, geraniums with the cabbages, and cauliflower, radishes and edible nasturtiums next to sprouts and beans. Leeks and carrots were planted near the lavender. This companion planting helped with germination and managing pests, but both Harry and May had a fondness for flowers. Harry also grew peas, pole and bush beans, parsnips, onions, lettuce, spring onions/scallions and rhubarb. However, his onions had to be grown from seed – which was in short supply. Neighbours who were 'digging for victory' and breaking new ground would have had disappointing onion crops for the first year or two, because onions need well-cultivated soil to grow well. Onions were so hard to get that they were a welcome gift or a popular prize.

One moonlit night, Harry remembered being in the Anderson shelter when enemy planes flew overhead. He saw his dad, silhouetted against the sky, in his shirt sleeves, in the shelter's doorway. He held a large enamel mug of tea, topped up with whisky. Harry said later:

In that moment, I felt as if Dad was guarding me and I was safe. I didn't know any better and thought the planes were thrilling.

While Harry Senior was at the steelworks, training and volunteering for the AFS and growing the family's fruit and vegetables, May and Harry Junior were working out how to manage their daily lives. May was slight and under five feet in height, and the daily shop was a physical struggle. Harry could not bend in the middle, so his father found an old carriage pram and extended it with a length of board for him to lie on and fixed a shallow wooden crate under it, so May could manage her nearly five-year-old son and the shopping.

A traditional baby carriage.
Image from Pixabay Content Licence by No-longer-here.

Each time May and young Harry went out, women stopped to ask May questions, treating Harry as if he was a deaf mute.

> *'Do they think he's going to live?', 'When are you putting him in a Home?', 'Shame he won't ever work or have a family', 'How long have you got him back for?', 'Will he walk again?'. And there I was, listening to it all. It's no wonder I became a people watcher.*

His mother gave the women and their insensitive questions 'short shrift', but it was an ordeal for them both.

> *I was called a cripple. It was a descriptive word then. I didn't take umbrage: it's what I was.*

At home, Harry felt 'in a whirl' without the strict rules of the hospital. It did not help that the household routine revolved around his father's rotating 12-hour shifts, on 'early, late or nights'. Harry Senior worked Monday–Saturday.

> *It was such a different way of life at home. Once I came downstairs for the day, I was forbidden to go back upstairs until night-time.*

Slowly, Harry got to know his parents, but it was made more difficult because he had seen how negated and powerless they had been when he was in hospital. The damage was probably made worse by medical staff criticising his mother for not giving him infection-free milk. It could have been made worse still if Harry felt unable to talk to his parents about experiences which were frightening, humiliating or degrading. If this were the case, it might have caused a further division between them, one they would never completely breach.

Dad was a positive man, a natural philosopher, with no airy-fairy reasoning. He was always practical.
He made sure we had a fire of an evening. One day, he went to work on the tandem and brought home a huge log tied to where the passenger should be. It fed the fire for a week. To improve his garden soil, Dad regularly scraped up horse manure from the roads with a shovel he carried on the back of his push bike.
Dad was a bit thin on books and education, so he couldn't progress at the works. Later, I tried to teach him the mathematics he needed to know, but he said he couldn't take it in. But he wasn't ignorant. He knew how to make the most of his networks, resources and circumstances.

He took notice of the lectures on street corners on the evils of drink. He was a skilled working-class man.

Harry was confident 'they would never starve'.

Although Dad grew up in the city, he knew how to feed us from the countryside. He cycled everywhere and collected mushrooms, apples and duck eggs. I always wanted to know what was in his saddlebags, and where the rabbits, hares, winkles and bruised fruit came from. He would pick up bargains from the wholesale fish market. Sheaf Market and Castle Hill Market were the places for meat, poultry, game, vegetables and fruit when the traders were packing up. Brains, heart, liver, kidney, tongue and tripe could be on the menu and, like my mother, he knew how to cook everything.

The Stork Margarine Cookery Service issued pamphlets to help housewives adapt their recipes to take the wartime shortages of ingredients into account and gave suggestions for foods some had not cooked with before. The recipes in these pamphlets were approved by the Ministry of Food.

SAVOURY TRIPE

1 lb. tripe	1 oz. margarine
Cold water to cover	1 tablespoonful flour
1 pint milk or milk and water	2 tablespoonsful sweet chutney
Salt and pepper	

This is a useful recipe when onions are scarce.

Wash the tripe, cover with cold water and bring slowly to the boil. Remove and cut into pieces. Simmer gently in the milk for 1½-2 hours in a covered saucepan. Drain and keep the milk hot. Melt the margarine and add the flour, stirring until it bubbles. Add the milk and stir until boiling. Add the chutney, the seasoning and the tripe and re-heat.
Serves 4 portions

Savoury Tripe. *Cookery Notes No 57. Liver, Heart, Kidney, Tripe, &c. / Stork Margarine Cookery Service.* London: Stork Margarine Cookery Service, 1944. Source: Wellcome Collection.

OX HEART SHEPHERD'S PIE

1 lb. ox heart	1 lb. cooked mashed potatoes
2 onions 2 carrots	Pepper and salt
¼ pint stock in which heart was cooked	

Wash and slice the heart, add 1 pint cold water and simmer until the heart is tender, about ¼ hour. Peel the onions and carrots and add to the heart when the water boils. Drain, saving the liquid, and chop heart, onions and carrots into small pieces. Fill a baking dish with the chopped ingredients, season with pepper and salt, pour over ¼ pint of liquid in which the heart was cooked, cover with mashed potatoes, and bake for 30 minutes in a moderately hot oven (Regulo Mark 6).
Serves 4-5 portions

Ox Heart Shepherd's Pie. *Cookery Notes No 57. Liver, Heart, Kidney, Tripe, &c. / Stork Margarine Cookery Service.* London: Stork Margarine Cookery Service, 1944. Source: Wellcome Collection.

SAUSAGE AND LENTIL TOAD-IN-THE-HOLE

1 lb. sausages
½ lb. lentils
1 onion or leek

1 teaspoonful salt
Pepper
Cooking fat

Soak the lentils and cook as instructions, adding onion or leek as soon as the water is boiling. Just before the lentils are cooked, add 1 teaspoonful salt. When the lentils are soft, strain off water, chop up the onion or leek and mix it thoroughly with the lentils and add pepper. Grease a meat tin and spread the lentils over the bottom. Lay the sausages on top of the lentils, pushing them down a little into the lentils, and brush them over with a little melted cooking fat. Bake in a moderately hot oven (Regulo Mark 6) for 45 minutes, but after 20 minutes turn the sausages over so that they get browned all over. Serves 4 persons.

Sausage and Lentil Toad-in-the-hole. Cookery Notes No 46. *How to Make a Little Meat Go a Long Way: And Some Pudding Recipes Too.* London: Stork Margarine Cookery Service, 1943. *Source: Wellcome Collection. Recipes approved by the Ministry of Food.*

RECIPES

BATTER OR YORKSHIRE PUDDING

Some people prefer the type of Yorkshire Pudding which is very puffed up with a lot of air holes, whereas others prefer the more substantial kind. This depends on the amount of egg used to a given amount of milk. The secret of a good batter is the beating. Batters using dried egg can be made with plain or self-raising flour, but you must be sure to follow the instructions carefully.

¼ lb. flour
1 tablespoonful dried egg

½ pint milk
Pinch of salt

Note: Use 2 tablespoonsful dried egg to get a more puffed-up result.

Sieve the flour, dried egg and salt into a basin. Make a hole in the middle and gradually stir in the milk, keeping the mixture free from lumps, and when all the milk has been added beat well for five minutes. Do not let the mixture stand but put into the oven immediately. While you are making the batter, melt a good-sized knob of cooking fat in a baking tin which should not be too big for the half pint mix, or use some dripping from the meat tin if you have a joint cooking. See that the fat is really hot, then pour in the batter. It is important that the fat should be smoking hot. Place it on a shelf just above the middle of the oven, and bake in a hot oven for 40-45 minutes (Regulo Mark 7).

Batter or Yorkshire pudding. *Cookery Service Notes No 51. How to Use Dried Eggs.* London: Stork Margarine Cookery Service, 1944. *Wellcome collection.*

CURRIED MARROW OR PUMPKIN

1 lb. marrow weighed without peel or seeds
½ lb. tomatoes or carrots
1 medium-sized onion
½ cooking apple or bottled apple
1 oz. margarine
Salt and pepper
¼ lb. any kind cooked meat
1 tablespoonful flour
1 dessertspoonful curry powder
1 tablespoonful vinegar
¼ pint vegetable stock, or water

Cook the marrow in boiling salted water for 10 minutes (pumpkin will need longer). Drain and save the water to make the sauce. Melt the margarine, chop the onion and apple and fry lightly. Stir in the flour and curry powder, and cook on a low heat for 5 minutes, stirring all the time. Draw off the heat, and add the chopped-up meat, tomato, marrow, the stock, and the vinegar. Season, and bring to the boil, stirring all the time, then cover, and leave to simmer on a very low heat for 30-40 minutes. Serve with a border of plain boiled rice, or mashed potatoes. Serves 3-4 portions.

NOTE: If carrots are used instead of tomatoes, cut in cubes and cook for 10 minutes with the marrow.

MARROW TOAD-IN-THE-HOLE

1½ lbs. peel and sliced marrow
1 lb. sausages
4 ozs. flour
2 level tablespoonsful dried egg
Salt and pepper
Fat for baking

Cook the marrow in boiling salted water, drain, press through a sieve and put back in the pan. Add the flour and egg and mix with the marrow. Cook for 5 minutes over a low heat, stirring all the time. Season. Melt the fat in a meat tin, and pour in the batter. Arrange the sausages in the batter, and bake on the second shelf from the top in a hot oven (Regulo Mark 7) for 30-35 minutes. Serves 4-6 portions.

Marrow recipes. *Cookery Service Notes No. 55. Marrows, Cucumbers & Pumpkins.* London: Stork Margarine Cookery Service, 1944. *Wellcome Collection.*

Dad put all the whelks and mussels under the sink in a white enamel bucket of water so their digestive tracts were cleared and we wouldn't get an upset stomach.

He cooked a lot and used vinegar and sugar to preserve foods. If there were apricots left in a bowl, he'd put them in a pan and they would become part of a sauce.

Harry noticed his dad made porridge every morning and took four thick doorstop slices of bread spread with rendered pork dripping to work. Harry said:

> *That's all he had for a 12-hour shift. Pork was much fattier then and you could buy the salted dripping from pork butchers, who cooked the meat on their premises. The butchers operated more like a charcuterie really, but they didn't have a name like that.*

Before work, Harry Senior put 'a measured amount of tea, what sugar could be spared, and condensed milk' in a white enamel can with a blue rim. At break time, he filled it with near-boiling water from the steam tap at work.

> *You couldn't look like a gentleman at the rolling mill. I couldn't recognise my father's features when he came in black from mill soot.*

After Harry had washed and changed at the end of each shift, he sat on the back step of the house, day or night, and had two, one-pint enamel mugs of tea while drinking in the sight of his beloved garden.

Harry discovered his dad read the newspaper every day, but he did not buy it. When others finished theirs, they left it in the workshops and barber shops around the city. In turn, when he had read it, he passed it on, too.

Harry already knew his mother was good company, and she had a lightning-quick mind. He said:

> *She would start a sentence, but a different person could finish it. A conversation with my mother was never dull. I think in my*

youngest years, a lot of what she talked about was based on her grandmother Eliza's wisdom and life experience.

May belonged to the traditional Mothers' Union, but she was also intensely curious, and often asked herself and her son 'What if ...?'. She believed in 'bettering herself'. She was a voracious reader who used the library at Firth Park. May made 'holiday' money knitting jumpers and cardigans which her husband sold at the steelworks.

Although Harry could now get about using crutches, his mother did not want him to be caught up in the rough and tumble of boys' games, 'in case he got hurt'. Harry added, 'People with disabilities were kept away from "normal" people. We were feared. What if the disability was catching? So, they didn't take kindly to us appearing among them.' He was occasionally allowed to be with his cousins. His cousin Beatrice Moore, née Lycett, said, 'Little Harry was fab, and I named my favourite doll after him.'[131]

May, who would not advocate for herself, nevertheless persistently badgered the authorities to give Harry a chance of an education. He was admitted to Beck Road Council School on 1 October 1939. Harry did not remember attending infant school. He thought he had been 'written off' when he went to Rivelin, and said that it was a nationwide policy not to 'have cripples at school'. Society wanted 'us out of sight', where they had 'no intention to make progress with us' as it 'wasn't worth educating cripples'.

Beck Road Council School, Beck Road, Shiregreen.
Official Opening, Thursday 12 May 1938 by Councillor J. Gill, Deputy-Chairman of the Education Committee.
Copied from: Official Opening Programme, Local Pamphlets Vol. 339 Ref. 042 S. Licensed from ©Picture Sheffield (Image m00108).

The Sheffield Cripples Aid Association's visitor for Shiregreen was alerted about his release from Rivelin, and Harry endured a regular visit to the house by an Association volunteer every month he was home. Contrary to his acceptance of the label, he rejected this way of seeing himself:

I didn't need Cripple's Aid. In my head, I wasn't a cripple.

The Sheffield Cripples Aid Association was established in 1909. It was a Christian organisation known to Harry as the 'Sunbeam Club', with the motto 'By love, serve one another'. The hymn below, which Harry remembered having to sing, might give a flavour of how children were expected to behave, regardless of the inevitable trauma and the exclusion they experienced from their community.

> Jesus wants me for a sunbeam
> To shine for Him each day;
> In ev'ry way try to please Him,
> At home, at school, at play.
>
> Chorus:
> A sunbeam, a sunbeam
> Jesus wants me for a sunbeam,
> A sunbeam, a sunbeam
> I'll be a sunbeam for Him.
>
> Jesus wants me to be loving,
> And kind to all I see
> Showing how pleasant and happy
> His little ones can be.
>
> Chorus
>
> I will ask Jesus to help me
> To keep my heart from sin;
> Ever reflecting His goodness,
> And always shine for Him.

Adult Harry had a clear memory of being patronised by the charity volunteers from a young age. He found the visits 'excruciating', but he was not allowed to escape to his bedroom.

We were inspected regularly, hair, teeth, eyes and fingernails, and encouraged to keep clean. It was insulting.

However, Harry said he later learned that the second decade of the 20th century had seen a surge in neglected and mistreated children. He went on:

There was still a horror of working-class children being neglected or mistreated. The visitors were middle-class women who expected to be treated with respect but who didn't know what their inadequacies were.

They'd pat you on the head and ask you questions, wanting to know if your parents were mistreating you. They didn't understand they were insulting your family, your home and your community. They were arrogant, with the wrong tone of voice, that of people who 'knew best'. They certainly didn't come across as friendly or helpful.

Harry thought the visitor should have been checking if he was getting an education that would help him support himself in adulthood. As an adult, he believed the volunteers were 'doing the right thing on their terms', but what he and his parents sorely needed was someone to help them build the secure emotional attachments that had been broken by their separations and to restore the security that had been torn from him. Sadly, this kind of help was decades away.

Harry thought what the middle-class female volunteers needed most was the ability to read social hierarchies, to recognise who the community leaders were and to understand that the 'working class' covered a wide spectrum of people, who had their own values and pecking order.

Sometimes, after the monthly ordeal ended, Harry was expected to show gratitude for the handout of a pair of thin grey socks, which he saw as an insult to his parents' ability to provide for him. I would like to think May received some benefit from the visits, but she, too, may have experienced them as a patronising intrusion, something necessary that she had to comply with. It is doubtful that May and Harry saw the after-care committee visits as making the best use of the association's funds.

In 1932, the closest year to Harry's admission to hospital, the annual report of the Cripples Aid Association recorded its patrons as the Duke and Duchess of Norfolk, the Duke and Duchess of Portland, the Earls and Countesses of Fitzwilliam and Wharncliffe, and the Lady Mary Wortley. The association included trustees, a large council, an executive and finance committee, a convalescent home committee, and the district and after-care committee. From the association's point of view, 'the most important section of our work, visiting our members in their own home, has been continued satisfactorily. Our visitors have become more efficient and better able to give advice and help.' In 1932 there were 18,274 visits.[132]

During these years, May and young Harry occasionally stayed with Harry's maternal grandparents, Leonard Turner and Elizabeth, or 'Lizzie', née Bunting. They lived in a council property at 99 Cookson Road about three miles away, similar to May's own. Their marriage was an unhappy one. A family story has it that Leonard married on the rebound. Although Leonard was known to be a drunk, Harry said he did not know him in that way. Leonard was a 'little mester', an independent craftsman who worked alone or employed a few workers and apprentices; many had their own workshop, but others rented space in a bigger establishment. He worked for himself from Tuesday to Saturday as a hollowware stamper, turning sheet metal into dishes, bowls, cups, vases, candlesticks, trays and other articles of household silver.[133] He was too hung-over to work on Mondays. Leonard was an educated man and a talented silversmith. However, according to Harry, he was the black sheep from a middle-class family, an outcast maverick who put any mail on the fire unopened. It was common knowledge that he had a long love affair with a woman in Bardney, Lincolnshire, where he went fishing regularly. Soon after war broke out, Leonard signed a Ministry of Defence contract to drop-stamp petrol tanks for Spitfires because he knew he could press them without weaknesses.

When Harry Senior had time off, he often said to his family, as he had said to May when they were going out on the tandem, 'Let's get lost.' May made sandwiches and the family either started walking or caught a bus from outside the house. They often hiked for 10–15 miles or more on the Moor – the Rivelin Valley; the River Don, Blacka Moor; Burbage Moor; Padley Gorge; Forge Dam; and Ringinglow were favourite places.

If you're walking that far, you needed refreshments. Dad often asked, 'Does anyone do tea?' The answer would be, 'Yes, Mrs So-and-So on the corner, she'll do you a tray with sandwiches for half-a-crown.' Some people put a card in their window offering tea and sandwiches. It often cost coppers.

When Harry had walked a few miles on crutches, huge blisters appeared under his armpits. But he experimented over time and made customised pads, which helped him walk more comfortably. Although Harry was always 'skinny', he built up his upper body strength and kept up with his parents.

The only people I knew in paid work were working-class men who were strong, like my dad. The least I could do was strengthen what muscles I could when I had the opportunity.

Harry regularly went walking with his mother when his father was at work. One time, in Fulwood after dark, she pointed out the house where she had been in service. The curtains were open, and the Jewish family was eating a Shabbat meal. May told Harry, 'That's where my life began. Before that, I was a skivvy for my parents, trapped at home.' At other times, May and Harry Junior would get on a bus for one stop, for the fun of it. He said, 'Public transport had superior upholstery. They were much more comfortable than cars.' However, Harry could only sit on one part of his right cheek.

On Sunday mornings, Harry listened to a popular musical request radio show, *Forces Favourites*. Harry said that comic songs were his father's favourite. Harry said, 'People sang at home doing the washing-up, on the street, everywhere, and we all knew the same songs.'

Discharge on the Outbreak of War

People made music everywhere; Mum and Dad burst into song throughout the day, all their lives.

We went to community singing at the weekends in the town centre. There was standing room only, but I found community sing-songs boring. Alongside hymns were folk songs and sea shanties, and everything in-between. You could buy words for the songs from the newsagents.

I preferred organ music. It was complicated and you could get lost in it.

One old music-hall song Harry remembered from this time was 'Hear All, See All, Say Nowt', recorded by Sandy Powell in 1939. Another favourite was the Yorkshire folk song 'On Ilkla Mooar Baht 'at' (On Ilkley Moor Without a Hat, *c.* 1850; see Appendix C for the lyrics). The 1928 song 'Together' ('We'll stroll the lanes together') was also popular. It was re-recorded in 1945.

Harry found words endlessly enticing, even if he did not always understand the songs on radio programmes like the wartime comedy *It's That Man Again*. No doubt May tuned into *Children's Hour*, which was broadcast from 5 pm to 6 pm every day of the week.

One wartime snippet was his parents taking in a 'woman of colour' who was in need. 'She slept on the floor in the sitting room for some time. Then I went back into Rivelin. When I came out, she was gone. I never knew why she was there or what happened to her. Perhaps she was a friend of Mother's who had been bombed out.'

Harry's abiding memory of Christmas at home was having a tree up on his birthday, making paper chains to hang around the sitting room and hanging a Christmas stocking at the end of his bed. On Christmas mornings, he found a pillowcase full of gifts under the tree.

In Rivelin, Harry was anonymous, unstimulated and ignored, and he wanted to be with his family. But at home, he was watched closely, smothered and micromanaged. He found it difficult when his parents interrupted his thoughts with endless instructions delivered with basic vocabulary – 'Put wood in the 'ole' [shut the door], 'Shove over', 'Pick that up', 'That's going to fall off there' – and sometimes he longed for the simplicity of life in the hospital, where he knew the rules and could live in his head.

6

Back to Rivelin

In later life, Harry found it difficult to talk of the war years. Apart from taking his children to visit some of the world war cemeteries in France and Belgium, he avoided reminders of war, including films, museums and exhibitions. However, a slightly older contemporary of Harry's later reflected: 'There began a fatalistic attitude to life. As children, we were surrounded by death, immersed in death – in the sky, on the films, in the papers, on the radio and in the street. Very often in our own street, or in a street down which we walked or cycled on the way to school or a playground. Death coming to members of our family, or the family of our school friends, or people we had known or seen, friends of our parents. In the accepting way of children, we accepted. We didn't know any different. But we were affected.'[134] Another contemporary said: 'I think those years installed in me a sense of frugality, an appreciation of things hard-earned and striven for … a gradual realisation of the horrors of war – not at the time, as my feelings were more of excitement at everything that was happening, but later in life. The deprivation, the drabness and the danger were all somehow character-building.'[135]

Harry expected to be sent back to the hospital in the Rivelin Valley, but he did not know what would trigger the decision. His condition was carefully watched through regular outpatient appointments, which may have been paid for through the Penny in the Pound scheme.[136] These appointments took place at the Tuberculosis Dispensary in Sheffield City Centre, at 51 Queen's Road, on the corner of Duchess Road, where Dr Pattison held clinics every Wednesday and Friday afternoon.[137] The pain from Harry's damaged femur grinding on his hip bone increased and Dr Pattison arranged for him to return to hospital on 6 July 1940 for what turned out to be another 11 months.[138] He was six and a half years old. Harry said, 'It was gruesome to get the plaster off', but that being in the hospital had its advantages: 'Home was uncomfortable. I felt powerless.' At Rivelin, Harry stopped being the observed and relaxed into being the one observing again. Looking back, Harry reflected:

> *I resented Mum and Dad, though I knew they meant everything kindly. In hospital, I knew who I was. I was my own man. I had my own space, my bed might be in a different place, but neither it, my bedside locker, nor the ward changed. I could live in my head. I knew who people were and how to get things done. I knew what I could control and where the possibilities might be. I had to live by the rules, but sleeping in the day and talking to the nurses at night made it tolerable.*

To be in the hospital away from his parents during wartime must have brought additional challenges for Harry. If 'former evacuees appear to be at greater risk of having insecure attachment styles and therefore lower levels of psychological wellbeing',[139] it seems likely that Harry and his fellow patients also struggled.

While he had been institutionalised rather than evacuated, there may be something to be learned from studies which discovered that early separation experiences are often related to mental health issues in adulthood.[140] This research also noted the child's lack of control over events and the potential change in the quality of care whilst separated; the lack of explanation given to many evacuees; the uncertainty about how long the separation would last; and the concern expressed by many of them over the safety of their parents. These are all experiences also believed to be common to Harry and the children in the hospital.[141] We know children with a healthy attachment to their parents seek closeness when they feel stressed or in peril. All Harry could do was to find ways to be seen by the adults around him and hope they would protect him.

Hitler made threats to invade Britain, and by 1 July 1940, German forces were occupying Guernsey and Jersey. Hitler's directive on 16 July 1940 read: 'As England, in spite of the hopelessness of her military position, has so far shown herself unwilling to come to any compromise, I have therefore decided to begin to prepare for, and if necessary to carry out, an invasion of England.'

While the Luftwaffe failed to secure the air superiority needed to invade, Harry remembered living in fear throughout the war as he had been told people with disabilities had been killed in Germany and occupied Europe. He did not exactly remember how he knew, but said it was common talk in the hospital. Harry's fears were justified. The Nazis passionately believed the Germanic people were part of the Aryan 'master race'. Those with physical and mental disabilities were viewed as 'useless' to society, and a threat to Aryan genetic purity. Therefore, despite Germany sending a delegation to an international conference at the beginning of the Second World War which helped lay the groundwork for later disability rights movements, those with mental or physical disabilities were murdered in what the Nazis called the 'T-4', or 'Euthanasia', Program[142] in which an estimated 260,000 people were killed.[143] Beginning in October 1939, children were the first to be killed, by gas and later poison or starvation, starting with infants and toddlers, and extending to youths up to 17 years of age.[144] According to the online Holocaust Encyclopaedia, 'By 1941, the supposedly secret Euthanasia Program [was] known about in Germany,' as various public figures and clergy had denounced the killing of people with physical and mental disability.[145] For example, on 3 August 1941 Bishop Clemens August Graf von Galen of Münster delivered a third public sermon against the elimination of people with mental and physical disabilities, whom the Nazis considered 'unproductive'. The British broadcast portions of the sermon on radio stations that could be heard in Germany, and Allied forces printed the sermon on leaflets and dropped them across Germany and other European countries.[146]

Harry could not have known that Hitler had indefinitely postponed Operation Sealion, the invasion of Britain, because the international force involved in the Battle of Britain had dealt the Luftwaffe a blow from which it never fully recovered.[147]

When Harry returned to Rivelin, May could no longer use Harry's ration book. The hospital was licensed and received food for their patients on the same lines as households, although they were often given priority if something was scarce.[148] Children's rations, generally speaking, were half those of adult portions, but they did have relatively higher proportions of fats and proteins.[149, 150]

An example of a poster May might have seen as she waited at an outpatient appointment with Harry. *Civil Nursing Reserve poster licensed from the IWM_ PST_014524_B. ©Crown copyright.*

Tomatoes and onions, which had been mostly imported from overseas, were controlled by the government, who created a distribution scheme. From 1941 to 1943, no onions could be imported from France, Spain, Bermuda, and the Channel Islands, so the Onion Distribution Scheme was introduced in the autumn of 1941. Under the scheme, onions were distributed during the autumn and winter in selected urban areas.[151] The allocations varied from 2 lb to 4 lb a head, according to the area. The number of points people needed for each foodstuff varied throughout the war depending on the supply. For example, in 1942, four points had to be given over to obtain a net pound of canned tomatoes.[152]

Food	Present Points Value per lb. net unless otherwise stated	Initial Points Value and Subsequent Variations
Canned Vegetables		
Beans, baked in tomato sauce ..	6	1941: Dec. 1-4; 1944: Dec. 10-3; 1945: April 28-4; 1946: Mar. 3-6; 1947: Sept 14-8; 1948: Jan. 30-6.
Beans, baked, in gravy ..	—	1941; Dec. 1-4; 1942: Mar. 9-2; June 1-1; 1943: Jan. 10—removed from Points Scheme.
Beans, dried, in brine	—	1942: Feb. 23-2; June 1-1; 1943: Jan. 10—removed from Points Scheme.
Peas	—	1942: Feb. 23-4; Nov. 29—retail sale suspended; 1943: April 4-4; 1944: Feb. 6-3; 1945: Aug. 19-4; 1946: Nov. 10-2; 1948: Jan. 31-4; Aug. 15-2; 1949: Jan. 30—removed from Points Scheme.
Tomatoes	4	1942: Feb. 23-6; Nov. 29—retail sale suspended; 1943: April 4-6; 1946: Feb. 3-8; 1948: Feb. 29 -4.

Points for canned vegetables.
Extract from 'Our Food Today No. 1', Ministry of Food Rationing in the United Kingdom, page 30. Wellcome Collection.

Onions were often raffle prizes or given as presents. 'One "aunt" on *Children's Hour*, wishing "A Happy Birthday and lots of presents" to one small listener, added, "I did hear of a lucky girl the other day who was given some onions, but we can't all expect a lovely present like that!"'[153]

Harry enjoyed the unchanging weekly menu in the hospital, particularly the 'velvety' vegetable soups and tasty perpetual stew thickened with oats which bubbled away in the kitchen. He described the powdered scrambled egg he was given for breakfast as 'beautiful'. Salty bread and dripping were still served for elevenses. 'If I was lucky, there'd be a bit of bacon or beef essence in it'. Supper was a cold meal prepared by the cooks and left for the nurses to give out. Lunch on Sundays might be thick slices of beautiful Yorkshire ham and fruit, but there were no bananas, as Britain stopped importing them in 1940.[154]

The nurses got fed up with the children being slow to eat. Harry suggested to them that seconds were given to those that ate quickly. From then on, he always got double helpings.

With Harry back at Rivelin, May could volunteer for the war effort.[155] No doubt she turned to the *National Service Guide* to consider the few options open to her. The guide exhorted women to become nursing auxiliaries and care 'for the young, the sick and the elderly'.[156] This role was for women aged 18 to 55 without prior nursing experience. Women volunteered primarily through the Civil Nursing Reserve and received two weeks' hospital-based training covering first aid, home nursing and practical hospital work.

May's training was paid for by the government and took place at the City General Hospital, two and a half miles from home, where she was assigned to nurse.[157] Her role was full-time for 48 hours per week. May worked nights so she could combine volunteering with cleaning and cooking for her parents and in-laws. She said she did not get the bus to and from the hospital. The transport system had been the pride of the city, particularly after the Sheffield Blitz and a month of the worst snowfall on record. Perhaps she walked to save money or because she wanted to free up a seat for other essential workers, but it meant she had to navigate through the blackout. May might have been comforted that 'there were quite a lot of people in town' and 'their mishaps in the dark were cheerfully met'.[158]

May wore a Second World War nursing auxiliary uniform and apron. The sleeves of the dress were slightly puffed with folded-back cuffs above the elbow. The uniform fastened with two removable buttons (taken off when the garment was washed) at the back of the neck and one at the bottom rear of the skirt. Her simple white apron was fixed with safety pins to the front, and two buttons at the back.[159] Over time, May was recognised as an assistant nurse, that is, one who has 'had a satisfactory period of nursing experience'.[160]

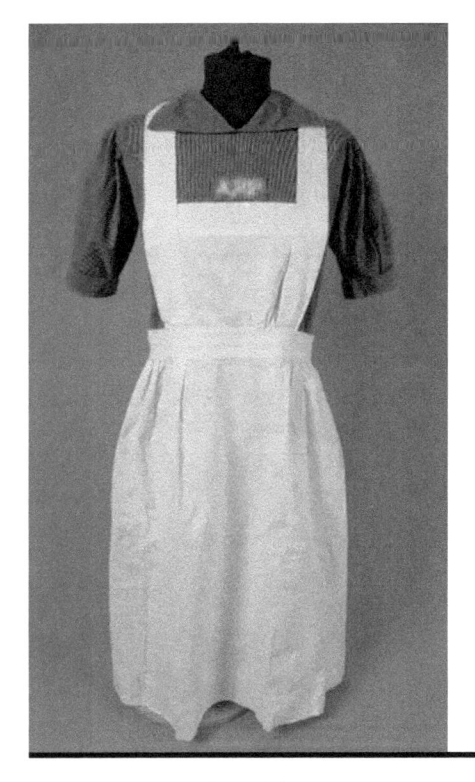

LEFT: Second World War Nursing Auxiliary Uniform and Apron – ARP Pattern 46.

RIGHT: Second World War Nursing Auxiliary Great Overcoat. Many nursing reserve members were issued with the grey/blue gaberdine greatcoat with fleece lining.

LEFT: Civil Nursing Reserve raincoat.

RIGHT: Civil Nursing Reserve Overcoat embroidered badge. An embroidered badge was sewn to the left breast of the Civil Nursing Reserve greatcoat. The design of the badge mirrored that of the enamel Civil Nursing Reserve badge, but with a red scarlet background.[161]

Images courtesy of www.ww2civildefence.co.uk.

As well as doing heavy cleaning, and some washing and cooking for her parents, May helped her in-laws, Urban Drabble, aged 71, and wife Emily, aged 61, with their cooking, washing and ironing. The couple had a volatile marriage. Harry Senior said his father, Urban, would throw his cap in the house and if Emily did not throw it back out, it was safe to go in. They lived at 71 Wallace Road, Neepsend, four miles from May and Harry's home. Apparently, May walked both ways.

May sometimes took a pig's head to her in-laws to make brawn.

> *I watched her strip it and cook it for a long time over the fire. When it was tender, she put it in a basin with a heavy weight on it. The next day, she sliced it. We would eat it with homemade bread and pickles. It was very good.*

Harry later described his grandmother Emily, who died in 1956, as having had a tough life. Two of her children had died before 1911. He found her intimidating. She weighed over 20 stone, and it is possible she had an undiagnosed thyroid condition. In a rare, unfiltered moment, Harry described her as 'quite aggressive, a slow thinker and pig ignorant'. It was the only unkind remark I heard him make about anyone, though he added, 'She was not a religious woman, but a woman of her time and place, doing the best she could with the hand she was dealt.' He found it hard to make conversation with her. Emily slow-cooked the family food in a large enamel bowl in a range. Hot water was always available for tea. Like many women, she had no food preparation surfaces, so she cut and buttered bread against her chest. Emily fed the family in sittings. For some years Emily cooked take-away pies and sold them to workers through a window. She stopped after changes were made to weights and measures.

Young Harry might have been safer in Rivelin during the Sheffield Blitz, but he still heard the air raid siren warning on the hospital roof and the sounds of the bombing reached the valley. The most devastating attacks on Sheffield took place on the nights of 12/13 December and 15/16 December 1940. When the wail sounded, a nurse pushed Harry's bed back into the ward from the terrace. Each of the children's beds was covered with an old mattress. He said of it, 'It wasn't much, but it looked as if they were doing something to protect us.' No doubt he worried about his parents.

On 12 December, over 330 German aircraft are believed to have attacked Sheffield. Perhaps because the main industrial part of the city was hidden by fog, the districts of Norton Lees, Gleadless, Abbeydale, Brincliffe Edge, Moorhead, Glossop Road, Park Hill, Millhouses, Sharrow, Broomhill, Crookesmoore, Walkley, Owlerton, Burngreave, Meersbrook, Wybourn and Neepsend were bombarded.

The Moor was devastated, whilst every building in Angel Street was bombed or fire damaged. King Street was also badly hit. 106 out of a total of 154 of the city's schools were damaged, with 8 being completely destroyed.[162]

There were about 1,800 auxiliary firefighters by the time the Sheffield Blitz took place. The AFS were housed at 20 stations across the city. When the sirens sounded, the men rushed to the city centre but soon found themselves overwhelmed by the numerous blazes raging across Sheffield.[163]

Two nights later the bombers returned and attacked the industrial east of the city, particularly Attercliffe, Grimesthorpe and Burngreave. Brown Bayley's steelworks was hit, as was Hadfield's steelworks at Helca, and the East Helca Works, Arthur Lee and other industrial sites. Almost 700 people were killed during the air raids. Over 82,000 of the city's 150,449 houses and shops had to be repaired, while 2,906 were obliterated or too badly damaged to be brought back into use.[164]

Many steelworks had their own air raid shelter, but Harry Junior probably never knew that an 18-year-old and a 31-year-old man died at his father's workplace in Osborn's shelter on 12 December 1940.[165] There is no family story that Harry Senior had been in the work's shelter that night. A father from another company told his children he found it terrifying: as each bomb dropped, the heavy steel doors were forced open and the draft caused by the bomb blast would pass through the labyrinth of corridors in the shelter at a terrific speed, and then the doors would clang back into their frames again until the next explosion.[166]

Bombs also fell on Sheffield 16 times between 1940 and 1942 in a campaign codenamed Operation Crucible, during which 1,121 high explosive bombs and 25 parachute mines fell.[167] Did Harry feel more vulnerable when his paternal grandparents were bombed out of number 71 Wallace Road? Or was he simply told they had moved? It is unlikely his grandparents shared that one of their near-neighbours died on the night of 12/13 December 1940, but they could not shelter him from a coming family tragedy.[168]

7

Life Begins

Harry was discharged on 16 August 1941 from the King Edward VII Hospital (among 25 other children that year).[169] One child died in the hospital that year.[170] When he got home, he found the Morrison shelter was gone. His father had dismantled it and arranged for the corporation to collect it.[171] The family continued to use the neighbour's Anderson shelter. The 'T' by the door had been turned into a white square on the wall, showing there was no longer a Morrison shelter on the property. As Harry accompanied his mother around the city, he saw some of the devastation from the bombing raids he had heard in Rivelin.

Did his mother tell him that a parachute mine had killed her oldest brother on 14 March 1941?[172] Harry's 35-year-old uncle, Harold Turner, was the father of three young children, and his wife, Elsie, was three months pregnant when he died. He had been fire-spotting at the top of Moonshine Lane, at 37 Southey Hill, two doors away from his family home. He ran towards the parachute, presumably thinking it was a German pilot who had ejected. House numbers 41 and 43 were destroyed, killing both families.

'Yet': A Story of Triumph Over Childhood Separation, Trauma, and Disability

ABOVE: Example of bomb damage, Sheffield City Centre 'Debris in High Street'. *Photograph taken by the police on 12 December 1940. Licensed from ©Picture Sheffield (Image s01145).*

LEFT: Harold Turner, 1906–41, as a boy. *With thanks to Frank Turner.*

Harry saw there were other changes. The local farm no longer delivered the family's milk. The new milkman was smartly dressed, and the milk arrived in clean, wide-necked glass bottles. May saved the wax discs that sealed them, and Harry carefully cut out the centres and wrapped scraps of wool around the disks to make woollen pom-poms. The milkman also sold oatcakes and pikelets, which were a thinner, yeast-free version of crumpets. From 12 October 1941, his mother May had to register with a supplier, as milk became a controlled item.[173]

Rationing continued. The Ministry of Food issued a guide for mothers to help children get a balanced diet, and advised: 'Some foods, which many mothers have always considered to be essential for their children, such as fruit and sugar, are now either scarce (rare to find) or unavailable. However, for both fruit and sugar, no harm will come if suitable replacements are given.'

May added to their income by running catalogues from home and earning commission, and they fascinated Harry. Freemans featured only clothing and, during the war and up to March 1949, housewives had to pay for their orders accompanied by the coupons introduced when rationing started.[174] Littlewoods was the one Harry preferred to flick through. It had started in 1932 and, by the end of the war, it produced millions of copies a year. It included clothing, electrical household items, kitchen appliances, furniture, furnishings, jewellery, toys and gifts all of which were available for interest-free credit. 'Mum would tell people when their order had arrived, then they popped in and had a chat while they examined the shirt or whatever they had asked for. They were rarely disappointed.'[175]

Food Guide for Children of All Ages

APPROXIMATE QUANTITIES PER DAY

	Food.	9 months to 1 year.	1—2.	2—6.	6—12.	12—18.
	Milk	1–1½ pint	1 pint	1 pint	½-pt. + school milk	½-pt. + school milk, or ½-pt. after leaving school
Per day	Potatoes	1 tablespoon	1 tablespoon	1–2 heaped tablespoons	2–5 heaped tablespoons	5–8 heaped tablespoons
per day	National bread	1 slice	½–1 slice	1½–4 slices	4–7 slices	7–14 slices
per day	Salad or raw vegetable	Orange juice or b'kcurrant puree or rose hip syrup	Fruit juice or 1½-oz. raw vegetable after 18 months	½–1 oz.	1–2 oz.	2–3 oz.
Per day	Green vegetable	1 tablespoon	1 tablespoon	1–2 heaped tablespoons	2–3 heaped tablespoons and or	2–3 heaped tablespoons and
	or Root vegetable	or 1 tablespoon	or 1 tablespoon	or 1–2 heaped tablespoons	2–3 heaped tablespoons	2–3 heaped tablespoons
per day	Margarine & Butter	½-oz.	½–½ oz.	½–¾ oz.	Full ration	Full ration
per week	Egg (if available)	2 per week	2–3 per week	4 per week	1 per week	1 per week
per week	Cheese	—	1–1½ oz.	1½–3 oz.	3 oz. (or full ration)	3 oz. (or full ration)
per week	Meat	Liver (only) 1 tablespoon	3 tablespoons (1 liver)	3–5 tablespns.	5–10 tablespns (or full ration)	1 lb. raw wt. (or full ration)
per week	Fish (if available)	2 tablespoons (fresh)	3 tablespoons (fresh)	3–4 tablespns (fresh or salt)	4–9 tablespns (fresh or salt)	1 lb. raw wt. (fresh or salt)
per week	Bacon	1–1½ oz. bacon fat	1–2 oz.	2–4 oz.	4 oz. (or full ration)	4 oz. (or full ration)

Food Guide for Children of All Ages.
This table was produced by the Ministry of Food (MOF) c. 1945, to help mothers plan meals for their children.[176]

Harry discovered his grandparents, Urban and Emily Drabble, had moved to a very recently built two-bedroom semi-detached council house at 20 Cowper Crescent. It was two-and-a-half miles away from his home. To May's relief, her in-laws could manage their cooking better on a new gas stove. Harry said, 'Granddad Urban never had very much, but one time he visited he gave me a tiny tin of salmon and told me "make sure you eat it all yourself".' This was likely grade III salmon, but it was still a sacrifice, as a small tin would have needed 12 of his 16 coupons a month to purchase it. Harry occasionally slept at his grandparents' house, perhaps when May worked as a volunteer at the hospital.

Despite their loving nature, Harry still struggled to form an attachment to his parents. Subconsciously, he likely resisted his need for them, uncertain of when he might be returned to Rivelin. Psychiatrist Dr John Bowlby would later recognise this form of denial as a defence mechanism.[177] The deterioration of the relationship between a mother and child, along with the intense rage or despair that often accompanied a child's separation from their parents, eventually became a well-documented psychological phenomenon. But the information came too late to ease Harry's or his parents' excruciating distress, or to mitigate the social, emotional, behavioural and health outcomes that persisted in hospitalised children even decades later.[178] 'Exposure to childhood adversity is associated with a lack of empathy, impulsivity and anger, and the emergence of behavioural problems, including delinquency and social alienation.'[179] One contemporary of Harry's, admitted to another hospital in 1948, described the lack of emotional care as being 'un-personed'.[180] He said, 'For many years, I felt I was part of an ongoing battle with unseen antagonists.' Another barrier was that Harry somehow heard how he had contracted TB and had mixed feelings about being with his parents, for 'some years', to his later regret, 'wrongly' blaming them for his infection and subsequent treatment.

May continued to do her best for Harry. She approached Beck Road Council School to inform them that Harry was back home. The headmaster refused to accept him, citing the school's many stairs and his need for crutches. The Education Committee later sent a letter to his parents stating that he would instead attend one of the first schools for children with disabilities. This was a converted building in the Attercliffe slums, with the words 'Home for Idiots and Imbeciles' carved above the entrance. It had no outdoor space, not even a yard. Harry received no lessons there. The environment certainly did not provide the supportive atmosphere where students with disabilities could gain the skills needed to navigate adult life in the wider community. Harry later described the bleak wards filled with non-verbal children with misshapen heads and twisted bodies strapped into padded seats. I can picture six-year-old Harry, hungry to learn, but with one leg shorter than the other and an arm he couldn't straighten, raging against the education committee's decision to further exclude him from his community in this inappropriate setting. Harry's protest worked. His mother took him home and refused to take him back.

May gave Harry jobs to do around the house. It became his responsibility to keep the linoleum gaps between the carpet and wall free of dirt, hair and dust, the brass stair rods polished and the stair paintwork pristine. He said he took pride in his contribution, but as an adult, he had wall-to-wall carpet and fitted stair carpet as soon as he could afford it. Harry spent many evenings by the fire with his mother 'repairing socks, zips, jumpers, everything really'. He also enjoyed the challenge of creating knitting patterns for the clothes his mother continued to sell. One day he watched his mother unpick his father's heavy overcoat, having washed and ironed it, and made him new warm wide-legged trousers from the material. Harry was delighted he could finally hide his leg-brace and his shorter, rake-thin leg, and take attention away from his built-up shoe.

May wrote to the education committee again, and Harry, a largely unsocialised child, was enrolled in Hartley Brook School Junior Department, aged 7, on 2 February 1942. The teaching was disrupted by air raids and the children's drills and evacuation exercises. The many sandbags at first aid post no. 19 at the school were a constant reminder that the country was at war.[181]

The quadrangle, Hartley Brook Junior School, Shiregreen.
Official Opening, Monday 30 September 1935 by the Rt. Hon. Oliver F.G. Stanley, President of the Board of Education.
Copied from: Official Opening Programme, Local Pamphlets Vol. 128 No. 6. Licensed from ©Picture Sheffield (Image m00104).

Harry remembered it as a miserable time. To his dismay, the staff decided that, as he was on crutches, he should sit with the girls for poetry and needlework while the boys learned woodwork. Although it was probably kindly meant, Harry said that it 'put a target on my back'. The children echoed adult attitudes and told Harry, 'You're a cripple, you should be in a home, not here with us.' The boys and girls regularly threw things at him and, after every school day, a group of boys waited for him outside the gates and thrashed him. Something he did not know at the time was that Sheila Gough, a girl in the infant school, had noticed him. When they met as adults in Rivelin, they became lifelong friends.

Harry often refused to go to school. 'Nobody cared, as it was thought I wouldn't be home long. I manipulated it, really.' The physical violence continued until Harry's father advised him to retaliate, much to his mother's dismay. His dad explained if he 'didn't give back as good as he got', he would always be a target. Harry unleashed his pent-up rage and attacked the next group that went for him. With wasted muscles from long years flat on his back in plaster and faced with several boys, Harry used his right crutch as a weapon. He was reluctant to retaliate against the girls, but occasionally snapped. The obvious solution was to become one of the school bullies. By becoming part of a gang, with his reputation as a fighter and his ability to move faster than the other children on his crutches, especially up and down stairs, he stopped being a target. He said, 'It was a relief. It didn't make me a nice person, but I was desperate. I still had an angry core I didn't know what to do with.'

A few weeks later, Harry was expelled, but he was not taken off the school register until September 1944, when the school was informed he was to be readmitted to Rivelin. 'The teachers didn't know what to do with me, so they ignored me. I couldn't cope with the expectations of school. Nor did I know the social rules everyone else took for granted. On every level, I was always trying to catch up with the other children my age.' No other education opportunity was offered, so he was not entered for the 11-plus grammar school entrance exam, which had been introduced in 1944.

Back at home, he watched how carefully his mother managed the house, and shopped for, prepared and cooked their meals. He said May's shopping list, despite rationing, invariably included: 'butter, lard, margarine, matches, eggs, bacon, and cigarettes,' but she would never know what they would come away with when they finally got to the end of a queue. When she went shopping without him, he was always excited to see his mother return and discover what she had bought. As he unpacked everything, he may have noticed a paper bag advertising the national wheatmeal bread. Most people preferred the nutritionally inferior white bread, but Harry had a fondness for the national one as it kept its shape when he soaked it in the gravy his parents made to accompany their dinner.

A paper bag advertising national wheatmeal bread, better for you and the same price as white bread, designed by the Ministry of Food.
In copyright. Source: Wellcome Collection.

Harry was keenly aware that every scrap of food had to be used. He watched his mother cut off the fat from meat, shred it and frizzle it in the frying pan when she made bubble and squeak with mashed potato, chopped cooked cabbage, and a little onion, if she had any.

WAYS WITH RAW FAT

Cut off excess fat from your meat before cooking and shred it finely. Use it as suet for puddings, suet pastry, dumplings and so on.

or - Shred it and frizzle it in your frying pan for frying tomatoes, potatoes, vegetables, bread and so on. Serve the shrivelled fat with the food.

or - Shred it and add a little to milk puddings.

If you are frying meat, cut off the excess fat, shred finely, and frizzle in the pan before you put in the meat. This saves cooking fat ; will be more digestible.

If you cut off the rinds of bacon rashers before frying, frizzle them in the pan before putting in the rashers. Or save them for flavouring soup.

Ways with raw fat. Our food today. 2, Wise housekeeping in war-time [Ministry of Food].
In copyright. Source: Wellcome Collection.

RISSOLES. Roll vegetables or meat rissoles in the crumbs, which should first be tossed in a very little hot fat.

Rissoles. Bread into battle: a wasted crust can mean a wasted convoy.
In copyright. Source: Wellcome Collection.

Harry said the best thing that happened to him in childhood was the birth of his sister Margaret in 1943. He had 'wanted a sister from tiny' and when he was home from the hospital, he got into the habit of pulling a fourth chair out at the kitchen table when they sat down to eat, saying, 'I want a sister there'.

My parents didn't want to have another child because of the war. I suppose their other child didn't fill them with confidence, either.

Perhaps the government seeing mothers as 'domestic soldiers' contributing to the war effort helped young Harry's cause.[182] That the National Milk Scheme of June 1940 made subsidised or free milk available to all pregnant women or nursing mothers might have influenced them, too. Harry Senior reconsidered and Harry studied his mother's growing belly. He helped her whenever he could and waited for her outside her antenatal appointments.

Antenatal examinations: a first visit at sixteen weeks followed by further visits at twenty-four and twenty-eight weeks, then fortnightly to thirty-six weeks and weekly visits thereafter ... During the visits the uterine height and girth to be taken, the foetal heart listened for, and the urine tested. It was expected that only the first examination and those at thirty-two and thirty-six weeks would be done by a medical officer; the rest being completed by midwives.[183]

Harry noticed May's ration book was replaced with a green one which entitled her to concentrated orange juice, cod liver oil, vitamins A and D tablets, an extra pint of milk a day, an additional half ration of meat and another egg per week.[184]

Eight-year-old Harry was overjoyed when his mother finally returned with his sister Margaret after her two-week stay at Nether Edge Hospital, located seven miles south-west of their home. He spent a lot of time watching over and talking to her. He enjoyed going to all of his sister's clinic appointments, taking pride in each of her milestones. A family story had it that one day when May stepped out to talk to the next-door neighbour, baby Margaret started to cry. Harry thought she was hungry, so he fed her some homemade jam on a spoon. Harry and Margaret shared a warm, close, lifelong bond.

In 1944, some children were moved out of the King Edward VII Hospital to enable wounded officers to be treated. However, while the orthopaedic service concentrated on the treatment, rehabilitation and training of the war-disabled, some children were readmitted.[185] Harry needed acute treatment and was admitted on 16 September 1944.[186] (It would be his last stay in Rivelin until he returned at 17, and again at 20 years old.) When Harry arrived in 1944, the doctor ordered the same sadistic nurse to put him back in a full body plaster. The hope was his femur would fuse into his hip joint. He probably did not know that five children died at the hospital of bone and joint tuberculosis that year.[187]

It was a wrench for Harry to be away from Margaret and he longed to be with her, especially as siblings were not allowed to visit. Harry also remembered missing his exercise books from home.

> *I organised them well. They had lots of priceless information on the back, like perches* and kilos. In the hospital, I never had substance. I still need substance.*

*A perch (also called a rod or pole) is a unit of length equal to 16.5 feet (5.0292 metres).

As Harry became more skilled in embroidery, he asked for permission to finish what he was working on for the regular sales of work. When Matron finally agreed, it gave him a purpose outside of the occupational therapy hours, but more importantly to him, it authorised his having tools and yarns in his locker. His mother secretly added a crochet hook, thread and specialist embroidery needles to his precious collection. The staff did not appear to recognise these as different from the ones he had permission to have. Over time, he produced 'genuinely saleable items'. Besides embroidered pillowcases, cushion covers and handkerchiefs, he used silks to produce antimacassars. These were protective covers thrown over the back of a chair or sofa, named after Macassar, a popular hair oil for men used since the 19th century. Harry then successfully argued with Matron that he should be allowed to sell items to visitors. At nine years old, Harry asked his mother to smuggle in a darning needle. His mother had taught him to darn and he mastered the art of repairing the impoverished students' stockings, which allowed a unique connection to develop between him and the junior nurses. All he needed from them was the use of their nail varnish, which they were happy to loan in exchange for wearable stockings. However, Harry was careful not to impede a money-making scheme that a long-term adult patient, Billy Graves, had.

> *From a young age, I had a careful understanding with him I wouldn't sell stockings as Billy sold these and other items from a little shop in his locker. But I made more repairing stockings than I would have done selling them.*

Craft tools were not the only thing Harry's mother smuggled in for him.

> *Mother passed over salad, tomato and onion sandwiches made with her homemade bread and Dad's produce, wrapped in a damp cloth to keep it fresh. [The sound of greaseproof paper could have alerted the staff to his contraband.] I had to hide the treat and eat in secret. Anything brought in would be taken from you. My mother never broke the 'no sweets' rule, though.*

Open storage on roadside verges, 40-ton stacks of 4,000 lb GP bombs. West of Little Doubting Farm on Hartcliffe Hill Road, Penistone. The building to the right is Little Doubting Farmhouse.
OS Map ref: 232.012.[188]

Harry's favourite memory of the war was the feel of ice cream slipping down his parched throat on a hot day. The Hulley ice cream factory in High Greave could no longer sell ice cream to the public, but it supplied the American Forces at the Wortley Air Ammunition Depot at Scout Dike above Penistone.[189] Harry Senior cycled to the depot to tell the Commanding Officer about the local children in the isolation hospital and asked him if they could spare a batch of ice cream.

> *Father just turned up at the bottom of my bed with a big can of Hulley's lovely vanilla ice cream wrapped in newspaper. It had been a hot summer and though it was a little cooler in September; I was sweating buckets in plaster. There was enough ice cream for every child. Some of them hadn't tasted it before. Thinking about it, he must have collected it on a Sunday and cycled with it on the tandem.*

Before Harry left Rivelin as a child patient, he was the only youngster to accept an invitation to listen to a group of evangelists he was told visited under the Billy Graham banner. He accepted because it gave him the chance to join nurses and adult patients in their beds in the nurses' recreation room. He wanted to find out where the nurses lived so he could add it to his mental 'escape' map, which included bus stops and their service times. Harry was overwhelmed by the message of the evangelists and described it as 'mind-blowing' and 'a road to Damascus moment'. He desperately wanted to get his hands on a Bible to help him understand where he and his experience fitted in to 'the bigger picture'. When Sister Jones, who later became matron, came to his bedside and asked him what he got out of the meeting, he carefully considered how he should answer.

> *I knew if I asked directly for a Bible I would be told 'no', but the sister had asked me a question and was waiting for an answer. I said, 'I want to know more.' Like many of the nurses, she was a woman of faith and, in the end, she couldn't resist bringing me a King James Bible. It had a unique paper smell and a shiny, durable black cover, although it wasn't a hardback. Inside, the paper was very thin with gold edged pages. Its beautiful language could be read over and over. You could almost taste it. I broke the code of reading with that book, and then I wrestled to make sense of it. You can't take it in without having a serious aptitude for comprehension. After you understand it, everything else is easier to comprehend. I don't know if my mind would have survived without the sustenance of that Bible.*

Despite losing his faith as a teenager, towards the end of his life, Harry realised the Bible was the cornerstone of his values, and how, along with Shakespeare, it had helped him make sense of life and other people.

Before Harry was released again, an incident helped him see the night sister with new respect. There was a prisoner-of-war camp close to the hospital and there were various breakouts over the war years. Harry spoke of one escapee breaking into the hospital around 1944. Despite the restrictive life she had led in nursing, he was told the sister in charge apprehended him, fed him and then locked him in a room until she got off shift. She then escorted him to the local police station. It was the talk of the ward for weeks, but it increased Harry's feelings of vulnerability. He realised that even if he left the hospital, he did not want to risk meeting an escaped soldier.

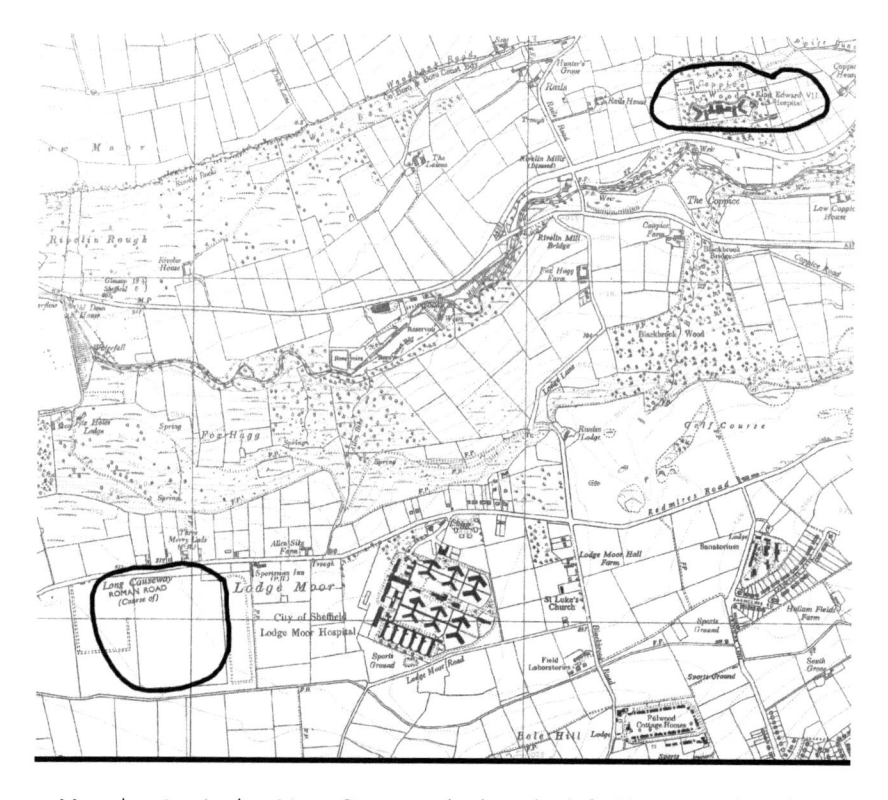

Map showing Lodge Moor Camp marked on the left. The King Edward VII Hospital for Crippled Children is circled top right.
Ordnance Survey 1956 cropped – Six Inches to a Mile (Sheet SK 28 NE).

Hopefully, young Harry did not know that Lodge Moor Camp near Redmires Reservoir was the largest of the 1,500 prisoner-of-war camps in Britain.[190] Here, German soldiers were interrogated and classified by their allegiance to the Nazi cause.[191] At its peak in 1944, the camp housed 11,000 German, Italian and Ukrainian prisoners-of-war, including some of the most fanatical.[192] The International Committee for the Red

Cross described it in 1944 as 'insufficient/uninhabitable', with half of the captives in huts and the other half in tents.[193] By September 1944, the rain turned the ground upon which many prisoners slept into mud. 'The prisoners who were fed food out of galvanised dustbins, had to stand outside in the mud, rain and cold for several hours a day during roll call, and since it was so overpopulated as a transit camp, they were squeezed into tents or the barracks with little personal space.'[194]

One morning a doctor said to a red-faced boy during his round, 'You're looking well. I think it's time you went home for a spell,' and Harry, who had just been told he could be up and about on crutches, thought a red glow might be what they were looking for. He moved as fast as he could to press a hot flannel on his face in the hope the doctor would send him home to his sister. He was disappointed that the doctor had left the ward when he returned, but this may have been around the time he had a rare chance to play when he and a few other boys raced each other up and down a corridor in adapted self-propelled wheelchairs.

At the end of three months, just after his tenth birthday, Harry found out he was to be discharged again.[195]

When I was up and about, I mustn't weight bear. So, a splint went on my left leg. I couldn't have rubber soles like other boys. The boot of the good right leg had an iron blacksmith trivet screwed on to it so that, as I walked, I couldn't inadvertently put any weight on my left leg. It clanged when I put it on the floor. It was an audible anomaly, underlining the fact that I was a cripple. Even in the best of times, I made a different sound to everyone else when I walked. I just had to accept it.

Harry asked if Old Tom would make the equipment, which forced him not to put pressure on his tubercular hip. 'The splint kept my hip joint rigid. It opened up at the bottom and back and the leather straps made it supportive and stable.' Harry explained that 'if your flesh was caught when the straps were tightened it was quite painful'. But if Tom made it, 'he put in a little flap of material that protected the skin, making it much more comfortable'.

He shuddered when he recalled having to make his own way to the ambulance that would take him home. He did not know why it was waiting for him at the bottom of the long drive, rather than coming to the back of the hospital as usual.

It was one of the many thoughtless expectations the staff had of us. They didn't seem able to see anything from our point of view. Later, I was told the staff believed that if your nurse thought you could do something, it gave you the confidence to do it.

But I was as weak as a kitten, having been on my back for so long. The staff didn't consider the muscle wastage. Once I was told I was going home, I was expected to get up and get moving on the crutches. No one even suggested I walk down the drive.

A nurse just pointed to the steps and walked away. It was frightening, making my way to the ambulance alone. I hadn't mastered the new crutches and, if I fell, I imagined finding myself in a broken heap at the bottom. Thinking of Margaret helped me focus on one step at a time.

The two flights of steps to the front entrance of the former King Edward VII Orthopaedic Hospital, Rivelin.
With kind permission ©Sheffield Newspapers/National World.

PART THREE

Timeline

DATE	AGE	EVENT
About 1947	12	Enrolled Hartley Brook Secondary (Modern) School, Hartley Brook Road
5 Jan. 1948	13	Enrolled at the Central Technical School (Building Department)
5 July 1948	13	Start of the National Health Service. The King Edward VII Memorial Hospital for Crippled children was renamed the King Edward VII Orthopaedic Hospital
Feb. 1949	14	Bought first violin from music shop on way to Central Technical School
About 1949	14	Lessons with John A. Harrison, Doctor of Music at 336 Bluebell Road
Aug. 1949	14	Camping holiday with family at Skegness
About Jan. 1951	16	Sheffield School of Art, Craft of silver-smithing, self-directed study
25 Jan. 1951	16	Received building diploma at Speech Day, Victoria Hall, Norfolk Street
Feb. 1951	16	Pain and lameness left hip (TB) [According to GP record]
1 May 1951	16	Silversmith Improver, H. Parkin & Son Ltd, Scotland Street, Sheffield
18 July 1951	16	Theory of Music Junior, London College of Music, 1st class, 100/100, Victoria Hall

Part Three

DATE	AGE	EVENT
12 Dec. 1951	17	Theory of Music Junior Honours, London College of Music, 1st class, 86/100, Victoria Hall
Jan. 1952	17	Admitted to the Royal Infirmary. Failed operation to stabilise hip
7 Feb. 1952	17	Transferred to King Edward VII Orthopaedic Hospital, formerly the Memorial Hospital for Crippled Children
19 July 1952	17	Intermediate Violin Playing, London College of Music, Honours 88/100 Victoria Hall
18 Aug. 1952	17	Admission to the King Edward VII Orthopaedic Hospital for 3 months' chemotherapy
1 Nov. 1952	17	Discharged King Edward VII Orthopaedic Hospital
Nov. 1952	17	Started the Beck Quartet providing music for dances in the mining villages, e.g. Pilley near Chapeltown
Nov. 1952	17	Referred for rehabilitation
12 Dec. 1952	18	Advanced Intermediate violin playing, London College of Music, Honours 86/100, Victoria Hall
25 Feb. 1953	18	Failed operation to stabilise hip at the Royal Infirmary. Graft could not be inserted
2 June 1953	18	Queen's Coronation. Harry watched it in a ward at the Royal Infirmary

'Yet': A Story of Triumph Over Childhood Separation, Trauma, and Disability

DATE	AGE	EVENT
19 June 1953	18	Discharged from the Royal Infirmary
June 1953	18	Credit Controller, Stock Allocation Clerk, Cost Clerk Brightside Foundry and Engineering Co.
16 Dec. 1953	19	Theory of Music Intermediate, London College of Music, 1st class, 88/100, Victoria Hall
26 Feb. 1955	20	Admission to the King Edward VII Orthopaedic Hospital for more chemotherapy
June 1955	20	Harry met nurse Doreen Parker
27 June 1955	20	Harry discharged himself from the King Edward VII Orthopaedic Hospital, with hip infection still discharging
12 Sept. 1955	20	Admitted to the Royal Infirmary for investigation. Hip spica cast removed
19 Sept. 1955	20	Sinus not discharging. Decided against debris clear-out at hip site
13 April 1956	21	Harry breaks left leg. Next 6 weeks in cast, followed by Thomas splint for 12 weeks
1956	21	Harry joins the costing department rising to section leader for Firth Vickers & Samuel Fox, Shepcote Lane Rolling Mill, Sheffield
1957	22	Credit controller, then stock allocation clerk, Bachelors Foods, Wadsley Bridge
19 July 1958	23	Married Doreen at St Mary's Church, Sheffield

8

Can't Do to Can Do

The British Broadcasting Corporation interrupted its scheduled radio programming on the evening of 7 May 1945 with a newsflash announcing that, following Germany's surrender that day, a national holiday would be declared for the following day, 8 May, to be known as 'Victory in Europe Day'.[196] The end of the war was in sight. May and the women of Butterthwaite Road pooled their ingredients and started baking. The men not on shift hauled trestle tables from the local churches and brought each family's chairs into the street. Children fetched, carried and ran around in excitement waiting for the big street tea party.

It might have been a difficult afternoon for May, though, as 10-year-old Harry told her he wanted to go back to live in the hospital. Harry said later he would never choose to leave his sister Margaret but, at that moment, the attention, uncertainty and noise of the celebrations overwhelmed him.

Adjusting to home life was difficult. His mother tried to protect him from the harsh and aggressive attitudes of the neighbourhood children by keeping him indoors but sometimes, instead of his father's prescribed walk, Harry went to play on the many bombed sites and building sites.

Victory in Europe Day party on Norwood Avenue, Shirecliffe: an example of a Sheffield council estate celebrating Victory in Europe. Norwood Avenue is 2.5 miles from Butterthwaite Road.
Licensed from ©Picture Sheffield (Image v04512).

I know Mother worried, but I would never have got hurt. I could look after myself. Other children didn't think. I was always an oddball.

At home, Harry's father rarely knew what to do with him. He was not the son he had expected. They each thought differently and they could not cycle or dig the garden together. Harry Senior often told him, 'Get your coat on and go for a walk.' Harry said, 'It was not thoughtless. He thought it was the best thing for me. The weather didn't make a difference. You dressed accordingly.'

Around this time, Harry regularly bought sweets and cigarettes in a cottage shop in Ecclesfield, where the items for sale were laid out on a sideboard. Harry said the place was run by a 'really old' woman. He then laughed and said, 'Well, I thought she was elderly but she was probably about fifty years old!'

His uncle George Drabble had a son, Brian, in 1941. Seven years younger than Harry, cousin Brian was the only child of the family Harry was allowed to play with. 'I regret I didn't treat him well. I didn't know how to play with other children, especially younger ones.' Harry also spent time with his uncle Walter: Walter Drabble, his dad's brother. He said, 'We sometimes went for meals and then not. There was no continuity. I don't know why.'

May struck up a friendship with Jackie Boules. The redhead had no children and ran a fish-and-chip shop called 'Jackie's', believed to have been on Shiregreen Lane. Her husband worked in a steel mill. Harry remembered the couple were often around when he came out of hospital. They spent a lot of time with him and, in around 1946, they took him on a caravan holiday to Whatstandswell. Jackie became very attached to him and said to May, 'I could take Harry off you, if you like.' No doubt it was meant well, but Harry said May immediately ended her relationship with Jackie.

Harry relished exploring the parks and gardens, museums and art galleries in and around Sheffield with his parents and sister. He also had strong memories of the local fields of primroses, followed by daffodils, that the boys played football on. Harry fished for 'ugly fish' in Blackburn Brook, and he said he 'tried to catch trout with a worm on a pin on the end of a piece of string'. He commented, 'It was a waste of bloody time.' Always curious and experimenting, he regretted the outcome when, aged around nine, he set a wasp's nest on fire with petrol to see what would happen.

Now that Harry had taught himself to read using the Bible, he went to the library regularly. Although his mother used the branch at Firth Park and it had a 'knowledgeable staff', Harry did

'Yet': A Story of Triumph Over Childhood Separation, Trauma, and Disability

not find the junior section 'attractive' so he caught a bus outside his house and visited the Sheffield City Library. In 1943 it had 11,000 children's books and 550 children's reference books.[197] Harry was most interested in how he could use the resources to make up for his lack of schooling. He knew that without an education he could not support himself. The library was open Monday–Saturday throughout the day and into the evening, and on Sunday, from 2 pm to 9 pm. He got to know the librarians, who were kind women and recommended mathematics and science books to him. Sometimes Harry left them a wishlist of books he had found out about elsewhere, and they did everything they could to find them for him. Craving, but starved of information, Harry also scanned the 38 newspapers, and the weekly and monthly women's magazines, hobby and craft magazines for men, and copies of *Reader's Digest* he found in the two reading rooms.[198] His respect for the printed word stayed with him.

The 1944 Education Act stated that every child should receive education suitable for their age, ability and aptitude, and obliged local education authorities to provide special educational treatment for those thought to need it.[199] However, by the time Harry was ten, he had missed a lot of schooling. People with physical, mental and sensory disabilities had been excluded from education, despite the growing numbers in institutions. Those with disabilities were commonly hidden in the home. Where provision was made, for example for children who were deaf or blind, the focus was on low-skilled work training rather than a full education. If the children were lucky, once they finished an apprenticeship, they were transferred into menial, low-paid, repetitive jobs in demeaning sheltered workshops.[200] The largest were funded by the British government and run by the Remploy group. Remploy was established by the British government to provide employment 'sheltered' from the competitive pressures of the open employment market.

May fought to get Harry back into mainstream education and he was accepted by Hartley Brook Secondary School, Shiregreen, in 1947.

North elevation, Hartley Brook Senior School.
Official Opening Monday 30 September 1935 by the Rt. Hon. Oliver F.G. Stanley, President of the Board of Education.
Licensed from ©Picture Sheffield (Image m00106).

As was usual, May made his school clothes from his father's cast-offs. Harry said, 'It was a sad period full of bullying and fighting. The staff and children didn't know what to do with me.' A male English teacher recognised his hunger for learning, and introduced him to fiction, including *Aesop's Fables*, *Alice in Wonderland* and *Gulliver's Travels*. The same English teacher also gave compulsory music appreciation classes, and a new 'universe exploded into being'. Harry glimpsed a structure in the sounds which he found magical and stayed after class to ask questions. The teacher often replied, 'I'll give that some thought,' and then came back to him another day with an answer. Harry achieved a B grade in the subject.

His female art teacher was also influential. Harry described her as an isolated, masculine oddball, with a completely different way of viewing the world. 'Her door was always open, and she had a knack for asking me the right question at the right time. She was always willing to give me advice if I asked her to. I wouldn't have stayed in school so long without her.'

His continuing self-directed learning and engagement at school paid off, and 12-year-old Harry ended his first year with an excellent school report. His only 'weak' subject was metal work – something he could not study in the library, but later excelled at. He was excused from physical training, but disappeared into his mind, rather than watch his classmates climb ropes, use the wall bars, beams and vaulting boxes, and complete drills or obstacle courses.

Hartley Brook Secondary School Report: IB 31 July 1947, signed by his father, Harry Senior.

The school-leaving age had been raised from 14 to 15 on 1 April 1947. The English teacher must have seen something in Harry because, one day in the autumn of 1947, he took Harry into an empty staff room, sat him at a small wooden table and told Harry he was to take some tests. It may be that he was hoping Harry would be selected for the engineering section at the Central Technical

School (CTS), rather than the building one. Harry commented that the mathematics and English papers were not memorable, but he said of the IQ reasoning tests:

> *It was just a big game. There were jigsaw pieces, and I was asked which ones went together. In another, I was asked which of the two lines were the longest. I measured them. Looking back, it was an aptitude test and all the questions explored my spatial awareness. The next thing I knew, my parents had received a letter to say I had been accepted at the technical school.*

Harry believed he had been expelled from Hartley Brook Secondary School, but he may have been confused because the intake for the Central Technical School for building was in January, not at the beginning of the school year. Harry Senior would have received the letter from the Education Committee in December 1947. If the template was the same as later years, it might have read as follows:

Examination for Entrance to the Central Technical School Building Department

I have pleasure in informing you that your son has qualified, on the results of the above examination, for admission to the Central Technical School (Building Department) as of January 1948.

The Central Technical School will re-open after the Christmas vacation on Tuesday, 3 January 1948.[201]

Along with the admission letter, there was a daunting list of items Harry needed to attend the course. Apart from the school uniform, he would need a boiler suit, a woodwork apron and drawing instruments, and a bag or satchel to carry his books. The uniform was a dark blazer with a badge. There were instructions about where the badge should be positioned and how the light-blue and grey cap should be worn. A tie was also compulsory. The cost would have been a stretch, but his parents could have dipped into May's holiday fund. Harry remembered being desperate to wear new, shop-bought, long grey flannel trousers, which hid the muscle loss in his left leg. May had to steel herself to visit the Army & Navy Stores to buy the boiler suit, which self-conscious Harry refused to try on in the store. However, he was delighted with the drawing instruments purchased from a shop opposite the Town Hall, and looked forward to learning how to use them.

The letter gave 13-year-old Harry hope, an invitation to belong, and the chance to avoid the 'humiliation of poverty'. What Harry Senior made of his son being offered a building course which could lead to a diploma is not known. Did he dare hope his son might find a way to earn a living?

The CTS gave boys a second chance to experience an education which combined vocational training with academic learning, with courses such as pattern making or foundry practice, and brickwork. The subjects covered included mathematics, technical drawing, plastering, English contracts, history, science (for example, water treatment), general plumbing, WCs (water closets, i.e. toilets), and carpentry and joinery. Music appreciation and singing lessons were also included. His new English master was Mr Dove, who championed the Hallé Orchestra and their concerts at the City Hall.

Former Central Technical School, West Street, originally built as Firth College.
Licensed from ©Picture Sheffield (Image s24526).

Full of optimism, Harry made his way to the rather grand Firth building.

Obviously, when I turned up on crutches, they knew there was a problem with me. Everyone stared. Some boys laughed and pointed at me; others turned their backs. A teacher said there must have been a mistake. I said, 'No,' and took out my letter to show him. 'Look, I've got the blazer, badge, cap, tie and satchel.' The man shook his head. 'You're to go home, Drabble.' I replied, 'No, I'm stopping.'

Harry's parents received a letter asking them to come to the school 'at once'. His dad was working, and May turned to Harry and said, 'If they're to talk about you, you'd best be there to hear it.'

She took him to the imposing education offices in Leopold Street, next door to the CTS. Harry remembered the momentous day clearly. He said that when they arrived, they were directed to a large, wood-panelled room that smelt strongly of beeswax. Four men in suits sat behind a long table. His mother was shaking, dressed in her Sunday best, which included a hat and white gloves. Beads of perspiration appeared on her forehead in the chilly room. One man flicked a finger at Harry, sending him to stand at the back.

The oldest gentleman (perhaps Stanley Moffat, the director of education) cleared his throat, looked down at a file in front of him and said, 'Your son was offered a place at the school, but we did not know he is a cripple. If we had known, we would not have offered him a place.'

May nodded.

'When the teacher told Harry he should return home, Harry refused to leave. You are here so we can explain the circumstances to you, so you can explain it to Harry and stop him from attending classes. You must understand that Harry would not be able to complete this course.'

May did not respond.

'Do you understand, Mrs Drabble?'

May paused before speaking. 'You think Harry can't do the course, sir.'

The spokesperson smiled.

'So, you will explain all this to him?'

The men appeared shocked when May responded, 'I will explain to Harry that if there is something he can't do, I will come and fetch him home.'

Self-efacing May won. Harry was in awe of what his mother had done for him.

I knew I had ground my mother down. I had thought I'd beaten her, but she still managed to fight for me. I don't know how she found the strength.

The Central Technical School gave Harry his first opportunity to learn something new at the same time as his peer group. But looking at his marks he achieved during the spring term of 1948, it must have challenged him. Given his poor grades, it would appear his teachers might have had higher expectations of him than the secondary school had done. (Harry's school reports can be found at Appendix E.)

Lessons took place all over the city as the pre-war classrooms had been bombed. Holly Street was the home of Harry's class, and was up several flights of stone steps. Townhead Street housed a science laboratory and an art classroom. Like most of the entrances, including the basic dining hall where a two-course meal was to be had, the classrooms in Queen Street were up many steps. The underground workshop known as Harold's (or Harry's) Tin Shop, on Arundel Street, later Tudor Way, between the Central Library and the Lyceum Theatre also had many stairs for Harry to negotiate. He became fast on the steps, and his crutches gave him an advantage when he rushed from one site to another as no time was allowed in the timetable for the pupils to reach their next lesson.

CITY OF SHEFFIELD EDUCATION COMMITTEE

CENTRAL TECHNICAL SCHOOL

Headmaster:
H. W. WADGE, B.Sc.
Telephone No. 26244

SHEFFIELD, 1

REPORT on the work of _Drabble Harry_
Form _1X_   Year _First_   for _Spring_   Term 19_48_

SUBJECT	Max.	MARKS Term	Exam.	REPORT	TEACHER'S SIGNATURE
English	50	27		Fair	——
French	50				
Geography	50	31		Good on the whole.	——
History	50	35		Showing progress.	——
Mathematics	100	65		G.	
Physics	50				
Chemistry and Metallurgy	50				
Applied Mechanics	50				
Building Science	100	63		Fair	——
Drawing I	50	22		Fair	——
Drawing II	50				
Art	50	20		Fair.	B.S
Engineering Workshop Practice	50				
Pattern Making and Moulding	50				
Carpentry and Joinery	50	23		Fair	——
Plumbing	50	30		Good	——
Bricklaying / Plastering	50				

TOTAL MARKS GAINED	296		
TOTAL MARKS POSS.	550	Grand Totals	

GENERAL REPORT—Position in Form _26_   No. in Form _30_
Age _13 yrs 3 mo._   Average Age of Form _13 yrs 5 mo._
Conduct _Fair_
Attendance—No. of times absent ____   No. of times late ____
Physical Education ____   Height ____   Weight ____
REMARKS :— _Poor result_

Form Master _S. Pillang_   _H. W. Wadge_ Headmaster
Next term commences on _12/4/48_

Central Technical School Form 1X First Term, Spring 1948.

However, Harry soon found he was 'streets ahead' of some of the boys in plumbing. He responded well to the kindness and good humour of the plumbing instructor, a First World War veteran and master craftsman. Harold Parkin had a great deal of experience, and was adept at working with different metals, but he had no formal teaching qualification. It was here that Harry first learnt to fashion objects from sheet tin. Harry became good at joining lead pipes. He explained:

> *When a pipe burst, you first marked it with plumbers' black so the solder would not settle around the pipe beyond the damage. Then you would clean it very carefully, give it nice square ends, build up your soldering in thin layers, wiping each time.*
> *It looked like a well-healed broken bone on an X-ray. I loved the plumbing department. (I later taught my wife to do it as well as any professional. There were a lot of burst pipes in the first property we bought at High Storrs.)*

He also recalled an instructor, Stanley Piling, a certified carpenter from whom he learned a lot despite the man's biting sarcasm.

Religious education (RE) was compulsory, but Harry had already joined the evangelical group Youth for Christ. He went further and joined the Scholars Christian Unit and was given a 'beautiful silver cross', which he wore on his lapel. The members were regularly given a question or text by a preacher and were asked to write a few words about the text. Members were asked to deliver these sermons to the school. Apparently, Harry was extraordinarily good at it, and towards the end of his course the head of religious education said, 'You could take it further, there's a place for someone of your talent in the church.' Harry realised with a lightning clarity why he could not pursue it, and replied, 'No, there isn't. I don't believe a word of it.' Looking back, he was sorry he did not let the man down gently, but in that moment, he was as shocked by this new epiphany as the teacher had been. He stopped going to the Scholars Christian Unit and the RE lessons.

Harry ended the first term in 26th place out of 30 boys. He remembered that someone in the class called him 'thick' and told him he could not do any better. Harry could never bear being told he could not do something, so, to prove the boy wrong, he knuckled down at the library and, with the help of librarians and teachers, he rose to tenth place by the end of the summer term. By the autumn term, he had reached fourth position. Having proved he could, Harry said he slacked off in the spring term of 1949. Fortunately, someone must have called 'present' when his name was called because nothing was said about his regular absences when, despite risking a caning, he took time off to watch the Hallé Orchestra rehearse.

If he had been unfortunate enough to be caught out, several teachers might have administered the punishment. The headmaster, Mr Wadge, was seen as a sadist by some. One anonymous writer on the Sheffield Forum wrote, 'In his room he had a stick wall cabinet where there was a selection of caning sticks, some thick, some thin, some cane, some solid wood and one wrapped in black tape. He opened the cabinet and chose his weapon of choice and then gave me six of his best.'[202]

Mr Gregory, a science teacher, also delivered corporal punishment. Harry's fellow pupil, Philip Seymour, described

Mr Gregory as a violent man when he lost his temper. Philip recalled: 'If someone tried to protect their behind with a textbook, the teacher soon spotted it and removed it. He then added more strikes to the punishment. Mr Gregory kept his cane in the chalk groove on his desk. One day, I bought a junior hacksaw from home in my schoolbag and sawed it in to one-inch pieces and returned it to the groove. Half an hour into the lesson, he saw what had been done and blew his top. No one dobbed me in, and because anyone could have done it before we arrived, there were no repercussions. After that, he carried around a length of the reddish flexible Bunsen burner tubing tied around his waist.'

Little Hill from Townhead Street, Playhouse Theatre, right.
Photo taken between 1940 and 1959.
Licensed from ©Picture Sheffield (Image s17629).

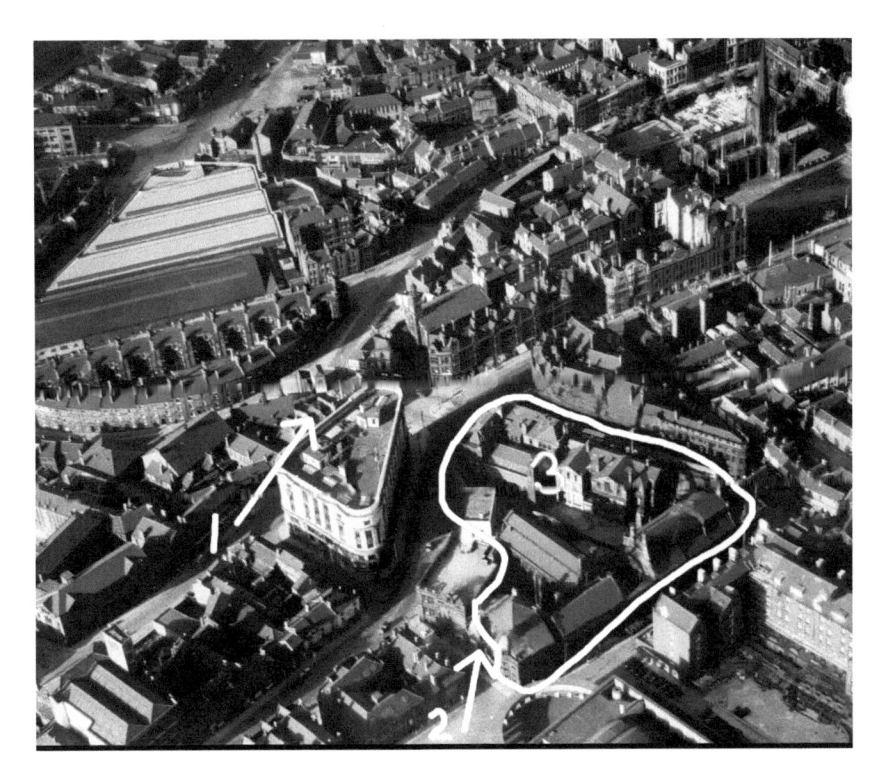

'Yet': A Story of Triumph Over Childhood Separation, Trauma, and Disability

An aerial photograph showing Little Hill (1), the Holly Street school building (2); and the education office and Central Technical School site (3). *Unknown photographer. Photograph taken taken prior to the bombing in December 1940.*

1) Little Hill. The building to the left on Little Hill is the Playhouse. Two classrooms were housed in the building to the right-hand side of Little Hill, adjacent to Townhead Street. Science and art lessons took place here. This was where Philip Seymour cut up Mr Gregory's cane.

2) The Holly Street building has two white dormer-shaped windows on the roof, the one further away from the half-moon shaped building (Sheffield City Hall), and the floor below it, is where the French lessons took place and a pupil was chained to the blackboard. In 1949, Mr Wadge gave the building and engineering students a lecture on how a television worked from the main hall stage, complete with a stripped-down TV.

3) The education office and Central Technical School site, now the Leopold Hotel and square where the Old Boys' Association meet twice a month.

Central Technical School, Sheffield, Class 6X, 1950.
Harry Drabble is the blond young man on the far right in the back row, gritting his teeth and balancing without his crutches. Harry could recite the register until his death. *In the author's collection.*

Other pupils are, Philip Seymour, third from the left on the back row; K. Marsh is seated in the middle row, fourth boy from the right (came third); G.W. Barge is the second boy from the right in the middle row (came fifth); P.J. Bennet is the third boy from the left in the front row; H. Schweizer (failed the course) is seated on third from the right on the front row; R. Ryalls is the second boy from the left in the front row (achieved the highest mark on the building section of the diploma course). The form master, Mr John Hunter, took woodwork. (Philip Seymour's father had been a master builder and had taught Mr Hunter joinery.)

Morning assembly included a minimum of one sung hymn, often with five verses or more. Hymns were sung at least 210 times a year and accompanied by a superb pianist, Mr Hughes. Herbert Wadge, the headmaster, read from the Holy Scripture, and reflected on the message of the reading, but also on 'the use of particular words and stylistic constructions'.[203] The school song was adapted by the headmaster.

The School Song (abridged)

From the Cheviots down to Dover

From the Wash to Milford Town

Yea and all the world over

Men are singing thy renown

Thy renown, O Spartan Mother

CTS our pride and boast

Here's good luck to one another

Here's a rousing loyal toast

Chorus – Flourish CTS forever

Pass the word along!

Here's a hand and there's the other

Friendships pledge to one another

Shake for Auld Lang Syne, my brother

Shout the good old song

Flourish CTS for ever – 'Sheffielders, Hurrah'!

Mr Dove, who took Harry's English lessons, concentrated on grammar, syntax and correct word usage. He taught Harry to say 'our books', and not 'us books', and so on, and shared English literature with a focus on plays, poetry, passages from books and selected texts.[204] *The Broad Highway* by English author Jeffery Farnol, and *How Green Was My Valley* by the Englishman Richard Llewellyn, became favourites.[205] Harry particularly enjoyed the challenge of Shakespeare's language and its gateway to explore the human condition.

Can't Do to Can Do

I had a broad Sheffield accent that wouldn't be understood even in most of Yorkshire, and The Broad Highway *reflected me and my character.*

Trigonometry was taught alongside other necessary mathematics. Philip remembered one lesson delivered by Mr Stanton, formerly of the RAF, where he explained to the class how trigonometry had allowed the 'Dambusters' raid on the German dams in the Ruhr Valley to succeed in dropping their bombs, allowing them to 'bounce' properly on the surface of the dam waters. 'The idea was that there would be two Aldis lights mounted on the nose and midships under the bomber. They would both shine a narrow beam spotlight downwards and off to the right of the aircraft. The two beams would become a single point of light at an exact point 60 feet below (and to the side of) the aircraft. The pilot then had to maintain a steady 232 knots and hold the aircraft level until the bomb aimer released the rotating drum bomb.'[206] Philip explained how this recent thrilling example made the lesson relevant and interesting.

By the September term of 1950, French had been added to the curriculum in Harry's form room. The pupils were early for the first lesson, and Philip remembered one of the class being chained to the blackboard on wheels. When the female teacher came in, she was 'flabbergasted' and demanded the culprit remove the chain immediately. Everyone played dumb, so she told them she would fetch the headmaster. While she was gone, the classmate was quickly unchained, and she came back alone to a quiet and well-behaved class. Philip could not understand why French was introduced to trainee builders, but Harry might have found it useful on his many holidays to France, Belgium, Switzerland and Luxembourg with his wife and children.

As Harry moved around the city, he passed Arthur Wilson, Peck and Co., Ltd, pianoforte, organ, and musical instrument dealers, in Beethoven House, on Pinstone Street. He stared at the violins in the window each time he passed. He never knew what drove him to go into the shop and part with his precious savings for the cheapest violin in stock.

Arthur Wilson, Peck and Co. Ltd., on the corner of Pinstone Street and Barker's Pool. By the 1940s, when Harry bought his first violin and bow here, it had moved to the opposite corner adjoining Leopold Street.' Image from *Sheffield and Rotherham up-to-date: A fin-de-Siecle review, 1897 (Local Studies Library: 914.274 SQ).*

For months Harry kept the instrument hidden under the bed, only getting it out of its case to stroke the wood. Eventually, he picked up the bow, put it on to his left shoulder and repeatedly played one note for hours at a time, listening carefully to the sound.

Understandably, his dad found this endless repetition difficult, and said, 'If it's in you, it'll come out right.' Harry disagreed, believing he needed to talk to a musician. His father suggested he visit a neighbour. Mr Hatter was a steeplejack and self-taught pianist. He was married to a pianist who had qualified as a teacher from the London College of Music. Harry used his pocket money to pay for his lessons with Mr Hatter. Sadly, Mr Hatter was to fall off a chimney and died from his injuries.

LEFT: Cover: *The rudiments of musical knowledge* by Charles W. Pearce, undated.

RIGHT: First page: *The rudiments of musical knowledge* by Charles W. Pearce.

In the author's collection.

Harry playing the violin, 1949, aged 15. (It was his bowing arm that he could not straighten.) *In the author's collection.*

Despite having only one good leg and one good arm, Harry completed the syllabus of the building course. He defied the children and adults he came across that insisted people with physical disabilities should be kept out of sight. However, finding somewhere to socialise was challenging. Harry sought places where he could take up space, and activities he could pursue. Like Derek Godbehere, Harry refused to see himself as someone with limitations. Derek said: *'I had crutches. I weren't disabled. I ran as fast as anyone. When the bottom of the crutch wore out, it was replaced. Mother were frightened with what I'd do on crutches. I could move.'*

Harry found a welcome at the neighbouring Methodist chapel, built in 1937, on Beck Road. He said, 'Methodists used straightforward, easy-to-read texts in an ordinary voice. The stories sounded sensible when they were told in a thick accent to a working-class audience – everyone could understand them.' When his voice broke, he joined several choirs, including the Beck Road Men's Choir, where he learned a lot from a man under five-foot-tall who had a wonderful singing voice. At 18 years old, Harry sang bass or tenor in the choir, depending on which they needed, although he thought he was probably a baritone. He could not sing the melody. The choirs were involved in many annual events throughout the year, for example, the Whit-Monday and Hymn Singing Festival of Joy in Firth Park.[207]

    Harry and his family often escaped to the cinema. In the 1940s cinemas were grand spaces which offered working-class families cheap entertainment, warmth, comfort and a touch of luxury. Female usherettes in uniforms reminiscent of domestic service in country homes showed people to their seats by torchlight. Harry loved the stimulating films with the soaring musical scores, but the seats were 'murder', as what was left of his hip did not bend. He found a way of perching on one bottom cheek and leaned backwards with his left leg stretched out. It was as painful as it looked. He ignored the people who told him he had no right to be there and that he would be in people's way if there was a fire. *The Great Caruso*, a 1951 biographical film made by Metro-Goldwyn-Mayer and starring Mario Lanza as Enrico Caruso, stood out. Harry said the cinema felt like an 'exceptional experience after the silence of the hospital'.

> *We went to the cinema three times a week and often sat in the 'Gods' at the Hippodrome. It was cheap, the seats were more comfortable than those at home. It was warmer, too.*

The Capitol Cinema was on Barnsley Road, less than two miles away at Sheffield Lane Top on the way to the City General Hospital. Its six doors led to a sophisticated art deco-inspired terrazzo floor with its confetti chips of marble, quartz, granite and glass sprinkled across a cream background, creating a constellation of pastel hues and sparkling accents that caught the eye. The interior designers completed the look with an understated pastel rose-and-green colour scheme, neo-classical in style, with high ceilings, alcoves, and statues. It was quite a contrast to the Drabbles' cosy council home.[208] The Capitol seated 1,700 people, 1,200 in the 4*d*, 6*d* or 9*d* seats, and 500 upstairs in the circle, where it cost 1*s*, or 1*s* 3*d* to sit.

Friday nights were variety nights. The acts ranged from a mixture of popular song and comedy turns to speciality acts incorporating acrobats and magicians. Although Harry did not talk specifically about those he saw, he later watched *The Good Old Days*, a BBC television light entertainment programme which ran for 30 years from 20 July 1953 to 31 December 1983. He particularly enjoyed the live orchestra and the extravagant language used to introduce the acts. The show was performed at the Leeds City Varieties, which recreated an authentic atmosphere of the Victorian/Edwardian music hall with songs and sketches of the era performed in the style of the original artistes.[209]

The New Capitol, Sheffield's Latest Cinema. Luxurious – with every Modern Equipment.
Photographer Stewart Bale approximate date 1940–1959. Licensed from ©Picture Sheffield (Image s02695).

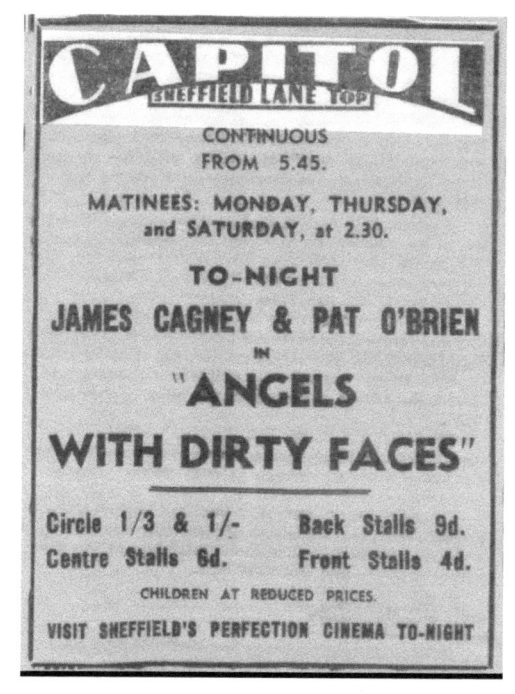

Ad for the film *Angels with Dirty Faces* appeared in the *Sheffield Evening Telegraph* – Monday 18 September 1939.[210]

'Yet': A Story of Triumph Over Childhood Separation, Trauma, and Disability

The Forum Cinema on Herries Road.
Licensed from ©Picture Sheffield (Image s21367).

The interior of Forum Cinema on Herries Road.[211]
Licensed from ©Picture Sheffield (Image s21367).

A 50-minute walk from home brought the family to the Forum Cinema on Herries Road, in the Longley Housing Estate around the corner from where Harry's uncle, Harold Turner, was killed. It opened in September 1938. The auditorium had seating for 1,814, and it was the largest cinema on Sheffield's housing estates.[212] The fuchsia, green and fawn paint with art deco-style panels impressed Harry.[213] The seats were covered in green crimped velvet, while 2,000 yards of special Wilton carpet added to the sense of luxury.[214] It had an organ and stage, and also hosted variety performances and musical concerts.

A third cinema was a bus ride away in the city centre. The Hippodrome had previously been a music hall and a venue to show early film reels; it became a permanent cinema in 1931, capable of seating 2,445 people. Unusually, the cheapest seats were at the rear and were nicknamed 'the Gods'. It was the Drabble family's favourite cinema. The matinee prices from here were 1s to sit in the circle, seats in the stalls cost 8d, and each seat in the gallery cost 4d. After 4 pm, the seats went up to 1s 6d, 1s and 6d, respectively.[215]

People queuing to see the latest film at the Hippodrome in Cambridge Street, Sheffield.
With the kind permission of ©Sheffield Newspapers/National World.

Harry said, 'An event might have been going out for a sit-down fish-and-chip supper. Sometimes, we had a drink in the dimly lit herbalist, with shelves crammed full of herbs in towering polished glass jars. It sold traditional botanical cordials, concocted with herbs, fruit, and spices like the medicinal-smelling sarsaparilla, the earthy dandelion and burdock, and a sweet blood-orange tonic.'

LEFT: Harry Senior, Harry, Margaret and May on holiday.
The pained expression on Harry's face reveals the physical difficulty he had balancing on one knee with the other straight as he tried to hide his disability.

RIGHT: Harry, May, Margaret and Harry Senior. Harry hides his damaged leg and raised boot. *In the author's collection.*

Few working-class families had an annual holiday outside of those organised through their place of worship, but 'Mother had worked for people with a much better lifestyle who had taste and education. They had nicer things than would ever be available to her.' So, May did all that she could to expand her children's horizons.

After the war, her knitting business paid for the family to go camping for a month each August. Harry's father bought an ex-army bell tent and equipment, and arranged for it to be collected from the house and sent by train and taxi to a farm in Skegness, to Blackpool and later to Paignton in Devon. The Drabbles followed on. Harry Senior would join them for the beginning and end of the holiday. Young Harry would help his father put up the tent, dig a moat around it, and pack up at the end of the holiday. Harry said, 'Holidays with the army bell tent wouldn't have been possible if Dad hadn't been doing the work he did. The tents and camping equipment were incredibly heavy in those days.'

We made our own mattresses with sheets sewn together stuffed with straw from the farm. I collected mushrooms in the early morning and brought back duck eggs. I caught rabbits with a snare, skinned them and spit-roasted them. Mum made tasty meals using foraged herbs. She was always trying something new.

His parents encouraged Harry's desire to educate himself and bought him a pocket dictionary.

A small pocket dictionary that May picked up for Harry while the family was on holiday in Paignton.
In the author's collection.
The dedication 'To Harry from Mum & Dad' is in May's writing.

Harry with his father. The photo was taken by a roving seaside photographer. Believed to be in Skegness.
In the author's collection.

Harry preferred camping life. Although it sometimes felt claustrophobic, it gave him the chance to roam and created 'windows of opportunity when you could spend some time with family'. Harry said it was a joy to talk to and teach his sister and 'best friend', Margaret.

Harry Senior, Harry, Margaret and May. With difficulty, Harry uses his left big toe to balance without his crutches. *In the author's collection.*

> *When we were on holiday, whether or not he knew them, my father was very good at entertaining adults and children with simple songs and humour. On holiday, he ate well and kicked and threw balls for the youngsters. He always had a gang of kids around him. Dad also dressed up in a borrowed skirt and blouse, or dress, in the music hall tradition and had people in stitches.*
>
> *It wasn't my humour. I preferred* The Goon Show *where, if you blinked, you'd end up on the wrong page. There were 'Kiss me, quick' funny hats, uneducated people being uneducated. Tea wasn't sophisticated. People talked, of course, but it was always about the same things. Although it wasn't to my taste, there was a sense of continuity and a kindness: apart from those who were disabled, people generally took each other as they were.*

Harry was not ashamed of his background, but he did not fit in. He preferred the entertainment at places like the Winter Gardens of Blackpool and Skegness, where visitors could listen to indoor live classical music and catch a theatre play, but his parents preferred the sing-songs. Harry loved watching Margaret engrossed in the puppet shows. The family went on long daily walks together.

In his teens, Harry often went camping alone or with friends. Still on crutches, he strapped an ex-army small half-tent to his rucksack, which he packed with a spade, a groundsheet, mess-tin, cup, matches and his cutlery. He carried a two-blade penknife with a can-opener in his pocket. One particularly memorable trip was camping at Monsal Dale, a valley in Derbyshire, with his friend

David Beeley from the technical school, who worked for the company Steel, Peech and Tozer. Harry said David was the best trumpet and cornet player he ever heard. The scent of 'lily of the valley takes me straight back there'.

Monsal Dale, steam train crossing The Viaduct Frith 67588, 1914.
In the author's collection.

On Wednesday afternoons, Harry skipped school, had a 'wash and brush up' in the superior rest rooms of a local department store, and climbed the stairs to the centre of the Grand Circle in Sheffield City Memorial Hall. He leaned his crutches against the railing. He was there to watch the Hallé Orchestra rehearse under Sir John Barbirolli, the principal conductor from 1943 to 1970. As they packed up, 'they were kind to this lad with the thick accent who turned up on crutches week after week to ask them questions'. Harry joined the Listeners Club, probably at the suggestion of Mr Dove, so he could attend exclusive concerts, including chamber concerts, and bought reduced tickets before they went on sale to the public. He studied the programme notes about the composer and pieces, and quizzed the orchestra before the concert started. He also belonged to the City Hall's Jazz Club – the second largest in England. For Harry, watching Humphrey Lyttelton, Nat King Cole, Johnny Dankworth, Louis Armstrong, Ella Fitzgerald and Count Basie play there were highlights. While he was interested in different forms of music, watching the Beatles had no appeal for him, although he respected them as folk artists/poets. Nor did Cliff Richard and The Shadows attract him.

Music is a magical, beautiful world where I can lose myself, no matter what is happening on the outside.

The snooker halls also had their appeal. Smoke-filled and often with a terrible reputation, snooker was a sport in which Harry could compete.

Snooker hall at the Walkley Community Centre. 'Originally, the charge to play was 6d, with 2d returned if the chalk was handed in at the end of the game.'[216] *Image provided by the Walkley Community Centre.*

There were halls all over Sheffield like Langtons, on Heeley Bottom, the hall under the Abbeydale Cinema and the Manor Cinema, where 15-year-old boys went for a 'penny bash' ('four of us paid one penny each'). 'We puffed cigarettes continuously and felt like 18-year-olds.' Harry added, 'There was always a man on the first table taking money off people, not me, though I watched to see how he got away with it.' Harry was not alone in bunking off school to watch or play a few games. Later in life, the televised games were a highlight of his year.

One of Harry's first musical experiences as a performer was playing for a football band. In around 1949, when he was about 15, he joined the Salvation Army band, pledging not to drink alcohol in return for the loan of brass instruments and basic instruction. He did not keep the pledge.

The players in the Grimesthorpe Brass Band were generous in allowing young people to join.[217] Was his father excited by Harry playing brass instruments? Harry Senior was certainly a long-time listener to the big brass band sound that Sheffield was famous for. Harry learnt to play nearly every instrument in the band, because they are all fingered the same as the cornet, but the trombone defeated him as his mouth was the wrong shape to make a pleasant sound. He often played alto sax E flat from a piano score.

The brass band met in a pub in an upstairs room. As Harry was the youngest, it was his job to collect the drinks from the bar. Seemingly impossible, Harry found a way to carry heavy trays up the stairs while on crutches. His first music stand comprised broken bits from a box which were offered to him by the bandleader, who had noticed he did not have one.[218]

Example of a Band of Hope pledge card promising total abstinence of alcoholic drinks. They acted as both rewards and reminders.[219]

John Harrison was also an important influence. He lived at Firth Park and was a Doctor of Music, though not a violinist like Harry. 'I heard Mr Harrison playing the piano, and I said, "I don't know what you were doing but it was marvellous and I want to understand why".' From December 1952, Harrison entered Harry for his music exams. Harrison started a Sunday group with Harry and others. Afterwards, they went to the pub for a couple of hours, then got the bus home with their music and instruments. This continued for years. Harry said, 'Some adults were supportive and kindly to aspiring young musicians. It was a working-class city, but everything I wanted to do I found a way to pursue it with other interested people.'

9

Emerging from Education and Battling Disability

Throughout his three-year building course, Harry was not sure he would graduate. He knew some of the teaching staff looked for an 'excuse to rid themselves of the cripple'. Other pupils occasionally sabotaged his work. He said, 'I don't know why they felt threatened by a boy on crutches, but it taught me to triple check everything.' Fellow pupil Philip Seymour recently explained that he and the other 14–16-year-old pupils did not understand why a lad with a disability would be on the course, but added Harry did everything demanded of him. Harry explained he was often aggressive and defiant, and having had so little schooling, he found it difficult to accept authority or recognise the hierarchy in the school system.

During the final bricklaying assessment, he was told to build three different walls. Harry thought they were not his best work. He 'lost it', and knocked them down before the examiner came to assess them. Maybe unconsciously, Harry was taking his failure into his own hands. Certainly, in his adult life, he gave himself a mental get-out by often choosing the 'impossible thing, because failure terrified me'. Towards the end of that examination day, the examiner caught up with him and said, 'Drabble, I saw your work and I have passed it.'

Harry did not know how well he had graduated until I gave him the results in 2022. He was delighted to learn he'd finished in 15th place out of a class of 51, ahead of the pupils who had dismissed and tried to humiliate him. A lad with only one good arm and one good leg, through determination and grit had earned himself a 2nd class Building Diploma. (Harry's Building Diploma can be seen at Appendix E.)

> The results as approved are as follows :-
>
> First Class Diploma   -   5
> Second   "   "   -   19
> Third   "   "   -   20
> Failed   -   -   7
>   TOTAL   51

Results for the diploma examination – Building Section – December 1950, Sheffield Central Technical School, page 1.

Sheffield Central Technical School
Diploma Examination – Building Section – December, 1950

NAME	Eng. Group Av.	Science Group Av.	Draw. Group Av.	Shops Group Av.	Mean Av.	Position	Result
Ryalls, R.	60	66½	73	61	65	1	1st
Bark, E.	59½	69	69	62	65	2	1st
Marsh, K.	67½	68	67	50½	63½	3	1st
Short, D.	70	58	64	57½	62½	4	1st
Barge, G.W.	57½	63½	63	57½	60½	5	~~2nd~~ /st.
Beardshaw, M.B.	63½	52	55	63½	58½	6	2nd
Cooke, P.	52½	55	62	61½	58	7	2nd
Baggaley, R.	56	57	61	56½	58	8	2nd
Foster, B.	55½	60	57	56	57	9	2nd –
Stevenson, W.	53	58	53	63	57	10	2nd
Seymour, P.C.R.	46½	46½	59	74	56½	11	2nd
Butcher, R.	48	52	61	62	55½	12	2nd
Cooper, D.	58	59½	59	46	55½	12	2nd
Colgrave, B.	48	55	59	58½	55	14	2nd
Drabble, H.	62½	56	54	46	54½	15	2nd
Watts, B.	52	58½	54	52½	54½	16	2nd
Binns, D.	54½	62	49	49	53½	17	2nd
Furniss, K.	61	61	51	37	52½	18	2nd
Williamson, J.B.	43½	51½	53	60	52	19	~~3rd~~ e. 2nd
Lister, G.	53½	58½	51	44	52	20	~~3rd~~ e. 2nd
White, B.	60½	63	44	39	52	21	~~3rd~~ e. 2nd
Fell, G.B.	56½	57	60	32½	51½	21	~~Fail~~ e. 3rd
Broadhurst, K.	44	50½	55	56	51½	23	~~3rd~~ e. 2nd
Boielle, J.E.	55	52½	48	48½	51	24	~~3rd~~ e. 2nd
Bennett, P.J.	62½	56	45	40½	51	24	~~3rd~~ e. 2nd
Staniforth, D.Y.	53	42½	57	50½	51	26	3rd
Bradbury, K.	47½	52	51	51½	50½	27	3rd

Results for the diploma examination – Building Section – December 1950, Sheffield Central Technical School, page 2.

NAME	MARKS				Mean Av.	Posi-tion	Result
	Eng Group Av.	Science Group Av.	Draw. Group Av.	Shops Group Av.			
Smith, J.	56½	45	45	51	49½	28	3rd
Thorpe, D.J.	50	47	49	50	49	29	3rd
Hornagold, G.T.	46	47½	49	53½	49	30	3rd
Beeley, D.G.	54	50	43	47½	49	30	3rd
Harrison, V.	51	45	47	53	49	30	3rd
Hartle, J.	56½	46	44	42	47½	33	3rd
Peat, N.H.	31½	42	59	53	46½	34	Fail
Sandall, P.	52	47	41	45	46½	34	3rd
Spittlehouse, R.	51½	45	41	47½	46½	34	3rd
Porteous, D.	44	40½	47	53	46	37	3rd
Bonnington, J.	47	40	48	48	46	38	3rd
Hudson, J.	43	47½	48	45	46	38	3rd
Ollerenshaw, Wm.	54½	39	40	47½	45½	40	3rd
Smith, J.	40½	37½	49	51	44½	41	3rd
Royston, J.	42½	38	42	49½	43	42	3rd
Hurman, R.	41½	40	39	49½	42½	43	3rd
Garlick, B.	43	43	38	43	42	44	3rd
Thompson, D.M.	44	41½	37	42½	41	45	3rd
Hayes, C.G.	36	39	37	52	41	46	Fail
Oakes, S.M.	38½	34	33	48½	38½	47	Fail
Tandy, G.F.	40	36½	35	43½	38½	47	Fail
Schweitzer, H.	38	37	33	41	37	49	Fail
Lambert, A.	37	32	35	41½	36½	50	Fail
Johnson, B.	35	32	29	34	32½	51	Fail

- 2 -

Results for each class for intake 1948–50, signed by H. Slack.
Extract from the Junior Technical School Diploma Examination Assessment Advisory Committee Minute Book, archive reference CA 626.22a.

On 25 January 1951, now aged 16, Harry performed 'Greensleeves' as part of a trio at the Technical School Speech and Graduation Day in the Victoria Hall, Norfolk Street, Sheffield. It had been arranged by his English teacher, Mr Dove, a violinist. If his parents were there, were they both bursting with pride (but perhaps, at the same time, worried whether he would find work)? The following day, Mr Dove kindly sent Harry a letter of congratulation commenting that the trio 'Rawson, Drabble and Staniforth' had been the best item in the programme, and he trusted he would see Harry at the City Hall concerts and at the Listeners Club.

Harry's time at the Central Technical School was a long period of stability, with loving support from his parents, a precious relationship with his sister, and a few influential teachers. He still found it difficult to manage his emotions, which led to mood swings and outbursts of anger. He said he found it easy to withdraw from social contact, push people away and rely on his own resources, but the positive experiences began to mitigate some of the damage that the separation from his parents had caused. Rather than remain detached, he formed a couple of relationships with fellow students. The headmaster signed a letter, presumably sent to his parents, which said that Harry had also 'proved himself to be a person of sound ability'.[220] Although Harry had had difficulties, he had figured out ways to overcome them. Harry had transcended his disability and earned his first qualification.

CITY OF SHEFFIELD
EDUCATION COMMITTEE

CENTRAL TECHNICAL SCHOOL

PRIZE DISTRIBUTION

Thursday, 25th January, 1951, at 7 p.m.

In the
VICTORIA HALL
NORFOLK STREET

Programme for the Prize Distribution, 25 January 1951, Victoria Hall. *In the author's collection.*

PROGRAMME

1. OPENING HYMN "O Beautiful my Country" . . *F. L. Hosmer*
2. CHAIRMAN'S REMARKS
   Councillor A. BALLARD, Chairman of the Governors
3. CHOIR (a) "Come, see where golden-hearted Spring" *Handel*
   (b) "Flocks in Pastures Green Abiding" *J. S. Bach*
4. HEADMASTER'S REPORT
   H. W. WADGE, B.Sc.
5. CHOIR (a) "Fine Knacks for Ladies" . . *John Dowland*
   (b) "No John" . . . . . . *Folk Song*
6. ADDRESS AND DISTRIBUTION OF PRIZES
   PROFESSOR ROGER ARMFELT
   (Professor of Education, University of Leeds).
7. (a) TRIO "Greensleeves" . . . . *arr. by Henry Geehl*
   (Piano—Rawson. Violins—Drabble and Staniforth).
   (b) PIANOFORTE SOLO "Prelude in G Minor" *Rachmaninoff*
   (Rawson)
   (c) CHOIR "Five Eyes" . . . . *Armstrong Gibbs*
8. VOTES OF THANKS
9. CHOIR "The Lord is my Shepherd" . . *Henry Smart*
10. HYMN "O Worship the King" . . *Sir R. Grant*
11. "GOD SAVE THE KING"

SPECIAL PRIZES

The School gratefully acknowledges the valuable encouragement and support indicated by the following annual donations for the provision of prizes:—

Sheffield and District Branch, Federation of Master Builders.
(Ten guineas).
Sheffield Building Trades Employers' Association.
(Twenty-three guineas).
Sheffield Lighter Trades Employers' Association.
(Ten guineas).
Mr. C. H. Firth. Annual Prize for Geography.
(One guinea).
Mrs. K. E. Blythe and Miss K. Blythe, M.A.
(One guinea).

This last prize is to be known as the "H. Bardill Blythe Prize for English." It is presented by his wife and daughter in memory of H. Bardill Blythe, Esq., M.I.P., A.M.I.B.E., who served Sheffield industry as a specialist in Furnace Design and who took a great interest in the work of the School. He died in October, 1948.

Interior pages of the programme for the Prize Distribution, 25 January 1951, Victoria Hall. *In the author's collection.*

'Yet': A Story of Triumph Over Childhood Separation, Trauma, and Disability

Harry could not stand, or walk, without crutches, and had a stiff, painful and unstable hip, so he could not take up a building trade. Following his father into the steel industry was out of the question. With little education and rooted in a working-class community, Harry could not see a path into non-physical work. According to a later candidate report for the Chartered Institute of Management Accountants, Harry went into training as a silversmith with the view he would take over his grandfather Leonard's company a couple of years later.

He was accepted on to a self-directed silversmithing course at the Sheffield College of Art in one of their many post-war satellite workshops in the still bomb-damaged city centre. The terms were 13 weeks long. He may have been pointed to the course as part of the local authority's support for those living with a disability. These initiatives, initially aimed at disabled ex-servicemen and women, were now being extended to the broader disabled population. Here Harry worked on design, turned a piece of metal into a bow, and created new moulds. He commented of the experience, 'Working on lead coffins was bloody good training.'

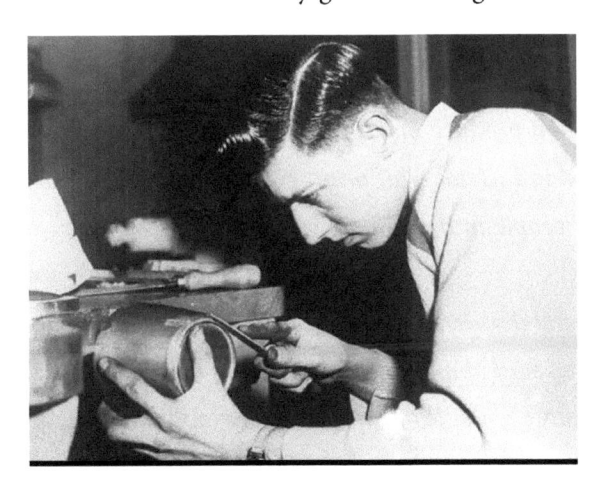

A student at the Sheffield College of Art. Unknown photographer.

Aged about 17 years old, Harry walked on crutches into the rear entrance of H. Parkin & Son Ltd in Scotland Street, in a slum area, and asked the foreman for a job. The man looked him up and down and asked, 'What can you do, lad?' Harry answered, 'Let me show you.' He was taken on as a silversmith improver: someone who did the work without having done a full apprenticeship – where he worked on silver tea sets. This was where he started drinking tea, as the chemicals in the air contaminated the taste of the water he had always drunk. Lunch was a loaf of his mother's bread with thin slices of cheese between each buttered doorstop slice. Despite his mother saying, 'What will the neighbours say?', Harry bought himself a pale blue suit. He said: 'It was incongruous in my situation. But despite my poor rate, I earned good money as a silversmith – twice as much as the men who were supposed to be teaching me – and I wanted to be seen as someone going places.'

> *I soon had the union on to me because I was outperforming the experienced men. It was decided I would start work at 10 am before the morning break. In my lunch hour I played the violin with the buffer girls, and I left at 3 pm. No team wanted to own me. They wanted me out. I didn't understand why they didn't adopt my methods and produce more, at a better quality, but I knew nothing about industrial relations then. There were 100 people in the company.*
>
> *The lowest in the hierarchy were the buffer girls, and they heard about what was being said about me. Nelly went in her [clothes protecting] rags to management to say they understood the men*

> had a problem with me, but said, 'This guy's work is the best in your shop. We take it in turns to buff it [and] because there is so little to do, the person who does it gets more of a bonus.' Those buffer girls had a heart of solid gold.

Socially, Harry did not fit in.

> One man was assertive. He wasn't popular, no one listened to him, but we got on alright. We used to chat on one side of the circle as the others talked their silly talk, all awful, small, meaningless noise. If one man had problems with his wife, no one would tell him it was because of his behaviour or say, 'Poor woman'. It was misogynistic. I wasn't part of it. Women just want to solve the problem. I've always been with the women, really.

During his time off, Harry enjoyed dressing smartly, and wore his father's long white silk scarf to concerts and operas, including those at City Hall, the Harrogate Opera House, and Ripon Cathedral. Invariably he left 'as drunk on the music as neighbours returning from the pub filled with alcohol on a Saturday night'. But once again, he was experiencing lameness and increased hip pain. Around January 1952, aged 17, he was admitted into the Royal Infirmary for an operation to fuse his hip.

A surgeon removed a long piece of bone from his right shin and wedged it into his pelvis in the hope it would stabilise it and reduce his pain. The operation was unsuccessful. He said, 'It was always a long shot. We were guinea pigs.'

Theatre, Royal Infirmary, Infirmary Road surgeons and staff with patient in the new operating theatre.
Licensed from ©Picture Sheffield (Image h00034).

Harry's hope of taking over Leonard's business ended while he was in hospital. His grandfather died on 5 February 1952 aged 75, and his tools were sold for very little. Harry needed a new plan. Despite his weeping wound, the Royal Infirmary discharged him. During this time, he continued with his music studies, and in July 1952, he passed the Intermediate violin exam with honours. On 18 August, Harry was readmitted to Rivelin, now renamed the King Edward VII Orthopaedic Hospital, for three months, to undergo an experimental two-drug chemotherapy. When Dr Herzog and the matron, Miss Elsie Jones, were appointed in 1952, they extended the visiting hours to a maximum of two hours on the afternoon of the first and third Sunday.[221] Harry said, 'Matron Jones visited my ward, and said, "I thought I'd seen the back of you. Remember, I'm watching you. You're not to use my staff for your own ends", and walked on.'

Matron Jones at King Edward VII Orthopaedic Hospital.[222] Cropped photograph from from 'King Edward 2008–2018' collated by Jean Bruce. *With grateful thanks to Margaret Miller.*

Specially trained senior nurses gave Harry a painful, expensive, deep intramuscular injection of 1 g of streptomycin daily, the first antibiotic cure for tuberculosis. Fortunately, the second drug, para-aminosalicylic acid, was swallowed, rather than injected, at a rate of 2–4 g, four times a day. Using both drugs reduced the development of drug resistance.

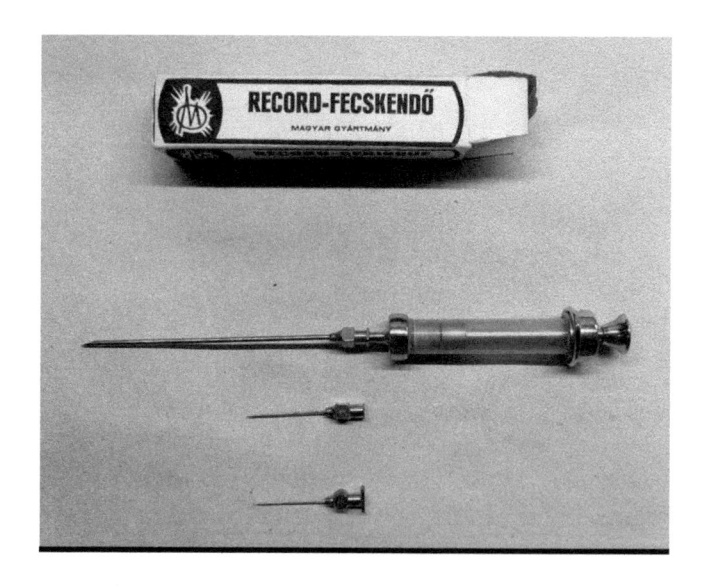

An example of a piece of Vintage Medical 2 ml Glass Syringe.
In the author's collection.

The side effects of the chemotherapy were grim. Lower doses of streptomycin can commonly result in decreased appetite; narrowing airways; chest discomfort; cough; permanent deafness; diarrhoea; dizziness; fever; headache; increased risk of infection; nausea; mouth and throat pain; renal impairment; skin reactions; altered taste; tinnitus and vomiting.[223] When he could, Harry distracted himself from the nasty side effects of the treatment by playing card games, such as rummy and pontoon. He often played solo whist for money with another three patients. When the pathology laboratory was free, he escaped the ward to practise the violin.

Favourite nurses brought Harry single bottles of stout and Player's cigarettes, which he paid for with the money he made mending stockings and selling his embroidery. He had got a taste for stout, which the hospital had provided as part of his treatment, but which was stopped to reduce costs. His smoking on the ward may seem strange, but although there had been early reports linking smoking with lung cancer, the *Nursing Times* reported, incorrectly, 'It certainly does good to tuberculosis persons and diabetics.'[224]

Not long after turning 18 in December 1952, Harry passed the Advanced Intermediate violin exam with honours. When he returned to his workbench later that month, he found his 'fabulous set of tools' had gone. He had worked on lead, tin and copper, but wanted to do the trickier stuff on the silverware side. However, he was put to work on Britannia metal, a pewter that was favoured for its silvery appearance and smooth surface. When Harry arrived, the shop steward, in charge of pewter, took one look at his crutches and shouted, 'You stand all day, and you've got no props!' Harry said, 'He hoped to drive me out. He warned me, "This is where your skills will be tested, lad." It was a very uncomfortable place to be.' Harry refused to be beaten. He was determined to show what he could do.

> *You had to strap the tankards to keep the seam straight, turn on the mandrel and then solder the whole joint. Pewter is soft, soft as you can get. I was given a proprietary solder that melted before the pewter did. You soldered with a little flame, and if you stopped, you made a hole. I found a nice turntable made for doing big presentation bowls in the stores. It was two feet across.*
>
> *I used to put all the pots I had to do on the turntable in a clockwise direction, so by the time I had done the first, the second was warm, and so on.*

Harry irritated the men around him. They did not like a youngster with disabilities taking to the work so well and showing them up. Harry could not bring himself to 'fall into line' in the hope he would be accepted.

The Georgian teapots, 12–20 at a time, were stamped out in a die, a flat piece of metal. If you did it the way I was shown, you had to trim the rubbish off. The way I did it was in two halves, with wires round the top and the bottom. It was absolutely right, no remedial work needed doing. It was hard soldering; we had a bloody great flame gun. You had to hold the piece in tongs, warm them with the flame, and when it was hot enough, solder it. Borax keeps the surface protected, so it doesn't oxidise. The standard practice was to solder the halves, acid off, then file off excess solder. The bottom has to be trimmed, so it's perfectly flat and you can put the bottom on. You'd mark out where the bottom should be, smooth the filing and dead smooth on the blocks that were nailed down on the bench.

I used carborundum. It was like a horizontal flat millstone; I invested a lot of time, and I brought my pot down at high speed. When I was ready to cut, I used shears I'd made from the rubbish bin; I had plenty of time. Big straight shears stretch cut material. I used what I called nibblers, tiny shears, which would give a rough edge. I didn't mark out as I did it by eye; my spouts never, ever dripped.

The men tried hard to rubbish what I produced but couldn't. One shouted, 'He's not measured it!', but when the foreman checked, it was spot on. Another tried to copy my technique, but the stone pulled the pot out of his hands and it smashed against the wall. I finally left, claiming that after the op I couldn't keep up with the work, but I saw the writing on the wall. Young people didn't want these products. I thought they'd be out of business soon.

In his spare time, Harry learnt to shoot at the Vickers Shepcote Rolling Mills rifle range, which had opened in 1914.[225] He stood or laid down to shoot the straw targets. Harry liked the cleaning and precision of guns.

The first thing you learn is not to fire in self-defence, and that knocking off things on a fence outside the range was a 'no, no'.

I decided shooting to eat is the only good reason to kill. I learned discipline and patience on the range.

In 1952, Harry started the Beck Road Quartet, and for the next ten years, they provided music for dances in the mining villages, like Pilley near Chapeltown. As was common, the band played a mixed repertoire, starting with traditional tunes the whole family knew, through to jazz and the current hits played for the younger adults at the end of the evening.

He discovered that the miners near Sheffield and in Derbyshire were open, warm-hearted and hospitable. Many were eager for culture and conversation. After performing, the event organisers usually invited the band members to their parlours for late-night discussions over copious cups of tea and homemade bread and jam. There, they talked about literature and poetry, including Shakespeare, religion, church music, jazz and the political news of the day. He rarely returned home before the early hours of the morning.

Being in a band was a way to make a little money, and widen his social group, but it also got Harry over the awkwardness of going to dances, avoiding the humiliation of not being able to dance and sitting on the sidelines. Although Harry drank a mixture of Guinness and cider (known locally as black velvet) at the dances where he played, he said, 'I wasn't drunk many times – drunk is when you are not in control'.

Beck Road Quartet, Tony Mills, pianist, Jack Beck, drummer and Brian Brownly, saxophone, c. 1952.[226] *Unknown photographer. In the author's collection.*

Church halls were cheap or free places for Harry and the band members to rehearse. He encouraged the church organisers to allow him to put on dances, with people paying a donation to the church on the door. The church organisers also agreed to put on plays to raise funds, often allowing Harry to arrange or provide the musical accompaniments.

Beck Road Methodist Chapel, Shiregreen, opened in 1937.
Licensed from © Picture Sheffield (Image arc01210).

The strong values of inclusivity, reason and social justice of the Unitarian Church appealed to Harry. He probably visited Upper Chapel in Norfolk Street the most.

Harry also played the violin in the orchestral pit in a city theatre for about a year. He found the orchestral work repetitive, boring and badly paid, and commented that playing Gilbert and Sullivan for two weeks put him off light opera.

Harry knew he could not keep doing physical work. His only hope to find a sustainable job and become a man capable of supporting a wife and children was to retrain for office work.

The Ministry of Labour had introduced a scheme for the training and resettlement of disabled persons in 1944. The National

Health Service Act of 1948 recognised the right of every person to access comprehensive facilities for treatment, rehabilitation and restoration of capacity for work.[227]

> 'To rehabilitate, is to bring back into the human circle, those whom disability has placed outside, and enable them to live a full, free and happy life … There is need, therefore, to consider what the disabled persons can do rather than what they cannot do, and so, on that basis to create the greatest possible opportunity for the disabled to take their places in the ordinary economic life of the country.'[228]

In November 1952, Harry was referred for rehabilitation, but instead of finding a gateway to clean, indoor work, he learnt over three long months to hate ineffective bureaucracy. The manager had no training in assessing people's potential and turned Harry down when he asked to join a course to become a bookkeeper.

He just wouldn't let me do it. I'd gone along and sat with the chap and did maths with him. I got every answer right, but he said, 'Oh you've done metal work, you can do that'. I said, I can't stand on crutches all day. I want to get into office work',
but no one listened.

Harry believed if he was stuck in the rehabilitation centre, he should use scrap metal to show other people practical techniques in metal work, ones that he thought employers would value.

> *I got into their bad books in the rehabilitation workshop. Everyone was doing it wrong, and I hated it. There were 20 in the metal workshop, so I showed them how to do everything properly.*
>
> *I was sent to the manager who told me, 'You don't realise we have problems getting contracts, so I need the work to last till the end of term. You need to slow down. Dismissed.' I was angry and frustrated. I believed if the workshop produced quality items, they would get better, more profitable contracts.*

Harry found it hard to work slowly and impossible to work badly. As he was left alone, he started making Christmas gifts using scrap metal from the yard. Despite being told he could make nothing worthwhile and should not waste his energy, Harry turned pieces of the old hot water tanks into ashtrays, trays, dishes and bowls with tricky, modern engraved geometric designs. Harry made these items to a better standard than was produced by the metal shop in the rehabilitation centre, and they were sold to raise money for the scheme.

He also made abstract pendants, believed to have been taught by William E. Bennett, head of the silversmith department at the Sheffield College of Art.[229]

Harry certainly described something remarkably similar to William Bennett's method, as described by gold and silversmith John Spencer:

> Just snip off random shapes of silver or gilding metal, tap them flat, load half of the units with a generous pallion of solder on one side and half with solder on both sides,

arrange any old how, then with a gentle flame let them fuse together while at the same time scattering silver or gilding metal filings on some of the units. Then saw-pierce around the edge and add previously melted beads.[230]

Jean Morrell (Cartwright) and A. Edward Cartwright are seated together front centre. Other staff members probably present in the picture included Kathleen M. Mills, Edith D. Bingham, J. Irwin Hoyland, W.E. Bennett and F.J. Brodie.[231]

A Jack Spencer abstract pendant, with grateful thanks to Jack for his permission to use the image. Technique attributed to William E. Bennett, head of the silversmith department at the Sheffield College of Art.

Harry's rough practice ashtray made of scrap metal. Not suitable for sale by the rehabilitation workshop, c. 1952, by Harry, aged 18.
In the author's collection.

'Yet': A Story of Triumph Over Childhood Separation, Trauma, and Disability

Close-up of an ashtray with Harry working out a design, therefore not suitable for sale by the rehabilitation workshop, c. 1952. *In the author's collection.*

Another rough practice piece made of scrap metal. Here, Harry experimented with the size of a new design, c. 1952. *In the author's collection.*

A brass dish made from scrap metal which Harry used to work out the dimensions of a new decorative motif. Not intended for sale, c. 1952. *In the author's collection.*

A brooch made from scrap. *In the author's collection.*

By the time Harry left the rehabilitation workshop, he had passed on some of his skills to the miners and soldiers on the 'fit to work' scheme, but had received no training to better his own circumstances. The hope of the Disabled Persons (Employment) Act of 1944 to provide vocational training courses to 'enable disabled persons to learn a new occupation which is suited to their disability and which makes full use of their capacity' had not been delivered.[232] No career guidance was forthcoming. Harry was given no hope of a course or a job, only a letter of referral to the labour exchange (a letter he did not present). Four years later, Harry found out he had been written up as 'an unstable dreamer who might suit the role of storekeeper or night watchman'.

> *I wasn't able-bodied, so I had no future in physical work, nor could I rely on what I could do with my hands if I had to stand all day, every day. I didn't blame the able-bodied people who said I was crippled and uneducated. They were right. I couldn't do more to improve my body, so my challenge was to educate myself and make the impossible leap into a profession.*

The Disabled Persons (Employment) Act of 1944 also arranged for the registration of disabled people, and insisted that 'any employer employing twenty or more employees is required to take a quota of about 3 per cent of disabled persons, and the Ministry has inspectors who make a number of inspections to make sure that this 3 per cent quota is maintained'.[233] In order to pay his way, Harry was forced to work for between a half and two-thirds of the rates paid to physically able stock allocation clerks at Brightside

Foundry & Engineering Company. He said, 'Clerks were paid less than people on the shop floor. They took the work because it was a clean job.'

The office manager at Brightside had the workers come together each month in a big circle to go through that month's figures. Everyone supposedly had a copy of the draft that was to go to the 12 members of the board of directors when it was approved. The first time Harry was included, the manager started to read the numbers. He added, 'Shout out if you've got a different number.' Harry heard a number that was not on his copy and thought fast. 'I'm the most junior, and in previous places people wanted me to keep quiet, but we've been told how we should act,' so he raised his hand. 'That's not the number I have, sir'. The manager responded, 'You're quite right. I read the wrong number.' Later, Harry found out from the typists that they were regularly instructed to produce incorrect copies. The manager used the test to find out who paid attention, and who was prepared to follow an instruction and speak out, even if it meant 'going against the herd'. Sometimes, the manager weeded out troublemakers who did not speak, but went to other people in the office to tell them a number was wrong. If they did this, they were fired. Harry was not given an incorrect copy again. He was later promoted and became a credit controller. He said, 'Later, as a manager, I didn't use devious tactics. I found if I explained why each task was important, people invariably worked harder and did the right thing.'

Early in 1953, 18-year-old Harry attended a clinic appointment where surgeon Frank Holdsworth said he was not recommending surgery to treat the long-standing, still discharging, TB lesion on Harry's left hip. The surgeon was 'well thought of and expected to receive a title'.[234] Disappointed, Harry went outside to have a smoke and considered his options. He concluded that, given how much his condition affected his life, he needed to 'further state' his case, so waited until Holdsworth finished his clinic and asked to speak to him. The outcome was that Harry was readmitted to the Royal Infirmary on 25 February. Again, a piece of bone was taken out of his left shin and wedged into his hip in the hope it would reduce his pain and make the hip stable. The operation was unsuccessful and left Harry with an open wound that drained into a bag tied to his leg. Again, he was put on a high dose of antibiotics. It helped for a while, but the infection returned.

On the men's ward, Harry noticed and thought about the other patients. An acutely depressed man had lost an arm and a leg when he was caught between two train wagons. He talked to Harry, fearful that his fiancée would leave him now that he could do nothing. Quietly, Harry taught himself to roll a cigarette with one hand. Once he had conquered the art, he passed the skill on and was delighted that this achievement turned around the patient's outlook. The man's fiancée responded to his new can-do attitude, and they planned their wedding. Harry also got talking to a boy who had a guitar with him. Harry borrowed it and taught himself to play chords to accompany people when they sang.

The man in the next bed to Harry had broken both ankles climbing and thought he would not be able to pursue his passion again. Harry encouraged him to reconsider the possibilities, and they planned a climb together. Harry regretted it did not happen, as his own operation failed. The climber was good at chess and taught him to play. They also pulled their beds together to play cards. About two weeks before he was discharged, Harry saw the Queen's Coronation. It was the only time he watched television in a hospital.

10

A Love Story Defies Expectations

Harry's dream was to marry and raise a family. However, there were many people who believed disabled people should not reproduce, and others who thought they did not have the right to have children. Eugenics, meaning 'good breeding', was a term coined in 1883 by Sir Francis Galton to describe 'the science which deals with all influences which improve the inborn qualities of a race'.[235] In Britain, at its worst, it sought to control the reproduction of those considered 'unfit'.[236] The Eugenics Society, started in 1907, became more concerned with 'curing' a variety of social and physical disorders among the poor, including tuberculosis.[237] The suggestion that Britain should endeavour to restrict the marriage of the physically and mentally unfit survived in a diluted form into the 1950s.

Harry said that people in his working-class community did not widely see or accept those with physical disabilities, and the thought of someone like him having children filled some with horror.

In his teens, Harry took a few girls out to the theatre, to see a film or attend a concert. The most memorable outing was when he impressed Maureen Middleton by rowing them both across the bay from Brixham to Torquay. Her father, Herbert, was part of Harry Senior's team at Samuel Osborn & Co., and the families socialised together. Maureen played the piano and Harry thought they might

'Yet': A Story of Triumph Over Childhood Separation, Trauma, and Disability

ONLY *HEALTHY* SEED MUST BE SOWN!

CHECK THE SEEDS OF HEREDITARY DISEASE AND UNFITNESS BY EUGENICS

This poster from the 1930s promotes the idea of 'positive' eugenics through the figure of the 'healthy' sower of seed, but also proposes unspecified 'checks' or 'negative' eugenic methods to prevent supposedly hereditary conditions and 'unfitness'.

be a good fit, but when he asked Mr Middleton if he could go out with his daughter, Herbert refused. The rejection bit, but Harry knew no father would want a disabled man courting his daughter.

On 26 February 1955, aged 20, Harry was readmitted to the King Edward VII Orthopaedic Hospital for the last time.[238] Doctors prescribed him three more months of chemotherapy and antibiotic injections for a weeping, infected wound but, he said, 'the Terramycin wasn't doing the trick'. Harry needed daily dressings and was in pain from the femur grinding in his pelvis. While he waited to see if his hip would respond to treatment, he reverted to sleeping during the day so he could talk to the night nurses. He met Sheila Gough when she was in charge of the men's ward. Harry often helped her to give her patients their earthenware hot-water bottles. They got talking and discovered they had both gone to Hartley Brook School. They became lifelong friends.

In April 1955, Harry met orthopaedic nurse Doreen Parker. He said:

I had an appalling reputation at Rivelin, and your reputation mattered a lot. You couldn't mention who I was without all the old stories coming out. Doreen was given a blow-by-blow of the latest gossip about what I had allegedly said or done, and who supposedly had said what. Talking about each other was the only entertainment most patients had. Gossiping never interested me.

Harry Drabble, aged 20, at the renamed the King Edward VII Orthopaedic Hospital, 1955. Believed to be the only photo of himself that Harry arranged to have taken. *In the author's collection.*

Doreen and Harry met because Jack Beckwith, who was in a neighbouring bed to Harry, 'went on about a nurse, Sybil Gough' (Sheila's sister). In vain, Jack tried to get someone to take a note to her.

'Yet': A Story of Triumph Over Childhood Separation, Trauma, and Disability

Believed to be Jack Beckwith c. 1955. *In the author's collection.*

Student nurses Doreen Parker and Sybil (known as Billie) Gough, in the grounds of the renamed the King Edward VII Orthopaedic Hospital, 1955. *In the author's collection.*

Jack's constant talk without action drove Harry 'mad'. He said, 'Write a note and I'll deliver it, if you'll just shut up about her.' Breaking the rules, Harry left the men's ward on crutches, hobbled around to the back of the building, and tapped on the window of the women's ward.

The former women's ward. The furthest window on the right was the one Doreen opened when Harry tapped to deliver Jack's note. Photograph taken by the author, 1 March 2022.

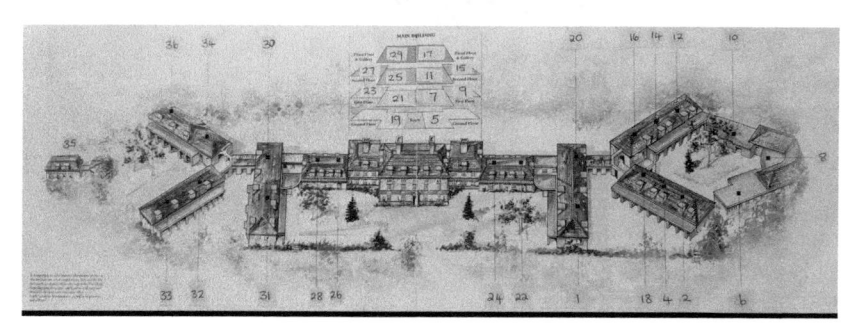

A marketing drawing of the King Edward VII Orthopaedic Hospital when it was being turned into apartments.

Seventeen-year-old Doreen Parker opened the window. Harry explained why he was there, passed over Jack's note, asked her name and said, 'Pleased to meet you. What time do you get off?' Doreen took Jack's note, but told Harry, 'I can't fraternise with patients,' and shut the window. He said, 'As it wasn't the thing to do, I packed up, left the hospital, and caught the bus to Malin Bridge, went into a phone box, and asked the operator to put me through to the nurses' home.' It was 27 June 1955.[239]

> **KING EDWARD VII. HOSPITAL FOR CRIPPLED CHILDREN**
>
> **PROBATIONER NURSES**
> there are few vacancies for well educated girls, aged 16—21; two years' training in Orthopodic Nursing; lectures given and certificates granted, salary £40–45 plus war bonus; uniform provided; liberal off duty—Apply for full particulars to the Matron.

Probationer nurses required, King Edward VII Memorial Hospital for Crippled Children
'Situations', Yorkshire Post and Leeds Intelligencer, 1942.[240]

The couple's first meeting was in Ecclesall Woods, which is made up of three large ancient woodlands. Here the couple spent hours sharing their lives and hopes with each other. Doreen planned to go to Africa when she qualified. Harry wanted a wife, a family and to travel.

A fortnight after their first date, Harry talked of marriage at Endcliffe Park. He said:

> *It was difficult to see the future, but I knew Doreen lived in poor conditions, and had much older parents who behaved as if they were in the previous century. As a student nurse, she didn't have the money to take part in what other girls were doing. I said to her, you could do worse than marry me. I'll give you a good house, transport and foreign holidays. She put all her eggs in my basket and trusted me to provide. She was a very good judge of people, no question about it, but I never understood why she took me on.*

Doreen had finished her first year as an orthopaedic probationer. Not accepting 'her lot', as her mother had had to, Doreen was desperate for independence. Aged 16, she had left her father Walter and mother Hilda in their severely dilapidated two-up, two-down blackened terrace in the centre of Sheffield to take up nursing.

LEFT: Doreen Parker aged about 17 years in her orthopaedic nurse uniform, c. 1955.

RIGHT: Doreen was given a King Edward Orthopaedic silver and blue uniform badge when she passed her final orthopaedic nursing exam. (The Latin, 'Ad Lucem', means 'To the light'.)

Both images in the author's collection.

Doreen's elderly parents had married late, and were 52 and 38 years old, respectively, when she was born. Despite her mother's kind, loving and gentle nature, Doreen experienced her as smothering, needy and clingy. Hilda's lack of education and her constant apologising also infuriated her. She tried to get close to her near-silent, Victorian father, but as a son of an alcoholic, he probably struggled to identify or convey his feelings.[241] He was strict, and although he was usually out of the house, he was emotionally absent when he was home.

As a child, Doreen was pleased when she was allowed to go up to her bedroom in the evening, so she could escape the claustrophobic combined kitchen and living room, and lose herself in a library book. Her only seat in the house was an uncomfortable, repaired wooden kitchen chair. Her father, Walter, sat in a wooden captain's chair with his feet propped on the range, while her mother relaxed in a tatty easy chair. Walter had slept in the front room since the outbreak of the Second World War. The house did not have a bathroom, so after dark Doreen used a stained, chipped chamber pot that sat under her narrow metal-framed bed. She had no linoleum or carpet on her bedroom floor, just a small rag rug by her bed that her mother had made her. The family shared an outside toilet with neighbours at the end of a small yard. Instead of the non-absorbent Bronco toilet paper, with its rough texture on one side and shiny surface on the other, the Parkers used old newspaper squares stuck on a rusty nail.

Despite living hand-to-mouth, Walter dipped into his precious savings for his daughter's Brownies and Girl Guides uniforms, though he never gave her the pennies the other girls had to buy chips on the way home. Doreen passed the 11-plus exam, and Walter bought her the required uniform for her to attend Greystones Secondary School.

As a Girl Guide, Doreen promised to 'help other people at all times' and obey the Guide Law, which included vows to be trusted, loyal and thrifty, and to smile no matter what difficulties beset her, but she found the social aspect of secondary school difficult. Many of the girls were spiteful to the 'slum' girl. Doreen worked hard to lose her thick Sheffield working-class accent as quickly as possible. The Parkers may have lived in poverty, but Hilda was resourceful and saved a little to give to her daughter as spending money occasionally.

LEFT: Doreen Parker's Girl Guides badge.

RIGHT: Girl Guide Illustrated, *An ABC of Guiding* by A.M. Maynard. In the author's collection.

A close friend, Ann Hill, née Wardley, said in 2001:

Doreen and I went dancing in Locarno Ballroom, Sheffield, and visited the Abbeydale Picture House. We were 'game for the lads' in an innocent way. We had so much fun. We went round in groups and would hook up with a group of boys, but it was so innocent compared to today.

LEFT: Doreen with friend Ann Wardley.

RIGHT: Doreen in the yard at Edmund Road, late 1950s. Doreen is wearing a hat Harry made her. She is standing beside the neighbours' garden, not her father's (which was probably planted with vegetables).
In the author's collection.

According to Harry, when Doreen was growing up, she was 'working completely on survival'. Knowing that qualifications would help her escape the grim slum house, Doreen worked hard at the kitchen table and her 1954 General Certificate of Education with passes in biology, English literature, geography and scripture knowledge gave her options. She tried office work, but found it did not give her the freedom from her parents that she craved. In the autumn of 1954, Doreen took up the offer of expenses and applied to train as an orthopaedic nurse at the King Edward VII Hospital in the Rivelin Valley.

The General Nursing Council approved the course for Part One of the preliminary state examination before general nurse training. According to newspaper adverts, the training allowance was around £220, with £100 deducted for board and lodgings.[242]

Doreen's monthly pay was about £8 a month (worth around £170 in 2024). There was no extra pay for working at weekends or for night duty and bank holidays, and no time off in lieu when a nurse, inevitably, ran over her working hours.

Harry would be Doreen's only boyfriend. He said that she was 'so positive, supportive of everything and everybody. She didn't have an agenda and always saw other people's point of view, before her own.' He added:

When I see a situation I don't like, my reaction is, 'I'm bloody well going to change it.' Doreen's was, 'This is the situation, how can I make it better?'

Doreen was easily frightened, but she was blowed if she would let it stop her from doing anything. She knew fear was part of life. People's needs empowered her, so being a nurse was a big help. It didn't matter what she felt; she rose to meet the challenge to help her patients.

Doreen said Harry challenged himself continually, and he was attentive, encouraging, responsive, patient, talkative, enthusiastic, and bursting with energy, ideas and plans, very different from the other youths Doreen had met. It was a heady cocktail, given how silenced, unseen, and unknown she felt with her father. Harry's confidence and the positive, empowering way he saw her was a revelation to Doreen. She never saw the easily triggered ball of anger within him, but she heard stories. Harry described it as an unexploded bomb he had carried around since he was first admitted to Rivelin. However, he said that on the day Doreen lightly touched his forearm:

'My reactiveness drained away. I knew everything was going to be okay; I had someone at my side. I never lashed out again, although I drew on the feeling "someone was going to pay" when I needed fuel to get things done. Without that hand on my arm, my behaviour would have landed me in jail, or dead.'

A few months after they met, Harry was admitted to the Royal Infirmary for a week-long investigation. To his relief, by the time he was discharged, he no longer had a weeping infected hip. He felt recovered enough to meet Doreen in the recreation room of the nurses' home at Rivelin. The nurses could invite their boyfriends, as long as they did not go upstairs to the bedrooms and they left by 10 pm.

The room didn't have much seating, not enough to entertain people or be useful. Doreen quizzed me. She'd heard all the stories, most of the adult patients and staff had heard of me, or knew me. All of them had something to say. There was so much gossip, I was notorious. It was not a nice feeling.

Doreen sat on my good knee as there was nowhere else for her to perch. It was innocent, no monkey business. People were artificially hysterical and tried to make the ordinary an exciting occasion. Someone turned the light out. Matron Jones came in and after she flicked the light switch back on, her gaze fell to her student on my knee. Matron made it clear this was a new low, even for me, and such behaviour was NOT acceptable.

As Harry was no longer a patient, Matron Jones could not penalise him, but there were repercussions for Doreen. Sheila Gough remembered 'how severely Matron told nurses off and the compulsory reading of various Bible quotes that followed'. **Romans 6:23** For the wages of sin is death; but the gift of God is eternal life through Jesus Christ our Lord and **Matthew 25:46** And these shall go away into everlasting punishment: but the righteous into life eternal, were common choices.

Doreen Parker with a staff nurse. Doreen is wearing the full apron of a student nurse over a winter cardigan. All the uniforms were second hand and passed around each new intake. The nurses were expected to make alterations in their spare time. Doreen's uniform had all the tucks unpicked, so she had three large pale stripes. The colour of the belt reflected the nurse's status. *In the author's collection.*

Harry's next big occasion was a drive to Peterborough to pick up Doreen from her aunt Min, her mother's sister, who lived with her Uucle Fred in a two-up, two-down mid-terrace at 264 Clarence Road. It was his first meeting with the extended family.

'Yet': A Story of Triumph Over Childhood Separation, Trauma, and Disability

Despite her father's condemnation of their relationship, Doreen had accepted Harry's marriage proposal. He did not have money for a ring. Instead, they made an appointment to see a local bank manager. He gave Harry 'solid advice' on how to become a reliable breadwinner and build a career. The manager later opened an account in their joint names and deposited their £1 in savings.

Harry's recent hospitalisation meant he was without work but, he said, 'I changed my circumstances quickly.' He joined Firth Vickers & Samuel Fox at Shepcote Lane Rolling Mill, where he worked in the costing department as a clerk. He was later promoted to Section Leader.

ORDER CLERK
Man, aged 20/30 years, required for this interesting and responsible position. Applicants must be adaptable and capable of learning processes involved in the production of Special Steels in the form of sheets and strip. Good standard of education required. 5-day week. Canteen and excellent sports facilities
Apply in writing or personally to:
Employment Officer
**FIRTH-VICKERS STAINLESS STEELS LTD.,
SHEPCOTE LANE WORKS,
TINSLEY, SHEFFIELD, 9.**

LEFT: An example of a job advertisement in the *Star Green 'un*, 7 October 1961, for an order clerk at Firth Vickers.[243]

RIGHT: H.L. Brown & Sons of 70 Fargate, Sheffield. H.L. Brown began trading as a watchmaker and jeweller at 29 Gower Street in Sheffield in 1867.
With the kind permission from the managing director, James Frampton, of H. L. Brown, Sheffield.

Certificate of insurance issued by H.L. Brown & Sons of 70 Fargate, Sheffield, for Doreen's engagement ring. The new job enabled Harry to buy Doreen an engagement ring in June 1956. In the author's collection.

If Walter was out of the house, Hilda would invite Harry in for a cup of tea when he dropped Doreen off for a visit. Hilda was accepting of him, glad that Doreen had found someone who loved her. She told him she did not care how much he earned, as long as he looked after her daughter. A gentle soul, she believed that 'if you can't say anything nice, say nothing at all'. Her thoughts, that Harry described as 'slow', he later explained were probably a symptom of her untreated, but diagnosed underactive thyroid. Walter told Doreen that he did not see any improvement when Hilda took hormone replacements, so she continued to suffer from the weight gain (especially in her legs), slow movements, exhaustion, sensitivity to cold, muscle pain and weakness, and depression common to the condition.

Despite Walter telling Harry that he did not want him to see his daughter, Harry continued courting the woman he was 'head over heels' for, and sent a pricey boxed Valentine to Doreen at the nurses' home in February 1956.[244]

LEFT: 'To my dearest Valentine' card, 1956.

RIGHT: Four surviving wooden puzzles made by Walter.
Both images are in the author's collection.

One day, Walter came home earlier than expected and found Harry sat at his kitchen table. He disappeared into the attic room and returned with a series of jumbled wooden puzzles and dropped them, in pieces, on the table in front of Harry. 'See what you can do with them', he said. Harry rose to the challenge. He did not leave the table until he had put each of them back together.

Doreen was not keen on music, and being regularly sleep deprived, she often fell asleep at the classical concerts she had been given free 'nurses' tickets to attend. After one concert, the couple ate in a restaurant where members of the Hallé Orchestra welcomed questions.

> *I asked them what their life was like. Not in my wildest dreams did I think their life was a good one. They were always on the road. They had no choice about what they ate or where they slept.*

A Love Story Defies Expectations

When Doreen was off duty, she went along to the dances Harry organised and played at as part of the Beck Road Quartet. Doreen collected the money on the door, paid for any drinks the band had consumed, and shared what was left between the band members. Harry put his share into their joint bank account. Occasionally, Doreen would dance while Harry was playing, but felt uncomfortable doing so, as she was mindful that Harry's damaged hip stopped him from dancing.

Often, Doreen could not see Harry as it was impossible for her to get back to the nurses' home before the door was locked at 10 pm. Buses were infrequent and there was quite a walk from the bus stop to the hospital. Harry found a motorbike where he could lean back, balance on one bottom cheek and still have his hands on the steering bars. He bought a 'doer-upper' with a sidecar to balance his awkward posture on the bike. It also gave Doreen somewhere to sit. Harry took the bike apart, cleaned it, and taught himself to maintain it. Now he could pick up and return Doreen to the nurses' home. Harry tapped on the roof of the sidecar when he saw a policeman, and Doreen became adept at slipping out of sight. He would have preferred to take his test, but they were suspended because of the fuel shortages during the Suez Crisis of 1956.

It could be cold on the motorbike and, in the winter, Harry could not talk until his face had defrosted. He wore a long Second World War motorcycle despatch rider's coat and an ex-army helmet. Unfortunately, he left the helmet in a phone box. He visited the lost property in the city police station for weeks, hoping to get it back.

'Yet': A Story of Triumph Over Childhood Separation, Trauma, and Disability

A BSA (Birmingham Small Arms Company) 1934 Sloper. Photo taken by the author at the Rural Life Living Museum, Farnham, Surrey, 2019 where Harry talked to the owner of the motorbike and reminisced about his own. The bike featured a saddle tank that gave a low seating position, improving the centre of gravity and handling. Its cruising speed was 55 miles per hour (89 km/h), with a top speed of around 75 miles per hour. *In the author's collection.*

An example of a 1940s leather half-bowl helmet as worn by Harry. *Unknown photographer.*

A Love Story Defies Expectations

An example of a 1944-dated British army despatch rider's coat as worn by Harry.
With kind permission of www.blightymilitaria.com

In 1956, Harry slipped and broke his left leg. He managed to get to a phone box to call Doreen to tell her he had broken it and could not pick her up for their next date. His friend David Beeley helped him home. The GP who visited the house examined it and told him he had strained it. Days later, the pain was getting worse. Finally, the GP arranged an ambulance to take him to have it X-rayed. Doreen rode with him in the ambulance, grasping his thigh firmly to reduce his pain as the vehicle jolted along the road to the casualty department. The X-ray showed he had fractured the upper third of his left femur.

On 3 April 1956, 18-year-old Doreen was issued a new cape and uniform and started a two-year Certificate of General Nursing at the Sheffield City General Hospital. Normally it was a three-year course, but she had had a year's training already. She rented a 'smelly, damp and grotty' basement flat with Patricia Grayson, a colleague from Rivelin, in a blackened terrace in the city. Harry continued to pick Doreen up, and their adventures continued.

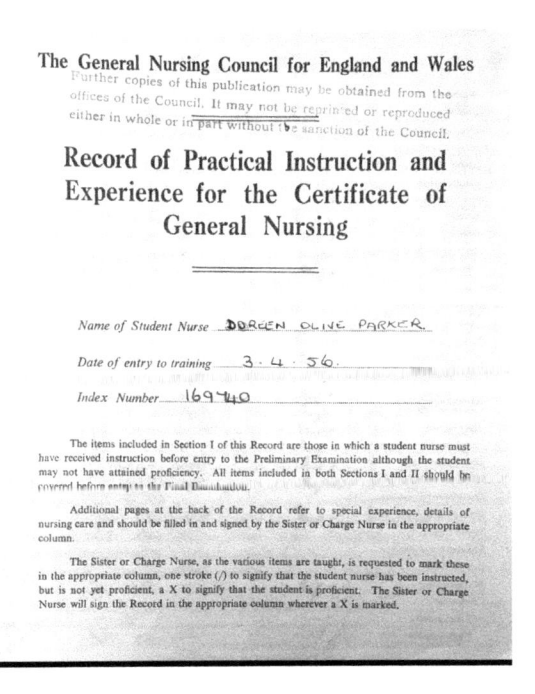

Doreen's record of physical instruction and experience for the Certificate of General Nursing. In the author's collection.

At the City General Hospital on 13 April, Harry went against the doctor's recommendation and insisted his leg was set in such a way that would allow him to sit, in a fashion, and stand barefooted with part of the ball of his left foot on the ground. It took 12 weeks to heal. He then set about teaching himself to walk without crutches.

> When I stopped using crutches, it was a buggers' muddle. I hadn't walked on my own since I was two years old, and I had to learn how to walk. I tried to make my gait look as normal as possible.

Harry and Doreen made the most of what little free time they had together. They asked each other, 'What shall we do? Where shall we go?' and had many day trips by bus, sometimes just getting on the next one leaving the station. Harry carried their food in a small canvas knapsack. Chatsworth and Derbyshire were popular haunts. They also picnicked on the moor, and walked along the

Pennine Way, to Forge Dam and Lady Bower, where Harry treated an ever-hungry Doreen to a bacon sandwich and a mug of tea.

According to Harry, Doreen became 'evangelical about children, particularly the boys, not having their hair cut in Rivelin, so I bought her a pair of scissors and a comb and said, "Practise on me until you're comfortable cutting the children's hair."'

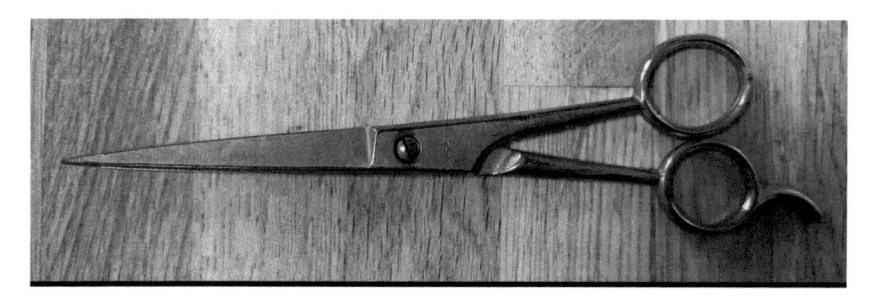

Doreen's hair-cutting scissors. She continued to cut Harry's hair until her death in 2002. *In the author's collection.*

Doreen practised giving injections by injecting oranges, but she hated the thought of putting needles into people, so I persuaded her to give me injections of sterile water. I gave her a report of what it felt like and, at one point, I had to have a series of antibiotic injections. I said 'I've got someone who can do that for me', and she was brilliant.

The State Registered Nurse training was gruelling. Despite Britain recruiting nurses from overseas, there was a national shortage, and the students were expected to do most of the heavy work. Doreen was woken somewhere between 6 and 6.30 am by a sister banging on the door calling her to morning prayer. Meals were taken in the dining room. The food was calorific and plentiful to enable the students to cope with their workload. A nurse found with a ladder in her stocking was instantly dismissed from the ward to put on another pair.[245] She had to make up time for her absence at the end of her shift.

Doreen worked the wards for a minimum of 96 hours each fortnight (not including meal breaks). All the students had to attend the compulsory day-time lectures in their time off. These were mostly delivered by a Sister tutor, who expected the attendees to listen closely and make copious notes. There were no handouts. The strict discipline, heavy responsibility on night duty, and the random practical training added to the difficulties the young women faced. The senior nursing staff were unmarried and with no children. They were sometimes bitter. Matrons were all-powerful and organised their nursing staff with military-style precision.

Some of the 18-year-olds who had started their nurse training appeared jealous of Doreen's orthopaedic qualification and experience, particularly those who had come from better living circumstances than Doreen's. A few of these young women were spiteful and made her life difficult. Towards the end of Doreen's training, she also suffered from systematic bullying from a senior nurse.

Harry and Doreen escaped for a romantic holiday in Wales in 1956.

Harry was determined to marry Doreen and for them to have children. To protect him from hurt, May tried to get him to be realistic. 'Why would an educated girl like Doreen have you? You have nothing to offer her.' But Harry already knew he had to better his prospects to give Doreen the life he had promised her.

A Love Story Defies Expectations

18-year-old Doreen in Colwyn Bay, North Wales, 1956. *The images on this page are in the author's collection.*

21-year-old Harry Drabble in Colwyn Bay, Wales, 1956.

Harry Drabble paddling in Colwyn Bay, Wales, 1956.

'Yet': A Story of Triumph Over Childhood Separation, Trauma, and Disability

Doreen sitting cross-legged on a beach.
This selection of images is in the author's collection.

Doreen on the beach with a view of Rhos-on-Sea, Wales, 1956. She is wearing a wedding ring two years before her marriage.

Christmas 1956 was spent with Harry's parents at 44 Butterthwaite Road.

A Love Story Defies Expectations

19-year-old Doreen Parker on Flamborough beach, 1957. *This selection of images is in the author's collection.*

19-year-old Doreen Parker on Flamborough Cliffs, Yorkshire, May 1957.

22-year-old Harry Drabble on Flamborough Cliffs, May 1957.

Doreen and Harry on holiday in Paignton c. 1957.
This was Harry's favourite photograph, because his shorter leg and
awkward gait are not obvious. *In the author's collection.*

At 23 years old, Harry was taken on as a stock allocation clerk, later becoming a credit controller, for Bachelors Peas at Wadsley Bridge, Sheffield.

> *As a cripple, I was paid less than the others. That's how it was. I 'gossiped' in the marketing section and got ahead of the game. The marketing department wanted shops to stock all the Bachelor range of peas, and my managing the stock was part of the plan. But it was never as successful as marketing said it would be.*

Harry looked into the order process and found the forms the small shopkeepers used to order from. He noticed that the factory encouraged small repeat orders of only a few products. The mainstay products were canned Marrowfat Bigga peas, dwarf peas (petit pois), and garden peas. Harry changed the forms, set up a fast way to check stock of the product and had small parcels made up and sent to the independent 30 or so depots around Britain. The new logistics improved orders.

Meanwhile, Doreen was struggling with the night shifts. She had always found the 12-hour stretches of night duty – 8 pm to 8 am – difficult. The nurses had a one-hour break for a main meal, and half an hour for a tea break. In reality, the students did not always get their breaks. Each nurse was meant to work the 14 nights by working five nights on and two off, then four nights on and three off, but Doreen's rota was deliberately set so that she regularly went 48 hours without sleep. Each period of night duty was for 12 weeks, usually on the same ward, but Doreen was given longer stretches.[246]

Harry said, 'Doreen was in a dark place, weeks away from qualifying, when she broke because of extreme sleep deprivation.' Unable to finish the course, she asked Harry if he was still serious about their marrying. When he said, 'Yes' she asked 'Can we get married in two weeks, then?' Harry said he would have been with Doreen under any circumstances and if a quick wedding was what she wanted, he would make it happen if he could. Doreen was under age, and her father refused his permission for them to marry, telling Harry, 'You don't breed from defective stock.' Harry understood Walter had been a farmer, was a Victorian at heart, and was trying to protect his daughter. However, he booked St Mary's Church and its community centre for the wedding breakfast. Doreen borrowed a wedding dress, veil and shoes. Friends gave practical gifts such as the wedding cake, the bride's bouquet and flowers for the buttonholes.

St Mary's Church, Bramall Lane.
Hebrides (talk | contribs) GNU Free Documentation Licence. Version 1.2.

Throughout the ceremony, the couple and many of their guests, including Doreen's mum, expected Walter to turn up and stop the ceremony.

A Love Story Defies Expectations

Harry Drabble and Doreen, née Parker, 19 July 1958, outside St Mary's community centre, Bramall Lane. *In the author's collection.*

'Yet': A Story of Triumph Over Childhood Separation, Trauma, and Disability

Doreen and Harry Drabble, with bridesmaids Ann Wardley, Harry's 14-year-old sister Margaret, and Harry's best man, David Beeley. David was on the same building diploma course as Harry. A friend of Harry's gave Doreen away. *In the author's collection.*

Doreen and Harry Drabble in the back of David Beeley's car. *In the author's collection.*

A Love Story Defies Expectations

Best man David Beeley recommended the couple go to Lathkill Dale, Over Haddon, the place where he and his wife had taken their honeymoon. While there, Doreen wrote to her in-laws, 'It's everything he said it was, it's beautiful.'

Harry and Doreen Drabble, in a high wind, sat on a stone bench in front of a drystone wall outside their honeymoon cottage in Lathkill Dale, Derbyshire, July 1958. *In the author's collection.*

Frith's postcard of Lathkill Dale, Over Haddon, c. 1960. *Copyright The Francis Frith Collection. With kind permission.*

They stayed in a cottage that was the home of Mrs Pocock. She moved in with relatives for the week to give Harry and Doreen the place to themselves, but came back to cook their breakfast and tea.

> *Someone once said to me, 'It was easy in your day.' They didn't have a clue. I wasn't thought capable of living independently. It was made clear that work, interests, a girlfriend, marriage and children – all the 'ordinary things' – weren't for the likes of me. I worked bloody hard all my life, in a hostile environment, in a society where disabled people were expected to be silent and take up as little space as possible, out of sight.*

With a loving, supportive wife at his side and the beginnings of a career, Harry set out to give Doreen the life he had promised her two weeks after they started courting. But the newlyweds started out in two derelict rooms, without plumbing, above a GP practice in Gleadless Road, Heeley. Doreen had found employment as an orthopaedic nurse and receptionist and talked her employer into giving them the rooms to live in with the promise, 'my husband will put in plumbing and when we leave, you can rent them out'.

Harry forged a strong reciprocal emotional connection with Doreen and learned to feel content in the company of other people. She overcame the lack of self-esteem she believed she experienced because of having an emotionally absent father. Both Harry and Doreen had grown up feeling, 'I'm better off taking care of myself', but together they found a healthier balance of intimacy and independence.

A Love Story Defies Expectations

Against almost impossible odds, Harry achieved his dream to love and be loved in return. He overcame the separation from his parents and the detachment from his family, community and class. The young nurses at Rivelin saved his sanity, and he found a welcome in the church and a way to nourish his soul through music and his relationship with his sister. Thanks to the free library system and the ever-supportive qualified librarians, he educated himself and found work despite the open discrimination in the rehabilitation centre and at work, and the rejection and sabotage he faced from his peers.

Each time Harry felt overwhelmed by the next rung of the ladder, he dismissed the 'little man on my shoulder and told him to bugger off, and come back next week'. When he was confronted with something he could not do, he reminded himself he couldn't do it '… yet', and worked out how to get from 'can't do to can do', and this he would do again and again.

APPENDICES

Appendix A
Bovine Tuberculosis – A Crime Against Society

There are two forms of tuberculosis. *Mycobacterium tuberculosis* (*M. Tuberculosis*), or pulmonary tuberculosis, is the form most people are familiar with. This contagious infection is spread when tiny droplets from the coughs or sneezes of an infected person are inhaled. Between 1851 and 1910 'nearly 4 million people are said to have died as a result in England and Wales. Three-quarters of those from tuberculosis of the lungs.'[247] *M. Tuberculosis* mainly affects the lungs, but it can affect any part of the body, including the stomach, the glands, the bones and the nervous system.

Mycobacterium bovis (*M. Bovis*), or bovine tuberculosis (bTB), commonly affected bones and joints, particularly those of young children, as they were the chief consumers of raw milk, the main cause of infection. Not all people who come into contact with bTB contract it. Approximately 5 per cent of infected people develop clinical symptoms within a year of infection, and between 5 and 10 per cent of latently infected people develop chronic progressive TB during their lifetime.[248]

Symptoms of bovine tuberculosis

The major symptom was pain. Muscle spasms were also common.[249] The damage caused by the infection could be considerable.[250] Children often favoured the non-affected leg when they could.

Crying out in the night was not unusual, because when the muscles relaxed during sleep, they contracted and rubbed the sensitive parts together.[251] The affected part might also be weakened and could fracture easily.

Bovine tuberculosis is a life-threatening disease. So long as the hip contains living tubercle bacilli, the patient risks dying of tuberculous meningitis.[252] There are various statistics for the number of deaths recorded as being from bTB, and they can appear confusing. One estimated that between 1912 and 1939, approximately 65,000 people in England and Wales died from bTB.[253] Another stated that in 1929 an estimated 5,565 people died of non-pulmonary TB (out of the 18,862 people who were infected with bTB in England and Wales; while in the same year, 57,274 had pulmonary TB).[254] However, a more recent investigation into the statistics by Peter Atkins, an Emeritus Professor of Geography, showed over 800,000 people died because of the transmission of tuberculosis from animals to humans in Britain between 1900–1950.[255] As Atkins states, 'Bovine TB was by far the largest, the most sustained, and the most deadly food-borne zoonosis in British history.'[256]

Perhaps because of the way industrialisation affected the population living in cities and suburbs, more northerners were affected.[257]

Conflicting advice

An article appeared in the *Sheffield Independent* in June 1933 letting mothers know of the country-wide Infant Welfare Centres. In each centre, a 'queue of mothers and perambulators wait in turn to have their charges weighed and "overhauled" by doctors and specially trained nurses ... they are advised about their baby's diet, clothing and general health. They are warned against the dangers of unsterilised milk.' The newspaper article explained that the existing powers of the authorities were ineffective and directed that boiled milk should be given to school-age children.[258]

Voluntary organisations provided many of the services for mothers and babies in Sheffield, with the help of some council-paid medical and nursing staff.[259] However, the city centre facility was criticised as overcrowded, bureaucratic and inconvenient for suburban mothers.[260] May was unlikely to have visited. However, there was a 'major political storm in the 1930s over the difficulties pregnant women and mothers from new estates had in getting to the central welfare clinics, and there were calls for the development of estate-based services'.[261]

Although many doctors recommended pasteurisation to make milk fit for human consumption, newspaper articles did not make it clear this was not happening. May was an intelligent and voracious reader, so it is likely she read the local newspapers. But the information they gave about the safety of milk was contradictory.

One article appearing in the *Sheffield Independent* in 1934 reported that a large proportion of milk was pasteurised:

> **Milk – A Nourishing Food**
>
> A large proportion of milk sold to-day is pasteurised, in other words heated to a temperature of between 145 and 150 degrees Fahrenheit, held at that temperature for half an hour and then immediately cooled by means

of refrigeration. This destroys harmful bacteria such as tuberculosis and has little, if any, effect upon the food value.[262]

The understanding that bringing infected milk to boiling point freed it from all poisonous germs did not lead to legislation in England. It did not become illegal to sell unpasteurised dairy milk in supermarkets or high street shops in England, Wales and Northern Ireland until 1985. It was outlawed in Scotland in 1983.[263] Pasteurisation was made compulsory in Canada in 1991.[264]

Pasteurised milk was available in Sheffield in Harry's youth, for example from the model dairy on Archer Road, Millhouses.[265] However, did Harry and other working-class children have access to it? The model dairy was eight miles from the council estate where the Drabbles lived.

Some farmers brought in medical care for their cattle. The Glaswegian vet James Wight, better known as James Herriot in the autobiographical fiction series *All Creatures Great and Small*, wrote about his experiences in a Yorkshire village in the 1930s:

> 'Screws' [tubercular cows] were all too common thirty years ago. ... Often they were good milkers and ate well, but they were killers and I was learning to spot them.[266]

An article in *Blyth News* (13 August 1934) stated:

> While tuberculosis is rife, pasteurised milk should be insisted on for infants. Such milk is heated sufficiently

to destroy disease-bearing germs, and then cooled and bottled ... Pasteurization has thus a great advantage, because it makes boiling unnecessary, and to boil milk is to destroy in it an essential element for human nourishment – vitamin C.[267]

In West Yorkshire in 1934, *The Todmorden & District News* recognised that a few drops of orange juice could make up for any lack of vitamin C in the boiled milk that should be given to young children.[268]

In 1935, it became government policy to establish TB-free attested herds, where cattle had passed the tuberculin test, which reduced the presence of TB in British herds from 40 per cent to just 1 per cent. But by 1939 only 50 per cent of milk was being pasteurised. Compulsory slaughter was finally brought in for TB-infected cattle in 1950. Despite this, it was estimated that raw milk from non-attested herds was still being supplied as late as 1960. Between 1921 and 1953, the number of deaths from non-pulmonary TB finally fell from 1,107 to 12. By 1955, it was believed that all such TB deaths were caused by bTB from infected milk.[269]

Another article in the same year reported a policy for the eradication of bovine tuberculosis, announcing that loans had been approved and that herd owners were co-operating in the scheme.[270] However, 'it was later argued that it was unreasonable that the county councils should be expected to adopt a scheme which would involve the county ratepayers' considerable administrative cost'.[271] While the Health Committee approved of the scheme and called for the sale of only Grade A milk, this labelling implied, incorrectly, that it was good-quality milk from tuberculin-tested cows. Infected milk continued to be sold.

In 1936, the year Harry was diagnosed, the *Sheffield Independent* reported that, every year, 2,000 people died from bovine tuberculosis, and between 7 and 10 per cent of cattle were infected. The 1935 Ministry of Agriculture and Food-launched voluntary testing scheme in England and Wales had failed. It was reported it had had 'no effect in reducing tuberculosis in cattle as it only empowered authorities to deal with animals in the advanced state of the disease'. In fact, it encouraged farmers to keep old cows.[272] Perhaps of greater concern was that 21 per cent of cases of tuberculosis in children under five years old were infected by *Mycobacterium bovis*, rather than the pulmonary infection that had been 'the single highest cause of death and disability in 19th-century Britain'.[273]

The infected milk Harry drank is believed to have come from Butterthwaite Farm.[274] It is probable the farm did not have to register as a supplier under the Milk and Dairies Amendment Act of 1922, because it provided milk to 'neighbours'.[275] Harry remembered milk being delivered to his home on Butterthwaite Road twice a day by a plodding horse and a crude cart driven by a woman with a 'terrible limp wearing a dirty waterproof coat'. May took out a jug to be filled from the metal cylinder with a tap. She did not know the drink encouraged for young children would disable her only child, take him away from his family, exclude him from education and probably from work. Harry remembered being told that an inspector went to the farm where the milk had originated, but the farmer had been tipped off and the infected cow was temporarily moved.

Pasteurising milk: A simple solution?

The path to pasteurisation was a long one in England. First, tuberculosis has a long incubation period in humans, so, initially, it was difficult to categorically link drinking unpasteurised milk with the disease.

The French chemist Louis Pasteur invented a process in 1865 in which milk was heated to a temperature of between 60 and 100 °C, killing most bacteria and mould.[276] But there was no robust knowledge of what time and temperature combinations would inactivate pathogenic bacteria in milk, and so, where pasteurisation was undertaken, several pasteurisation standards were in use. By 1900, a more stable knowledge concerning bovine tuberculosis had almost been achieved.[277] By the mid-1920s veterinary surgeons could routinely test cattle.[278] Those that displayed a skin reaction to the test were termed 'reactors'. Some farmers had herds free of the infection, but while testing was encouraged, it was voluntary. Any cows that were found to be infected would be slaughtered, but the compensation was not set at a level that encouraged farmers to have their herds tested.

There were delays, in part, because the National Veterinary Medical Association was relatively new, having been formed in 1919. There was also nationwide opposition for routine veterinary inspection as the best solution to the problem of bovine tuberculosis because vets had little power to act.

In 1931 William Savage (later Sir) a County Medical Officer of Health, cited several obstacles standing in the way of bTB-free milk:

> Farmers were not obliged to permit routine inspection of their cattle, nor even bring them in from the fields,

> unless there were good grounds to suspect a specific disease in the herd.
>
> Farmers were not bound to disclose changes in their herd or what became of tuberculous animals. Notification of disease was only required of the farmers when an animal showed gross symptoms of tuberculosis. (Often farmers waited until the cow had finished producing milk, so the value of the beast had fallen below that of the compensation offered for slaughter.)
>
> Even when tuberculosis was found, a dairyman could not be forced to change his methods, and the disease was therefore likely to recur.
>
> Udder tuberculosis was detectable most readily just after milking, but vets could not always be available at those times of day.[279]

Given these issues, Savage recommended improving the physical infrastructure of buildings and insisting on 'minimum standards of cleanliness, the use of microscopes and guinea pigs in the bacteriological detection of infected milk and pasteurisation.'

Opponents to pasteurisation, usually from the farming and veterinary worlds, supported by smaller dairy traders, saw these measures as intrusive. They argued there were doubts about the true extent of the disease and its impact upon humans and, 'they did not feel that it was worth threatening rural livelihoods by the increased costs of production that would inevitably flow from a slaughter policy or forced investment in new buildings'.[280] As late as the end of the Second World War, 'the average farmer looked with grave suspicion on the ... interest displayed both by the medical and veterinary profession in milk production'.[281] These attitudes led to policy paralysis and extended inaction in Britain. Many thousands of children, particularly in the working class who generally bought the cheapest milk, unnecessarily became lifelong casualties.

Milk legislation

The House of Lords discussed infected herds many times. For example, in 1922, during its second reading of the Milk and Dairies (Amendment) Bill, the Minister of Health, Sir Alfred Mond, said:

> Under Clause 5 it is made an offence for any person knowingly to sell milk from a cow with tuberculosis of the udder ... The penalties are purposely made severe because a person selling milk of that kind is retailing not food but poison. That is a crime against society, and society has a full right to protect itself against it to the best of its ability.[282]

But the Bill did not stop children being infected. According to *A Dictionary of Dairying*, Dr J.G. Davis noted: 'Probably no subject outside religion and politics has been the cause of more prolonged and bitter controversies than the proposal compulsorily to pasteurize all milk.'[283]

The resulting Milk and Dairies (Amendment) Act, which came into operation in 1925, and the Milk and Dairies Order that followed in 1926 did not protect Harry and his peers either. Although there were arguments about pasteurisation and the possible change of taste, a more compelling explanation for the delay was that the financial loss in slaughtering the 40 per cent of the dairy herd which was infected with tuberculosis was deemed to be too great. Small producers were protected, at the cost of children's lives, their health and their future ability to make a living.

In a debate in the House of Lords in 1931, a noted abdominal surgeon, Lord Moynihan, explained that in England 31.5 per cent of tuberculosis in children up to the age of 15 was of bovine origin; that in England 57 per cent of enlarged tuberculous glands in the neck and 33 per cent of bone and joint tuberculosis in children, and in Scotland 90.3 per cent of glandular enlargements of the neck and 61.2 per cent of bone and joint tuberculosis all owed their origin to the drinking of contaminated milk.[284] Later, Lord Moynihan emphasised, 'There are 100,000 farms in this country, and only 400 produce grade A, tubercular-free milk, or tested milk.'[285]

As it was impractical to slaughter tubercular cows as soon as they were identified, it was decided to free as many herds as possible from infection under a voluntary scheme over a period of four years so that, at a later date when the overall incidence of TB infection had been reduced to manageable proportions, it would be possible to introduce radical measures to get rid of the rest.

Under the Attested Herds Schemes (1935), herds which were free from tuberculosis, as judged by having passed three consecutive TB tests, could be registered as attested herds. The farm had to be approved as suitable for the maintenance of an attested herd, and the owner was required to give an undertaking to observe several rules designed to prevent, as far as possible, the chance of reintroduction of infection into the herd. A bonus of one penny per gallon was paid on milk from an attested herd sold through the Milk Marketing Board. The herd was tested at intervals and any reactors had to be isolated at once and removed from the premises within a stipulated time. What progress there was proved painfully slow, as the following newspaper clipping from 30 January 1935 shows.

> Tests urged AVOIDING TUBERCULOSIS Mr W. Tweed, chief veterinary surgeon for Sheffield, said the best method to get rid of tuberculosis would be for the farmers to have their herds undergo the tuberculin test. Last year he managed to get one Sheffield farmer to adopt this method, and now he was licensed to sell certified milk, he hoped to get others to follow the same line.[286]

By 1936, there were only 414 attested herds.[287] Tragically, the process of testing, as outlined in the Sheffield Ministry of Health's annual report in 1937, was insufficient.[288]

Was May confused by all the conflicting advice, or simply unaware of the dangers? Perhaps she was mindful of every penny and sought the cheapest milk available. Or maybe doorstep milk saved a daily walk to find pasteurised milk. I can understand how May might have trusted local authorities to do the right thing by requiring that 'all milk sold within their areas ... be pasteurised or certified free from the offending bacillus'.[289] I doubt she knew that 'the annual death rate from bovine tuberculosis [was] 3,000, with a larger number crippled'.[290]

While it was difficult to make a definitive causal connection between the presence of bacteria and people developing disability during the late 19th and the early 20th century, other countries decided the weight of evidence was enough to act. By 1941, every county in the US was free of bovine tuberculosis, whereas on the Continent, milk was boiled.[291] Britain would take another half-century to protect its children.[292]

'Competing and conflicting scientific, bureaucratic, professional, and commercial interests' ensured that levels of infection remained high in England until the 1950s.[293] The routine pasteurisation of milk finally stopped the risk of bovine tuberculosis spreading from infected cattle to humans, and it was declared to have been eliminated in Britain by 1960.[294]

Appendix B
About the King Edward VII Memorial Hospital

The King Edward VII Memorial Hospital was owned by the Sheffield Corporation. Its original full name, ending in 'for Crippled Children', reflects a term in common usage at the time, but it is now considered unacceptable.

The hospital opened in 1916 and admitted children mainly suffering from tuberculosis of the bones or joints. It had 130 beds. From 1931 the King Edward VII started treating children with congenital deformities, rickets and paralysis from polio. The hospital also acted as a sanatorium as patients were taken outside for open-air treatment.

A clause in the Sheffield Corporation Bill of 1939 allowed the admission of adults suffering from surgical TB, as well as other 'crippling' diseases. From 5 July 1948, the hospital was renamed the King Edward VII Orthopaedic Hospital.

The word 'orthopaedic' is derived from the Greek, and means 'appertaining to the straight child'.[295]

Appendix C
'On Ilkla Mooar Baht 'at'
(On Ilkley Moor Without a Hat, *c.* 1850)

Arnold Kellett says of the song, 'We can at least clear the ground by looking at the most widely accepted tradition that *On Ilkla Mooar* came into being as a result of an incident that took place during a ramble and picnic on the moor. It is further believed that the ramblers were all on a chapel choir outing, from one of the towns in the industrial West Riding.'[296]

Appendix D
Leonard Turner's Tragic Discovery

While there were family stories of Leonard being an alcoholic, it is not known what caused Harry's grandfather to drink so heavily. Did an early trauma, when he was 11 years old, make him more vulnerable?

One morning during Christmas week in 1887, Leonard was walking along Frog Walk just around the corner from his home in Washington Road. The wall along Frog Walk adjoins the General Cemetery. Here, in a hole in the wall, he found the body of a newborn baby wrapped in newspaper and calico. He reported his findings to the Cemetery officials, who told him to go and find a 'bobby'. Off he ran to the Highfield police station and told them what he had found. An inquest was held on Christmas Eve, where he repeated his tale. The Coroner concluded the baby was stillborn and abandoned, and Leonard was praised for his efforts.

THE DEAD BODY OF A CHILD FOUND IN FROG WALK.

This morning, about 10 o'clock, as a boy named Leonard Walker, 134, Washington road, was walking down *Frog* walk, he discovered in a hole in the wall the dead body of a newly-born child, which was wrapped up in a *Sheffield Daily Telegraph* newspaper, and placed in a tub near the snuff mill end of the walk. He at once reported the matter to Police constable Womeck, who took the body to the mortuary.

'The dead body of a child found in Frog Walk'.
Sheffield Evening Telegraph article, 21 December 1887.[297]

THE CHILD FOUND DEAD IN FROG WALK

INQUEST THIS DAY.

Mr. D. Wightman held an inquiry this afternoon, at the Mortuary, on the body of a newly-born female child, who was found wrappeed in paper on Wednesday morning, in Frog walk, by a boy who drev Detective Womack's attention to it. Mr. Arthur Hallam, police surgeon, who had made a *post mortem* exaimination of the body, stated that it had never had a separate existence from its mother, being born dead. Detective Womack said he had made inquiries, but— verdict to the effect "hat deceased was found dead, not having had a separate existence from the mother.

'The child found dead in Frog Walk'.
Sheffield Evening Telegraph article, 23 December 1887.[298]

APPENDIX E
Harry's Termly Reports and Diploma from the Central Technical School (CTS)

CTS First year Spring report, 1948.

'Yet': A Story of Triumph Over Childhood Separation, Trauma, and Disability

---

CITY OF SHEFFIELD EDUCATION COMMITTEE

CENTRAL TECHNICAL SCHOOL

Headmaster:
H. W. WADGE, B.Sc.
Telephone No. 26244

SHEFFIELD, I

REPORT on the work of **DRABBLE HARRY**

Form **IX** Year **1ST** for **SUMMER** Term **1948**

SUBJECT	Max.	Marks Term	Exam.	REPORT	TEACHER'S SIGNATURE
English	50	22		weak	
French	50				
Geography	50	41		Very good work.	
History	50	32		Good throughout.	
Mathematics	100	76		Improved	
Physics	50				
Chemistry and Metallurgy	50				
Applied Mechanics	50				
Building Science	100	57		V. Fair	
Drawing I	50	28		fair	
Drawing II	50				
Art	50	35		Good. He has worked well this term.	
Engineering Workshop Practice	50				
Pattern Making and Moulding	50				
Carpentry and Joinery	50	26		Satisfactory	
Plumbing	50	31		V good	
Bricklaying / Plastering	50				

TOTAL MARKS GAINED **348** Grand Totals **348**
TOTAL MARKS POSS. **550** **550**

GENERAL REPORT—Position in Form **10** No. in Form **30**
Age **13 yrs 8 mth** Average Age of Form **13 yrs 8**
Conduct **Satisfactory**
Attendance—No. of times absent **10** No. of times late **1**
Physical Education Height Weight
REMARKS: *A big jump in position*

Form Master **S. Pilling** **H. W. Wadge**, Headmaster
Parent's Signature Next term commences on **7th SEPT. 1948**

CTS First year Summer report, 1948.

253

Harry's Termly Reports and Diploma from the Central Technical School (CTS)

CITY OF SHEFFIELD EDUCATION COMMITTEE

CENTRAL TECHNICAL SCHOOL

Headmaster
H. W. WADGE, B.Sc.
Telephone No. 26244

SHEFFIELD, 1

REPORT on the work of **Harry Drabble**
Form **2X** Year **1st** for **Xmas** Term 19**48**

SUBJECT	Max.	Term	Exam	REPORT	TEACHER'S SIGNATURE
English	50	31	33	V fair	
French	50				
Geography	50	42	24	Very good	
History	50	45	33	Good	
Mathematics	100	72	69	V. good	
Physics	50				
Chemistry and Metallurgy	50				
Applied Mechanics	50				
Building Science	100	56	66	Excellent	
Drawing I	50	25	42	A very good exam. result	
Drawing II	50				
Art	50	28	34	Good. Has original ideas but is rather restless	
Engineering Workshop Practice	50				
Pattern Making and Moulding	50				
Carpentry and Joinery	50	34	21	Satisfactory	
Plumbing	50	28	40	Good	
Bricklaying / Plastering	50	30	—	Good	

Total Marks Gained
Total Marks Poss.   Grand Totals **763**

GENERAL REPORT—Position in Form **4R** No. in Form **30**
Age **14-10**   Average Age of Form **14-5¾**
Conduct **Very good**
Attendance—No. of times absent **9** No. of times late **0**
Physical Education   Height   Weight
REMARKS :— A very good report. Well done Drabble!

Form Master _____   _____ Headmaster
Parent's Signature _____ Next term commences on **10th Jan**

CTS First year Xmas term, 1948.

'Yet': A Story of Triumph Over Childhood Separation, Trauma, and Disability

---

CITY OF SHEFFIELD EDUCATION COMMITTEE

CENTRAL TECHNICAL SCHOOL

Headmaster:
H. W. WADGE, B.Sc.
Telephone No. 26244

SHEFFIELD, 1

REPORT on the work of **Harry Drabble**
Form **5x** Year **Second** for **Spring** Term 1949

SUBJECT	Max.	MARKS Term/Exam	REPORT	TEACHER'S SIGNATURE
English	50	31	V Fair	
French	50			
Geography	50	43	Very good work.	
History	50	31	Works well.	
Mathematics	100	64	Very Fair	
Physics	50			
Chemistry and Metallurgy	50			
Applied Mechanics	50			
Building Science	100	66		
Drawing I	50	27	Fair	
Drawing II	50			
Art	50			
Engineering Workshop Practice	50			
Pattern Making and Moulding	50			
Carpentry and Joinery	50	31	A little down on last term	
Plumbing	50	29	Very unsatisfactory	
Bricklaying	50	37	Very Satisfactory	
Plastering				

TOTAL MARKS GAINED	357	Grand Totals	357
TOTAL MARKS POSS.	550		550

GENERAL REPORT—Position in Form **21** No. in Form **31**
Age **14 yr 4 mths** Average Age of Form **14 yr 7 mths**
Conduct **Good**
Attendance—No. of times absent **3** No. of times late **5**
Physical Education _____ Height _____ Weight _____
REMARKS :— A fair terms work. Could improve his position with a little more care.
Form Master **H. Hollinski** **H.W.Wadge** Headmaster
Parent's Signature _____ Next term commences on **2.5.49**

CTS Second year Spring report, 1949.

Harry's Termly Reports and Diploma from the Central Technical School (CTS)

CTS Second year Summer report, 1949.

'Yet': A Story of Triumph Over Childhood Separation, Trauma, and Disability

CTS Second year Autumn report, 1949.

Harry's Termly Reports and Diploma from the Central Technical School (CTS)

CITY OF SHEFFIELD EDUCATION COMMITTEE

CENTRAL TECHNICAL SCHOOL

Headmaster:
H. W. WADGE, B.Sc.
Telephone No. 26244

SHEFFIELD, 1

REPORT on the work of **H. Drabble**
Form **6X** Year **THIRD** for **SPRING** Term 1950

Subject	Max.	Marks Term	Marks Exam.	Report	Teacher's Signature
English	50	33		Very fair	
French	50				
Geography	50	38		Good	
History	50	30		Very fair	
Mathematics	100	46		Weak – greater sustained effort essential	
Physics	50				
Chemistry and Metallurgy	50				
Applied Mechanics	50				
Building Science	100	65		He has been busy this term	
Drawing I	50	31		V. satisfactory	
~~Drawing II~~	50				
~~Art~~	50				
Engineering Workshop Practice	50				
Pattern Making and Moulding	50				
Carpentry and Joinery	50	35		Good	
Plumbing	50	25		Fair	
Bricklaying / Plastering	50	36		Satisfactory on the whole	

Total Marks Gained	339			
Total Marks Poss.	550	Grand Totals		

GENERAL REPORT—Position in Form **20** No. in Form **28**
Age **15.3** Average Age of Form **15.7**
Conduct **Not as settled as it should be for a boy of this year**
Attendance—No. of times absent **12** No. of times late **3**
Physical Education Height Weight
REMARKS:— **His "patchy" report is rather like his general behaviour**

Form Master **John R. Hunter** **H.W. Wadge** Headmaster
Parent's Signature Next term commences on **24 April**

CTS Third year Spring report, 1950.

CTS Third year Summer report, 1950.

Harry's Termly Reports and Diploma from the Central Technical School (CTS)

CITY OF SHEFFIELD EDUCATION COMMITTEE

CENTRAL TECHNICAL SCHOOL
DIPLOMA

This is to Certify that

Harry Drabble

after completing the Building Course has obtained a Second Class Diploma, having reached a PASS STANDARD in the following subjects:—

Mathematics, Building Drawing, Plumbing, Brickwork, Plastering,

with CREDITS in English, History, Building Science, Carpentry and Joinery.

and DISTINCTIONS in Geography

J. H. Bingham
Chairman of the Education Committee.

Director of Education.

H. W. Wedge
Headmaster.

Date December, 19 50

Harry's diploma.

18 Suggestions for Discussion

1. What were your initial impressions of young Harry's personality and character? Did you relate to him?

2. How did you feel reading about Harry's separation from his parents at such a young age? Do you remember a separation from your parents or caregivers?

3. Discuss the ways Harry tried to find meaning, purpose and connection during his long hospital stays. What coping strategies stood out to you?

4. What did you think about the hospital's policies around visiting hours and interaction with patients? How do you think they affected Harry?

5. Harry talks about observing and trying to make sense of the world around him. How do you think this shaped his worldview?

6. What were some of the biggest challenges and obstacles Harry had to overcome? How did he do so?

7. Discuss the role music played in Harry's life. Why do you think it was so important to him?

8. What did you think about Harry's defiant, rebellious nature? Could you relate to his feelings of anger and need for autonomy?

9. What did you think about Harry's drive to educate himself and gain qualifications despite his challenges? Where do you think this determination came from?

10. Discuss Harry's social struggles and efforts to find community. What relationships do you think were most meaningful to him?

11. How did you react to the discrimination and the obstacles Harry faced as a person with physical challenges? What do you think has changed over the decades?

12. What did you make of Harry's complex feelings about his disability and defiant attitude towards the limitations society placed on him?

13. How did you feel reading about Harry's ongoing health struggles alongside his efforts to make a living?

14. People with disabilities were paid less than their colleagues. Do you think more, or less, people with disabilities are in work in Britain now? Do you think there is still a pay gap?

15. What did you think about Harry's courtship of Doreen? How did marrying in church without Doreen's father's permission defy expectations of the period?

16. What from Harry's story stuck with you the most? Might his experience apply to your own life?

17. How do Harry's childhood experiences compare to depictions of disability and hospitalisation in society at the time?

18. Discuss how disability rights and care standards have (or haven't) evolved since Harry's childhood.

If you could ask the author a question, what would it be? (You can email your question to helen@helenparkerdrabble.com.)

Would you like to read what happened next? If so, please email helen@helenparkerdrabble.com.

From the Author

Thank you for reading Harry's story. Around 4 million new book titles are published each year, and reviews (especially on Amazon) are one of the few ways independent authors can be discovered, so I would be grateful if you left a review on Amazon, GoodReads or at your favourite store.

If you would like to read what Harry did next, please email me at helen@helenparkerdrabble.com or contact me through social media: LinkedIn: Helen Parker-Drabble; Facebook: @FactualTales; X (formerly Twitter): @HelenPDrabble; Bsky: @helenpdrabble.bsky.social.

Should enough people show an interest, I will continue his story, including how he used the Great Train Robbery of 1963 to empower disenfranchised working-class youths to gain their first professional qualification.

You can read articles and find more about my work at www.helenparkerdrabble.com, where you can also sign up to my newsletter.

Acknowledgements

This book would not have been possible without all my father shared with me. I am so sorry he did not live to read the final version. Heartfelt thanks are due to my brother Stephen, who shared his recollections and feedback on various drafts. Grateful thanks to our aunt Margaret for the photos and memories she generously shared with me.

I am indebted to Dad's lifelong friend Sheila Cousins, née Gough, and her daughter, Helen Darling, for sharing their memories. Thanks are also due to Doreen's friend, Ann Wardley.

It is always a challenge to fill in the gaps. The Sheffield City Archive and Local Studies Library, Picture Sheffield and the National Emergency Services Museum provided invaluable help. I also interviewed the late Derek Godbehere, a contemporary of Dad's, several times. Although this memoir is not what he might have expected, I am sure he would have approved with my raising awareness of the children who lost so much of their childhood in unimaginable circumstances and for getting his and Dad's memories 'out there'. I am in debt to Margaret Miller who generously shared her personal archive of the King Edward VII Hospital. Jack Spencer, silversmith and goldsmith, and his son John Spencer, goldsmith, helped me fill in the blanks of Dad's time at the Sheffield College of Art.

My appreciation goes to Gill Blanchard, Michelle Higgs, and Jo Morton whose expertise and advice was crucial in shaping this memoir. The work shared by Gill's writing group inspired my

Acknowledgements

own. Gill, Michelle and Jo also read multiple drafts, offered honest feedback and endless encouragement, which propelled me forward.

Facebook groups that have been enormously helpful include those of the Central Technical School Sheffield (Old Boys Association), and with particular thanks to Philip Seymour, who remembered Dad; Sheffield History; Sheffield History Group; Stannington & Rivelin Group; Sheffield Writers Network Group; Memoir, Autobiography and Non-Fiction Book Lovers; and We Love Memoir.

My heartfelt thanks go to Dad's students, particularly James Selby, Issac Britton and Vicky Voller, for sharing their memories of, and gratitude for, Dad as a holistic teacher.

I also appreciated the input of Dr Carole Reeves, Ann Shaw (The Children of Craig-Y-Nos), Dr Emma Sutton, and Dr Sarah Chaney, who provided valuable information, insight, and guidance.

I gratefully acknowledge the skill of Neil White of Restorapic.com in restoring a number of photographs so they could appear in this book.

ENDNOTES

1. Parker-Drabble, Helen. "How Key Psychological Theories Can Enrich Our Understanding of Our Ancestors and Help Improve Mental Health for Present and Future Generations: A Family Historian's Perspective." *Genealogy* 6, no. 1 (2022): 4. doi.org/10.3390/genealogy6010004.

2. Borsay, Anne. *Disability and Social Policy in Britain since 1750: A History of Exclusion.* Palgrave Macmillan, 2005, 55.

3. Westover, Tara. *Educated.* Penguin Books, 2022, 384

4. Chamberlain, Geoffrey. "British Maternal Mortality in the 19th and Early 20th Centuries." *Journal of the Royal Society of Medicine* 99, no. 11 (November 2006): 559–563. doi.org/10.1177/014107680609901113.

5. Rennie, John. *Report of the Medical Officer of Health, Sheffield City.* City Council, 1934, 101.

6. Teague, née Drabble, Margaret. Letter to Helen Parker-Drabble, December 12, 2023.

7. Mathers, Helen, and McIntosh, Tania. *Born in Sheffield: A History of Women's Health Services, 1864–2000.* Wharncliffe, 2000, 76.

8. Drabble, Helen. Childhood memory. n.d.

9. Mathers, Helen, and McIntosh, Tania. *Born in Sheffield: A History of Women's Health Services, 1864–2000.* Wharncliffe, 2000, 91.

10. Mathers, Helen, and McIntosh, Tania. *Born in Sheffield: A History of Women's Health Services, 1864–2000.* Wharncliffe, 2000, 94.

11. Rent approx. 10*s.* 6*d.* Owen, A.D.K. "A Report on the Housing Problem in Sheffield." Sheffield Social Survey Committee Pamphlet No. 2. Sheffield Social Survey Committee, 1931, 36. McIntosh, Tania. *"A Price Must Be Paid For Motherhood": The Experience Of Maternity In Sheffield, 1879–1939.* Thesis, University of Sheffield, 1997, 57.

12. Ordnance Survey Revision 1935, Shiregreen. OS 25 County Series 288.8.

13. Hayes, Dan. "Why George Orwell Hated Sheffield." *Sheffield Tribune*, December 5, 2024. www.sheffieldtribune.co.uk/why-george-orwell-hated-sheffield/.

14. Scree – Sheffield Hallam University Research Archive. Accessed April 20, 2025. http://shura.shu.ac.uk/10780/1/Bennett_&_Hock_(2013)_Scree.pdf, 51; "Orwell Memories On A Diamond Day." *Sheffield Morning Telegraph*, February 2, 1990.

15. Orwell, George. *The Road to Wigan Pier*. Secker & Warburg, 1959, 107.

16. See Appendix D for two newspaper reports about 11-year-old Leonard Turner finding a dead baby.

17. *The Motherhood Book for the Expectant Mother and Baby's First Years*. Allied Newspapers Ltd, 1933, 126–127.

18. *The Motherhood Book for the Expectant Mother and Baby's First Years*. Allied Newspapers Ltd, 1933, 206.

19. *The Motherhood Book for the Expectant Mother and Baby's First Years*. Allied Newspapers Ltd, 1933, 214–215.

20. *The Motherhood Book for the Expectant Mother and Baby's First Years*. Allied Newspapers Ltd, 1933, 435.

21. *Whites Directory of Sheffield & Rotherham*. Sheffield, 1905. Osborn, Samuel & Co (steel merch. & manuftrs. of crucible steel castings etc.). Address: Clyde steel & iron works, Wicker; 184 Brook Hill, Blonk Street, Rutland works.

22. Seed, T. Alec. *Pioneers for a Century 1852–1952: A History of the Growth and Achievement of Samuel Osborn & Co., Limited Clyde Steel Works*. Sheffield, 1952, 70.

23. Winch, Ken. "A Brief Guide to Dating Bartholomew Maps." n.d. Accessed February 16, 2025. Ken Winch, retired Bartholomew's Librarian and Map Curator.

24. Jolley, Michael Jeremy. *A Social History of Paediatric Nursing 1920–1970*. Thesis, University of Hull, 2003, 153.

25. Jolley, Michael Jeremy. *A Social History of Paediatric Nursing 1920–1970*. Thesis, University of Hull, 2003, 153–154.

26. Jolley, Michael Jeremy. *A Social History of Paediatric Nursing 1920–1970*. Thesis, University of Hull, 2003, 154.

27. Skinner, E.F. *Centenary of the Royal Hospital Sheffield, 1932*. United Kingdom, 1932. https://wellcomecollection.org/works/akrmg53h. Photographer A.L. Watson. Copyright previously held by British Medical Association and assigned to Wellcome in 2005.

28. Atkins, Peter J. "Bovine Tuberculosis: The Human Impact." In *A History of Uncertainty: Bovine Tuberculosis in Britain, 1850 to the Present*. Winchester University Press, 2016.

29. "Infected Milk Dangers." *The Sheffield Independent*, April 9, 1934, 5, column 5.

30. *The Motherhood Book for the Expectant Mother and Baby's First Years*. Allied Newspapers Ltd, 1933, 397.

31. Sheffield Hospitals' Council, *Annual Report 1930*, 13–17; McIntosh, Tania. *Social History of Maternity and Childbirth*. Routledge, 2012, 102–105; and Sheffield Survey Report, TNA MH66/1076, maternity section.

32. King Edward VII Memorial Hospital for Crippled Children (Ref. NHS11/4/1/2). King Edward VII Hospital collection.

Collection. Admission register, 2 Jun 1926–17 Dec 1938. Admission number 3280 admitted 19th July 1937.

33. Jolley, Michael Jeremy. *A Social History of Paediatric Nursing 1920–1970*. Thesis, University of Hull, 2003, 15.

34. Named the King Edward VII Memorial Hospital for Crippled Children before the introduction of the National Health Service in 1948.

35. Borsay, Anne. *Disability and Social Policy in Britain since 1750: A History of Exclusion*. Palgrave Macmillan, 2005, 53.

36. McIntosh, Tania. *"A Price Must Be Paid for Motherhood": The Experience of Maternity in Sheffield, 1879–1939*. Thesis, University of Sheffield, 1997, 68; Doyle, B. "Labour and Hospitals in Urban Yorkshire: Middlesbrough, Leeds and Sheffield, 1919–1938." *Social History of Medicine* 23, no. 2 (May 5, 2010): 374–392 [381]. https://doi.org/10.1093/shm/hkq007; Moore, Graham. "Standing Firm to Provide Healthcare during the Sheffield Blitz." Westfield Health, November 8, 2024. https://www.westfieldhealth.com/blog/standing-firm-to-provide-healthcare-during-the-sheffield-blitz.

37. Forrester-Brown, M. "The Splinting of Cases of Tuberculosis of the Hip." *Journal of British Surgery* 18, no. 69 (July 1, 1930): 54–77. https://doi.org/10.1002/bjs.1800186909; Kirkup, John. "Maud Forrester-Brown (1885–1970): Britain's First Woman Orthopaedic Surgeon." *Journal of Medical Biography* 16, no. 4 (November 2008): 197–204. https://doi.org/10.1258/jmb.2007.007044.

38. Kirkup, John. "Maud Forrester-Brown (1885–1970): Britain's First Woman Orthopaedic Surgeon." *Journal of Medical Biography* 16, no. 4 (November 2008): 197–204. https://doi.org/10.1258/jmb.2007.007044.

39. Rennie, John. *Report of the Medical Officer of Health, Sheffield City*. City Council, 1937, 126.

40. Rennie, John. *Report of the Medical Officer of Health, Sheffield City*. City Council, 1937, 112.

41. Jolley, Michael Jeremy. *A Social History of Paediatric Nursing 1920–1970*. Thesis, University of Hull, 2003, xv.

42. "Health | TB: The Sandbag and Fresh Air Cure." BBC News, December 14, 1999. Accessed November 25, 2024. http://news.bbc.co.uk/1/hi/health/564540.stm.

43. Odelberg-Johnson, G. "Different Types of Tuberculosis of the Hip in Children." *Acta Orthopaedica Scandinavica* 9, no. 2–3 (January 1938): 197–209 [198]. https://doi.org/10.3109/17453673808988902.

44. Odelberg-Johnson, G. "Different Types of Tuberculosis of the Hip in Children." *Acta Orthopaedica Scandinavica* 9, no. 2–3 (January 1938): 197–209 [209]. https://doi.org/10.3109/17453673808988902.

45. Foot, Samantha. "The Alexandra Hospital for Children with Hip Disease: 'For the Reception, Maintenance and Surgical Treatment of the Children of the Poor' Suffering from Tuberculosis of the Hip in the Nineteenth Century." Master's thesis, University of London, 2011, 27.

46. Herzog, Erich G. *A History of King Edward VII Orthopaedic Hospital Sheffield*. Sheffield, 1986, 4.

It was edited and photographs added by Peter Dean. This history of King Edward VII Hospital was dictated by my father-in-law, the late Dr Eric Herzog at some time in 1985–1986, after he retired as Superintendent in 1972. I believe he intended it for publication and he appears to have selected a number of illustrations, which were referenced in the text. The only surviving copy is a typewritten version on which he has made a number of corrections. Unfortunately, I have not been able to find the accompanying illustrations.

47. Houghton, Jemma. "'Digging for Drugs': The Medicinal Plant Collection Scheme of the Second World War." *Pharmaceutical Historian* 52, no. 3 (2022): 69.

48. *Smithsonian Magazine*. "How Humble Moss Healed the Wounds of Thousands in World War I." Smithsonian.com, April 28, 2017. Accessed December 12, 2024. https://www.smithsonianmag.com/science-nature/how-humble-moss-helped-heal-wounds-thousands-WWI-180963081/.

49. "Making Sphagnum Moss Dressings, Glasgow, Scotland: Educational Images: Historic England." Educational Images | Historic England. Accessed December 7, 2024. https://historicengland.org.uk/services-skills/education/educational-images/making-sphagnum-moss-dressings-glasgow-scotland-11939#:~:text=The%20moss%20was%20often%20collected,wounds%20during%20battles%20for%20centuries.

50. Sydenstricker, V.P. "The Impact of Vitamin Research upon Medical Practice." *Proceedings of the Nutrition Society* 12, no. 3 (September 1953): 256–269. https://doi.org/10.1079/pns19530056; Eggersdorfer, Manfred, Laudert, Dietmar, Létinois, Ulla, McClymont, Tom, Medlock, Jonathan, Netscher, Thomas, and Bonrath, Werner. "One Hundred Years of Vitamins: A Success Story of the Natural Sciences." *Angewandte Chemie International Edition* 51, no. 52 (December 3, 2012): 12960–12990. https://doi.org/10.1002/anie.201205886.

51. "History." Centers for Disease Control and Prevention, October 18, 2023. https://www.cdc.gov/tb/worldtbday/history.htm#:~:text=In%201943%2C%20Selman%20Waksman%2C%20Elizabeth,%2C%20and%20rifampin%20(1966); "For Beautiful Mouths." *Sheffield Daily Telegraph*, March 1, 1932, 6, column 4: "Mrs. Mellanby and Dr. Lee Pattison have shown in Sheffield that cod liver oil checks decay in the teeth of children–the tests were made with children in Sheffield and elsewhere whose teeth were already formed–but the Research Council hopes this year to announce even better results in children who had not cut their teeth when the doses of vitamin D began. At King Edward Hospital, Sheffield, Mrs. Mellanby and Dr. Lee Pattison are investigating the effect on decayed teeth of a diet rich in vitamin D but without bread, porridge, or puddings."

52. Singh, Widhilika, and Kushwaha, Poonam. "Potassium: A Frontier in Osteoporosis." *Hormone and Metabolic Research* 56, no. 5 (February 12, 2024):

329–340. https://doi.org/10.1055/a-2254-8533; "Health from Carrots." *Sheffield Daily Telegraph*, March 1, 1932, 6, column 4:

"Professor Mellanby has also been busy in Sheffield determining the value of vitamin A—an ingredient of some fresh vegetables—in checking disease. At Sheffield Royal Infirmary he and Dr. Roberts tested the effect on locomotor ataxy of vitamin A and carotene, which is the colouring principle of carrots.

Other Sheffield researches last year included work by Dr G.A. Clark on the secretion of insulin in the human body, and Dr C.G. Imric with Dr Marion Brown on the part played by phosphorus in the muscles. Minerals such as phosphorus and iron are proving to be far more active and necessary in the human system than doctors used to think."

53. Seymour Caton, Margaret Jane. *T.B. hip. Short plaster spica*. Photograph. Wellcome Collection, 183 Euston Road, London NW1 2BE, n.d. The photograph is part of a collection presented to the Wellcome Institute Library by the Rev. John P. Caton B.D., on 26 January 1989. The photographs were taken by Caton's late wife, Margaret Jane Seymour Caton, when she worked as a nurse at St Nicholas' and St Martin's Orthopaedic Hospital, Pyrford, Surrey, between 1935 and 1937. The hospital was later known as the Rowley Bristow Hospital.

54. Mohideen, M.A.F., and Rasool, M.N. "Tuberculosis of the Hip Joint Region in Children." *SA Orthopaedic Journal*. Accessed November 23, 2024. http://www.scielo.org.za/scielo.php?script=sci_arttext&pid=S1681-150X2013000100008.

55. Forrester-Brown, M. "The Splinting of Cases of Tuberculosis of the Hip." *Journal of British Surgery* 18, no. 69 (July 1, 1930): 54–77 [60]. https://doi.org/10.1002/bjs.1800186909; Owen, Edmund. *The Surgical Diseases of Children*. 3rd ed. Cassell and Company, 1897, 59.

56. Moon, Myung-Sang, Sung-Soo Kim, Sung-Rak Lee, Young-Wan Moon, Jeong-Lim Moon, and Seog-In Moon. "Tuberculosis of Hip in Children: A Retrospective Analysis." *Indian Journal of Orthopaedics* 46, no. 2 (April 2012): 191–199 [195]. https://doi.org/10.4103/0019-5413.93686.

57. Forrester-Brown, M. "The Splinting of Cases of Tuberculosis of the Hip." *Journal of British Surgery* 18, no. 69 (July 1, 1930): 54–77 [60]. https://doi.org/10.1002/bjs.1800186909; Owen, Edmund. *The Surgical Diseases of Children*. 3rd ed. Cassell and Company, 1897, 414.

58. Parker-Drabble, Helen. Derek Godbehere of 23 Thornbridge Road, Sheffield, S12 3AL. Personal, July 15, 2022. Derek gave permission for the author to use quotes from their interview and subsequent telephone conversations in her project to raise awareness of the experiences, and their consequences, of the children admitted to the King Edward VII Memorial Hospital of Crippled Children.

59. Fillet and spica plaster (1936). Accessed November 23, 2024. https://www.youtube.com/watch?v=Z77fNgHjQYI. From 8.41 minutes.

60. Forrester-Brown, M. "The Splinting of Cases of Tuberculosis of the Hip by a Visiting Surgeon to the Children's Orthopaedic Hospital, Bath." *The British Journal of Surgery* 18, no. 69 (July 1930): 54–77. https://doi.org/https://doi.org/10.1002/bjs.1800186909.

61. Parker-Drabble, Helen. Derek Godbehere of 23 Thornbridge Road, Sheffield, S12 3AL. Personal, July 15, 2022.

62. Adam. "The Lime Trees of Rivelin: Stunning Natural Monument: Awa Tree Blog." AWA Trees, March 21, 2018. https://www.awatrees.com/2015/11/20/the-lime-trees-of-rivelin/.

63. Herzog, Erich G. *A History of King Edward VII Orthopaedic Hospital Sheffield*. Sheffield, 1986, 3.

Edited and photographs added by son-in-law Peter Dean.

64. MacDonald, Betty Bard. *The Plague and I*. Akadine Press, 1997, 84.

65. Whitman, Royal. *A Treatise on Orthopaedic Surgery*. 2nd ed. Henry Kimpton, 1904, 342.

66. Jeddo, Salim, Chuan Wang Huang, and Ming Li. "Case Report on the Recurrence of Tuberculosis of Hip after 40 Years." SpringerOpen, November 6, 2014. https://springerplus.springeropen.com/articles/10.1186/2193-1801-3-662.

67. Griffith, A. Stanley. "Incidence of Human and Bovine Bacilli in Tuberculous Meningitis." *The Lancet* 223, no. 5783 (June 1934): 1382–1387. https://doi.org/10.1016/s0140-6736(00)56513-1; Wilkins, E.G., Griffiths, R.J., Roberts, C., and Green, H.T. "Tuberculous Meningitis Due to Mycobacterium Bovis: A Report of Two Cases." *Postgraduate Medical Journal* 62, no. 729 (July 1986): 653–655. doi:10.1136/pgmj.62.729.653. PMID: 3529067; PMCID: PMC2418736; "Father Note to Doctor: Trouble over City Child's Death." *Sheffield Independent*, August 7, 1937, 13, column 1.

Endnotes

68. "Spinal Anaesthesia During the 19th and 20th Centuries – Cocaine and Controversy." Association of Anaesthetists. Accessed December 10, 2024. https://anaesthetists.org/Home/Resources-publications/Anaesthesia-News-magazine/Anaesthesia-News-Digital-April-2021/Spinal-anaesthesia-during-the-19th-and-20th-Centuries-cocaine-and-controversy.

69. "Father Note to Doctor: Trouble over City Child's Death." *Sheffield Independent*, August 7, 1937, 13, column 1.

70. "Rivelin Sick Visits." *Sheffield Evening Telegraph*, March 6, 1939, 8, column 4.

71. Jolley, Michael Jeremy. *A Social History of Paediatric Nursing 1920–1970*. Thesis, University of Hull, 2003, 16.

72. Jolley, Michael Jeremy. *A Social History of Paediatric Nursing 1920–1970*. Thesis, University of Hull, 2003, 16–17.

73. *The Motherhood Book for the Expectant Mother and Baby's First Years*. Allied Newspapers Ltd, 1933, 735.

74. Robertson, James, and Robertson, Joyce. *Separation and the Very Young*. Free Association Books, 1989, 11.

75. Robertson, James, and Robertson, Joyce. *Separation and the Very Young*. Free Association Books, 1989, 33.

76. Robertson, James, and Joyce Robertson. *Separation and the very young*. London: Free Association Books, 1989, 18–19.

77. Robertson, James, and Robertson, Joyce. *Separation and the Very Young*. Free Association Books, 1989, 28.

78. Robertson, James, and Robertson, Joyce. *Separation and the Very Young*. Free Association Books, 1989, 22.

79. Stewart, John. *"The Dangerous Age of Childhood": Child Guidance in Britain, c.1918–1955*. Based on a presentation at the Department for Education, October 6, 2011. History and policy. Accessed December 10, 2024.

80. "Child Problems." *Sheffield Independent*, September 13, 1938, 4, column 2; "Anti-Social Children Aided." *Sheffield Independent*, October 20, 1938, 5, column 1.

81. "Obituary: June Jolly, Pioneer in Transforming Children's Services." *Nursing Times*, March 23, 2016. https://www.nursingtimes.net/opinion/obituary-june-jolly-pioneer-in-transforming-childrens-services-23-03-2016/.

82. Herzog, Erich G. *A History of King Edward VII Orthopaedic Hospital Sheffield*. Sheffield, 1986, 3.

Edited and photographs added by author's son-in-law Peter Dean, 4.

Herzog, Erich G. *A History of King Edward VII Orthopaedic Hospital Sheffield by E.G. Herzog Orthopaedic Surgeon Emeritus*, 1986, 7. An original copy of E Herzog's manuscript held by Margaret Miller, Director of Rivelin Court Limited, the Residential Management Company for the former King Edward VII Orthopaedic Hospital. Seen by the author on the 6 March 2022.

83. Herzog, Erich G. *A History of King Edward VII Orthopaedic Hospital Sheffield*. Sheffield, 1986, 5; Herzog, Erich G. *A History of King Edward VII Orthopaedic Hospital Sheffield by E.G. Herzog Orthopaedic Surgeon Emeritus*, 1986, 8.

An original copy of E Herzog's manuscript held by Margaret Miller, Director of Rivelin Court Limited, the Residential Management Company for the former King Edward VII Orthopaedic Hospital. Seen by the author on the 6 March 2022.

84. Sheffield History Guest, "King Edward Hospital." Sheffield History – Sheffield Memories, October 13, 2008. http://www.sheffieldhistory.co.uk/forums/index.php?/topic/3046-king-edward-hospital/.

"Life was hard for patients. Every day their beds were wheeled out of the individual rooms under the open colonnades that linked them, come rain or shine. The beds were covered with tarpaulins when it rained. Of course there were no antibiotics then, fresh air was the only cure for TB. Life was not easy for the nurses either. They all lived in the main building, up in attic dormitories, and were in fear of Matron and the doctors. They had one afternoon off a week, and used to go to the post office at the end of Rivelin Valley Road where it joins the Manchester Road, and buy bottles of pop and sweets. I heard this from two elderly ladies who came to look round the King Edward's estate, now converted into housing. They had been nurses at the Edward VII hospital during the war, and one had emigrated to Canada and it was the first time she had been back since."

85. Shuttleworth, Ann. "A History of Nursing in Britain: The 1930s." *Nursing Times*, August 26, 2021. https://www.nursingtimes.net/news/history-of-nursing/a-history-of-nursing-in-britain-the-1930s-26-08-2021/.

86. "The Lancet Commission on Nursing." *The Lancet* 219, no. 5663 (March 1932): 585–588. https://doi.org/10.1016/s0140-6736(00)91039-0.

87. Shuttleworth, Ann. "A History of Nursing in Britain: The 1930s." *Nursing Times*, August 26, 2021. https://www.nursingtimes.net/news/history-of-nursing/a-history-of-nursing-in-britain-the-1930s-26-08-2021/.

88. Originally middle-class medical social workers known as almoners acted as gatekeepers to hospital treatment weeding out those who could afford to pay for their care. During the 1920s and 1930s they operated the hospital means test. However, those in the job saw their role as much more nuanced and often spent more time with those who had difficult social problems than trying to get payments for the hospital. Social programmes were developed locally to meet the needs of the poor. During the Second World War the roles shifted further with one annual report not mentioning the extraction of money for care, but acknowledged the Almoner's Office pass all the types which go to make up the Hospital world, the lonely, the misfits, the discouraged and the difficult – all through sickness or poverty, in need of some help or advice.

Gosling, George. "Social Work and the Coming of the NHS." People's History of the NHS, March 15, 2016. https://peopleshistorynhs.org/encyclopaedia/social-work-and-the-coming-of-the-nhs/.

William Beveridge's report of 1942 *Social Insurance and Allied Services* identified five "Giant Evils" in society: squalor, ignorance, want, idleness and disease, and went on to propose widespread reform to the system of social welfare to mitigate these problems.

Abel-Smith, Brian. "The Beveridge Report: Its Origins and Outcomes." *International Social Security Review* 45, no. 1–2 (January 1992): 5–16. https://doi.org/10.1111/j.1468-246x.1992.tb00900.x.

89. Tripe is the stomach lining of beef cattle. It is a complete source of protein, meaning it contains all nine essential amino acids your body needs to function. It is rich in vitamin B12, selenium, zinc, calcium, and iron. Kubala, Jillian. "Tripe: Nutrition, Benefits, and Uses." *Healthline*, March 1, 2022. https://www.healthline.com/nutrition/tripe#nutrition.

90. Parker-Drabble, Helen. Derek Godbehere of 23 Thornbridge Road, Sheffield, S12 3AL. Personal, July 15, 2022.

91. Smith, M., Williamson, A.E., Walsh, D., and McCartney, G. "Is There a Link between Childhood Adversity, Attachment Style and Scotland's Excess Mortality? Evidence, Challenges and Potential Research." *BMC Public Health* 16, no. 1 (July 28, 2016). https://doi.org/10.1186/s12889-016-3201-z.

92. Herzog, Erich G. *A History of King Edward VII Orthopaedic Hospital Sheffield by E.G. Herzog Orthopaedic Surgeon Emeritus*, 1986.

An original copy of E Herzog's manuscript held by Margaret Miller, Director of Rivelin Court Limited, the Residential Management Company for the former King Edward VII Orthopaedic Hospital. Seen by the author on the 6 March 2022.

93 Parker-Drabble, Helen. Derek Godbehere of 23 Thornbridge Road, Sheffield, S12 3AL. Personal, July 15, 2022.

94. A collaborating account: "Hospital Life for Me." *Best of British Magazine*, November 2, 2010. https://www.bestofbritishmag.co.uk/hospital-life-for-me/.

95. Parker-Drabble, Helen. Derek Godbehere of 23 Thornbridge Road, Sheffield, S12 3AL. Personal, July 15, 2022.

96. Parker-Drabble, Helen. Derek Godbehere of 23 Thornbridge Road, Sheffield, S12 3AL. Personal, July 15, 2022.

97. Sheffield No. 3 Hospital Management Committee Annual Report, 17, 1 April 1957 to 31 March 1958.

98. Herzog, Erich G. *A History of King Edward VII Orthopaedic Hospital Sheffield*. Sheffield, 1986, 3.

Edited and photographs added by son-in-law Peter Dean, 8.

99. Herzog, Erich G. *A History of King Edward VII Orthopaedic Hospital Sheffield*. Sheffield, 1986, 3.

Edited and photographs added by son-in-law Peter Dean, 8.

100. Apparatus used on hospital beds to aid hip adduction. Hip abduction is the movement of the leg away from the midline of the body. Herzog, Erich G. *A History of King Edward VII Orthopaedic Hospital Sheffield*. Sheffield, 1986, 3.

Edited and photographs added by son-in-law Peter Dean, 8.

101. MacDonald, Betty Bard. *The Plague and I*. Akadine Press, 1997, 164–165.

102. Stevenson, G.H. "Some Aspects of Osteomyelitis." *Glasgow Medical Journal* 27, no. 12 (December 1946).

103. "Woman Hairdresser." *The Star*, January 31, 1939, 8, column 1.

104. Maartens, Brendan. "To Encourage, Inspire and Guide." *Media History* 21, no. 3 (July 3, 2015): 328–341. https://doi.org/10.1080/13688804.2015.1053386.

105. "Premier's Broadcast on National Service." *Sheffield Daily Telegraph*, January 21, 1939, front page, column 5.

106. "Premier Opens Defence Drive 'Show What People Can Do.'" *Sheffield Daily Telegraph*, January 24, 1939, front page, column 5.

107. "Prudent Course." *Sheffield Daily Telegraph*, January 25, 1939, 8, column 2.

108 Maartens, Brendan. "To Encourage, Inspire and Guide." *Media History* 21, no. 3 (July 3, 2015): 328–341. https://doi.org/10.1080/13688804.2015.1053386.

109. According to www.kenleyrevival.org/content/catalogue_item/national-service-booklet-1939.

110. *Sheffield May Special*. Film. Pathe, 1939. URN: 91337. Film ID: 3305.11.

111. Maartens, Brendan. "To Encourage, Inspire and Guide." *Media History* 21, no. 3 (July 3, 2015): 328–341. https://doi.org/10.1080/13688804.2015.1053386.

112. Sheffield City Archives, King Edward VII Hospital collection (Ref. NHS11/4/1/2). Admission register, 2 Jun 1926–17 Dec 1938. Discharged 3 September 1939.

113. Goodman, Susan. *Children of War: The Second World War through the Eyes of a Generation*. John Murray, 2006, 93.

114. NHS11/4/1/2–4 King Edward VII Memorial Hospital for Crippled Children admission registers (indexed), Jun 1926–Dec 1958. Ref. Admission number 3280; Central Ambulance service; *Sheffield Year Book*. Sir W. C. Leng & Co., 1939.

115. Robertson, James, and Robertson, Joyce. *Separation and the Very Young*. Free Association Books, 1989, 41.

116. Robertson, James, and Robertson, Joyce. *Separation and the Very Young*. Free Association Books, 1989, 16–17.

117. Parker-Drabble, Helen. Derek Godbehere of 23 Thornbridge Road, Sheffield, S12 3AL. Personal, July 15, 2022.

118. Harvey, Peter. *Sheffield in the 1930s*. Sheaf Publishing in association with the Star, 1993, 3.

119. Harvey, Peter. *Sheffield in the 1930s*. Sheaf Publishing in association with the Star, 1993, 3.

120. Assistant Roller 2nd Hand Heavy Worker, according to the 1939 National Register; Schedule of Reserved Occupations (Provisional) Presented by the Minister of Labour to Parliament by Command of His Majesty, January 1939, page 20. "The occupations listed in this Schedule are those in respect of which in the general national interests restrictions will be placed in peace time on the acceptance of volunteers for certain forms of enlistment or enrolment for service in time of war", page 3.

121. Harvey, Peter. *Sheffield in the 1930s*. Sheaf Publishing in association with the Star, 1993, 25.

122. Rationing in Britain during World War II – Faculty of History. Accessed April 20, 2025. https://www.history.ox.ac.uk/::ognode-637356::/files/download-resource-printable-pdf-11. "A Time to Dare and Endure." Address given in the Free Trade Hall Manchester, January 27, 1940. Published in R.S. Churchill (ed.), *Into Battle: Speeches by the Right Hon. Winston S. Churchill*. London, 1941, 164–165.

123. "Rationing in the United Kingdom." Wikipedia, December 14, 2024. https://en.wikipedia.org/wiki/Rationing_in_the_United_Kingdom.

124. Moseley, Katrina. Waste Not, Want Not: Feeding the British Home Front: Women's Interconnectivity in the Second World War. The Recipes Project. Accessed December 18, 2024. https://recipes.hypotheses.org/tag/second-world-war.

125. Minney, Nicola. "How Did Rationing Work in the Second World War?" The Museum of English Rural Life, October 28, 2024. https://merl.reading.ac.uk/blog/2022/05/everything-you-wanted-to-know-ration-books/.

126. Anderson, Neil. *Sheffield's Date with Hitler: The Story of the Blitz*. ACM Retro, 2010.

127. Cooper, Tim. *The Story of Sheffield*. The History Press, 2021, 222.

128. Anderson, Neil. *Forgotten Memories from a Forgotten Blitz*. ACM Retro, 2012.

129. Harvey, Peter. *Sheffield in the 1930s*. Sheaf Publishing in association with the Star, 1993, 25.

130. *Your Anderson Shelter This Winter*. Ministry of Home Security, 1940, 1–2.

131. Email to Helen Parker-Drabble. From Brother Stephen Drabble – Info from author's second Cousin Tracy, March 19, 2006.

132. *Annual Report.* Cripples Aid Association, 1932, 7.

133. Tools of the trade silver, hollowware, E.P.N.S.* trade hawley ... Accessed April 20, 2025. http://www.hawleytoolcollection.com/uploads/PDF/Silver%20Trade.pdf.

134. Goodman, Susan. *Children of War: The Second World War through the Eyes of a Generation.* John Murray, 2006, 320.

135. Goodman, Susan. *Children of War: The Second World War through the Eyes of a Generation.* John Murray, 2006, 324.

136. Doyle, B. "Labour and Hospitals in Urban Yorkshire: Middlesbrough, Leeds and Sheffield, 1919–1938." *Social History of Medicine* 23, no. 2 (May 5, 2010): 374–392. https://doi.org/10.1093/shm/hkq007; Moore, Graham. "Standing Firm to Provide Healthcare during the Sheffield Blitz." *Westfield Health*, November 8, 2024. https://www.westfieldhealth.com/blog/standing-firm-to-provide-healthcare-during-the-sheffield-blitz.

137. Bayleaf, Sheffield History Admin, and Author. "Sheffield Yearbook 1939", 39, 208. Sheffield History – Sheffield Memories, August 7, 2012. https://www.sheffieldhistory.co.uk/forums/topic/13064-sheffield-yearbook-1939/.

138. Sheffield City Archives, King Edward VII Hospital collection (Ref. NHS11/4/1/3). Admission register, 1 Jan 1939–30 Dec 1953. Admission number 347 confirming his admission on July 6, 1940.

139. Foster, Diane. *The Evacuation of British Children during World War II: A Preliminary Investigation into the Long-Term Psychological Effects.* Thesis, University of London, 2000, 128.

140. Foster, Diane. *The Evacuation of British Children during World War II: A Preliminary Investigation into the Long-Term Psychological Effects.* Thesis, University of London, 2000, 130.

141. Foster, Diane. *The Evacuation of British Children during World War II: A Preliminary Investigation into the Long-Term Psychological Effects.* Thesis, University of London, 2000, 130.

142. "Fourth World Conference of Workers for Cripples 'Care of Crippled Children'." *The Scotsman*, June 22, 1939, 10, column 5.

143. United States Holocaust Memorial Museum, article The murder of people with disabilities. Accessed December 18, 2024. https://encyclopedia.ushmm.org/.

144. The History Place – Holocaust Timeline: Nazi Euthanasia. Accessed January 25, 2025. https://www.historyplace.com/worldwar2/holocaust/h-euthanasia.htm; Parent, Stefan, and Shevell, Michael. "The 'First to Perish.'" *Archives of Pediatrics & Adolescent Medicine* 152, no. 1 (January 1, 1998). https://doi.org/10.1001/archpedi.152.1.79; Hudson, Lee. "From Small Beginnings: The Euthanasia of Children with Disabilities in Nazi Germany." *Journal of Paediatrics and Child Health* 47, no. 8 (January 31, 2011): 508–511. https://doi.org/10.1111/j.1440-1754.2010.01977.x; United States Holocaust Memorial Museum. Accessed January 25, 2025. https://encyclopedia.ushmm.org/content/en/article/euthanasia-program; "Child Euthanasia in Nazi Germany." Wikipedia, December 9, 2024. https://en.wikipedia.org/wiki/Child_euthanasia_in_Nazi_Germany#cite_note-7.

145. The History Place – Holocaust Timeline: Nazi Euthanasia. Accessed January 25, 2025. https://www.historyplace.com/worldwar2/holocaust/h-euthanasia.htm.

146. Evans, Richard J. *The Third Reich at War: How the Nazis Led Germany from Conquest to Disaster*. Penguin, 2009, 97–99.

147. "8 Things You Need to Know about the Battle of Britain." Imperial War Museums. Accessed December 18, 2024. https://www.iwm.org.uk/history/8-things-you-need-to-know-about-the-battle-of-britain.

148. *"Our Food Today No. 1"*: "Rationing in the United Kingdom". Ministry of Food, Public Relations Division, 1950, 19.

149. Ox. Accessed December 18, 2024. https://www.history.ox.ac.uk/::ognode-637356::/files/download-resource-printable-pdf-11.

150. *"Our Food Today No. 1"*: "Rationing in the United Kingdom". Ministry of Food, Public Relations Division, 1950, 25.

151. *"Our Food Today No. 1"*: "Rationing in the United Kingdom". Ministry of Food, Public Relations Division, 1950, 18–19.

152. *"Our Food Today No. 1"*: "Rationing in the United Kingdom". Ministry of Food, Public Relations Division, 1950, 30.

153. thewartimekitchencom. Accessed December 18, 2024. https://thewartimekitchen.com/?p=238.

154. "Our Food Today No. 1": "Rationing in the United Kingdom". Ministry of Food, Public Relations Division, 1950, 15.

155. There is also a family story that May worked in a cafe. It is not known if this was before Harry was born, was one of the many mobile cafes during the war, at a British Restaurant or after the war. Originally called 'Community Feeding Centres', the name British Restaurants was chosen by the Prime Minister. The national feeding network was administered by the wartime Ministry of Food (MOF). They were public dining rooms offering price-capped and nutritious food to help people who had been bombed out of their homes, had run out of ration coupons or otherwise needed help. They closed in 1947.

156. *National Service.* His Majesty's Stationery Office, 1939, 20.

157. The City General Hospital and the Fir Vale Infirmary were run as separate institutions until 1967 when the Hospital (then with 654 beds) and the Infirmary (then with 682 beds) were amalgamated under the title of the "Northern General Hospital." *Sheffield's Hospitals.* Sheffield Libraries Archives and Information, 2008–2016 (v.1.3).

158. Walton, Mary, and Lamb, J.P. *Raiders Over Sheffield: The Story of the Air Raids of 12th & 15th December 1940.* Sheffield City Libraries, 1980.

159. "WW2 ARP Nursing Uniforms and Insignia." WW2 Civil Defence Uniforms, Insignia, Helmets and Equipment. Accessed December 18, 2024. https://www.ww2civildefence.co.uk/nursing-uniforms.html.

160. *National Service.* His Majesty's Stationery Office, 1939, 20.

161. "WW2 ARP Nursing Uniforms and Insignia." WW2 Civil Defence Uniforms, Insignia, Helmets and Equipment. Accessed January 3, 2025. https://www.ww2civildefence.co.uk/nursing-uniforms.html.

162. Sources for the Study of the Sheffield Blitz of 1940. Sheffield Libraries Archives and Information 2010–2016 (v.1.3), 4.

163. Shepherd, Helen. "Remembering the Sheffield Blitz." 999 Museum, December 11, 2020. https://www.visitnesm.org.uk/post/remembering-the-sheffield-blitz.

164. Sources for the Study of the Sheffield Blitz of 1940. Sheffield Libraries Archives and Information 2010–2016 (v.1.3), 4.; Walton, Mary, and Lamb, J.P. *Raiders Over Sheffield: The Story of the Air Raids of 12th & 15th December 1940.* Sheffield City Libraries, 1980, 138.

165. "Samuel Osborn." Sheffield War Memorials. Accessed December 18, 2024. https://sheffieldwarmemorials.weebly.com/samuel-osborn.html.

166. "WW2 People's War – Wartime Childhood in Sheffield." BBC. Accessed December 18, 2024. https://www.bbc.co.uk/history/ww2peopleswar/stories/50/a3785150.shtml.

167. "Sheffield – UXO City Guide." 1st Line Defence, October 30, 2024. https://www.1stlinedefence.co.uk/resources/uxo-city-guides/sheffield/.

168. "Roll of Honour of Civilian War Dead of Pitsmoor Area – Sheffield 1939–45." Accessed December 18, 2024. https://www.chrishobbs.com/sheffield/pitsmoorwardead.htm.

169. Rennie, John. *Report of the Medical Officer of Health, Sheffield City.* City Council, 1937, 29.

170. Rennie, John. *Report of the Medical Officer of Health, Sheffield City.* City Council, 1937, 35.

171. Ref. NHS11/4/1/3. Admission register, 1 Jan 1939–30 Dec 1953. Admission Discharged under admission number 347 and discharged August 16, 1941.

172. CWGC. "Find War Dead." CWGC. Accessed December 19, 2024. https://www.cwgc.org/find-records/find-war-dead/.

173. *"Our Food Today No. 1":* "Rationing in the United Kingdom". Ministry of Food, Public Relations Division, 1950, 12.

174. "Timeline." Delivered by Freemans. Accessed December 19, 2024. https://www.deliveredbyfreemans.com/timeline.

175. "Record." Search Results. Accessed December 19, 2024. https://archives.ljmu.ac.uk/Record.aspx?src=CalmView.Catalog&id=LW%2F5.

176. "Rationing." St Albans Museums, April 30, 2020. https://www.stalbansmuseums.org.uk/rationing.

177. Békés, Vera, Aafjes-van Doorn, Katie, Spina, Daniel, Talia, Alessandro, Starrs, Claire J., and Perry, J. Christopher. "The Relationship between Defense

Mechanisms and Attachment as Measured by Observer-Rated Methods in a Sample of Depressed Patients: A Pilot Study." *Frontiers in Psychology* 12 (September 27, 2021). https://doi.org/10.3389/fpsyg.2021.648503.

178. Reisz, Samantha, Duschinsky, Robbie, and Siegel, Daniel J. "Disorganized Attachment and Defense: Exploring John Bowlby's Unpublished Reflections." *Attachment & Human Development* 20, no. 2 (September 27, 2017): 107–134. https://doi.org/10.1080/14616734.2017.1380055.

179. Smith, M., Williamson, A.E., Walsh, D., and McCartney, G. "Is There a Link between Childhood Adversity, Attachment Style and Scotland's Excess Mortality? Evidence, Challenges and Potential Research." *BMC Public Health* 16, no. 1 (July 28, 2016). https://doi.org/10.1186/s12889-016-3201-z.

180. Jolley, Michael Jeremy. *A Social History of Paediatric Nursing 1920–1970*. Thesis, University of Hull, 2003, 149.

181. "Sandbag Thefts at ARP Posts." *Sheffield Evening Telegraph*, December 13, 1939, 7, column 4; "ARP Orders: Medical Section First Aid Posts." *Sheffield Daily Telegraph*, February 11, 1939, 3, column 7.

182. Davis, Angela. "Wartime Women Giving Birth: Narratives of Pregnancy and Childbirth, Britain c. 1939–1960." *Studies in History and Philosophy of Science Part C: Studies in History and Philosophy of Biological and Biomedical Sciences* 47 (September 2014): 257–266. https://doi.org/10.1016/j.shpsc.2013.11.007.

183. Ministry of Health. "Memorandum on Antenatal Clinics: Their Conduct and Scope," July 1929.

184. Davis, Angela. "Wartime Women Giving Birth: Narratives of Pregnancy and Childbirth, Britain c. 1939–1960." *Studies in History and Philosophy of Science Part C: Studies in History and Philosophy of Biological and Biomedical Sciences* 47 (September 2014): 257–266. https://doi.org/10.1016/j.shpsc.2013.11.007.

185. Osmond-Clarke, H. "Half a Century of Orthopaedic Progress in Great Britain." *The Journal of Bone and Joint Surgery. British volume* 32-B, no. 4 (November 1950): 620–675. https://doi.org/10.1302/0301-620x.32b4.620.

186. Sheffield City Archives, King Edward VII Hospital collection (Ref. NHS11/4/1/3). Admission register, 1 Jan 1939–30 Dec 1953. Admission number 1158 confirmed his admission on September 16, 1944.

187. Rennie, John. *Report of the Medical Officer of Health, Sheffield City*. City Council, 1944, 40.

188. Scout dyke. From the Langsett & Midhope at war website. Accessed December 19, 2024. http://www.langsettandmidhopeatwar.co.uk/scout-dyke/. No longer active.

189. "Wortley." American Air Museum. Accessed December 19, 2024. https://www.americanairmuseum.com/archive/place/wortley.

190. "News." The University of Sheffield, May 22, 2024. https://www.sheffield.ac.uk/archaeology/news/remains-britains-largest-prisoner-war-camp-uncovered-archaeologistsey.

191. https://www.atlasobscura.com/places/lodge-moor-pow-camp-ruins.

192. UGC. "Lodge Moor POW Camp Ruins." *Atlas Obscura*, February 15, 2013. https://www.atlasobscura.com/places/lodge-moor-pow-camp-ruins.

193. "UK's Biggest Second World War Prisoner Camp Unearthed in Yorkshire." *The Guardian*, July 4, 2019. https://www.theguardian.com/world/2019/jul/04/biggest-second-world-war-prisoner-camp-unearthed-in-yorkshire-lodge-moor.

194. Dominic. "Britain's Biggest WW2 Prisoner of War Camp Uncovered in Yorkshire." Vox Historia – History Learning Blog, March 15, 2023. https://historylearning.com/blog/britains-biggest-ww2-prisoner-of-war-camp-uncovered-in-yorkshire/#:~:text=%E2%80%9CThe%20prisoners%20were%20fed%20food,barracks%20with%20little%20personal%20space.%E2%80%9D.

195. Sheffield City Archives, King Edward VII Hospital collection (Ref. NHS11/4/1/3). Admission register, 1 Jan 1939–30 Dec 1953. Discharged under admission number 1158 on December 9, 1944.

196. "What You Need to Know about VE Day." Imperial War Museums. Accessed December 19, 2024. https://www.iwm.org.uk/history/what-you-need-to-know-about-ve-day.

197. *Sheffield Year Book*, 1943.

198. Bayleaf, Sheffield History Admin, and Author. "Sheffield Yearbook 1939", 47, 208. Sheffield History – Sheffield Memories, August 7, 2012. https://www.sheffieldhistory.co.uk/forums/topic/13064-sheffield-yearbook-1939/.

199. Barnes, Colin. *Disabled People in Britain and Discrimination: A Case for Anti-discrimination Legislation.* Hurst in association with the British Council of Organizations of Disabled People, 2000, chapter 2. https://disability-studies.leeds.ac.uk/wp-content/uploads/sites/40/library/Barnes-disabled-people-and-discrim-ch2.pdf.

200. Disability in Time and Place, English Heritage Disability History Web Content, Simon Jarrett, 2012. Accessed April 20, 2025. https://historicengland.org.uk/content/docs/research/disability-in-time-and-place-pdf/; Humphries, Stephen, and Gordon, Pamela. *Out of Sight: The Experience of Disability, 1900–1950.* Northcote House, 1992, 122.

201. Russell, Terence M. *"Forty Years On": Life and Work at the Central Technical School, Sheffield. A Reminiscence for "The Old Boys' Association."* Pickard Communication, 2003, 25.

202. PopT. "Central Technical School." Sheffield Forum, August 18, 2012. https://www.sheffieldforum.co.uk/topic/4816-central-technical-school/page/56/.

203. Russell, Terence M. *"Forty Years On": Life and Work at the Central Technical School, Sheffield: A Reminiscence for "The Old Boys' Association."* Pickard Communication, 2003, 93.

204. Russell, Terence M. *"Forty Years On": Life and Work at the Central Technical School, Sheffield: A Reminiscence for "The Old Boys' Association."* Pickard Communication, 2003, 29.

205. "Welshness and Britishness: The Case of Richard Llewellyn." The Social History Society, 2020. https://socialhistory.org.uk/shs_exchange/welshness-and-britishness-the-case-of-richard-llewellyn/.

206. Sabaratnam, Devan. "Dambusters – on Triangulations and Forgotten Boffins." May 25, 2020. https://devan.codes/blog/2020/5/19/dambusters-and-forgotten-boffins.

207. Libraries, Archives and Information. *Sources for the History of Shiregreen.* Sheffield City Council, 2016.

208. Higginbottom, Mike. "Sheffield's Perfection Cinema." Mike Higginbottom Interesting Times, October 24, 2021. https://www.mikehigginbottominterestingtimes.co.uk/2014/01/09/sheffields-perfection-cinema/.

209. "BFI Screenonline: *Good Old Days, The* (1953–83)." Accessed December 19, 2024. http://www.screenonline.org.uk/tv/id/788925/index.html#:~:text=BFI+Screenonline:+Good+Old+Days,+The+(1953-83)&text=An+evening+of+variety+and,the+Leeds+City+Varieties+theatre.&text=In+-January+1953,+a+programme,on+a+weekly+variety+bill.

210. "Picture Sheffield." *Sheffield Evening Telegraph*, September 18, 1939, 3, column 6.

211. Ward, Richard. *In Memory of Sheffield's Cinemas*. Sheffield City Libraries, 1988, 53.

212. "The Forum Cinema, Herries Road, Sheffield 1938–1969." Accessed December 19, 2024. https://www.chrishobbs.com/sheffield/forumsheffield.htm.

213. "Essoldo Southey Green." Cinema Treasures. Accessed December 19, 2024. https://cinematreasures.org/theaters/25709; Ward, Richard. *In Memory of Sheffield's Cinemas*. Sheffield City Libraries, 1988, 52.

214. Ward, Richard. *In Memory of Sheffield's Cinemas*. Sheffield City Libraries, 1988, 52.

215. Ward, Richard. *In Memory of Sheffield's Cinemas*. Sheffield City Libraries, 1988, 67.

216. "A History of the Rooms." Walkley Community Centre. Accessed January 4, 2025. https://www.walkleycommunitycentre.org/a-history-of-the-rooms.

217. Humphries, Stephen, and Gordon, Pamela. *Out of Sight: The Experience of Disability, 1900–1950*. Northcote House, 1992, 124.

218. Now owned by his cello-playing granddaughter, Louise.

219. Band of Hope. *Band of Hope Post 1948 Pledge*. In the public domain.

220. Wadge, Herbert Willan Wadge, MBE Willan. Letter to Whom it May Concern from the headmaster of the Central Technical School, September 25, 1959. In the author's collection.

221. Herzog, Erich G. *A History of King Edward VII Orthopaedic Hospital Sheffield*. Sheffield, 1986, 5.

It was edited and photographs added by Peter Dean.

222. Bruce, Jean. *King Edwards 2008–2018*. Sheffield, 2018.

223. "BNF Is Only Available in the UK." NICE. Accessed December 19, 2024. https://bnf.nice.org.uk/drugs/streptomycin/; Waters, Mitchell. "Streptomycin." StatPearls [Internet], July 4, 2023. https://www.ncbi.nlm.nih.gov/books/NBK555886/.

224. "History of *Nursing Times*: The 1930s." 101, no. 19 (May 10, 2005): 28.

225. "Vickers Rifle Range." *Sheffield Independent*, May 1, 1914, 5, column 4.

226. "Jack Beck was a lovely person, good looking, died of peritonitis, because of bad nursing. Your mother went to see him, she never forgave them." Harry Drabble.

227 Osmond-Clarke, H. "Half a Century of Orthopaedic Progress in Great Britain." *The Journal of Bone and Joint Surgery. British volume* 32-B, no. 4 (November 1950): 620–675 [630]. https://doi.org/10.1302/0301-620x.32b4.620.

228. "Disabled Persons (Employment) Bill." Hansard, December 10, 1943. Accessed December 19, 2024. https://api.parliament.uk/historic-hansard/commons/1943/dec/10/disabled-persons-employment-bill.

229. Spencer, John. Email to Helen Parker-Drabble. Form Submission – Contact – Jack Spencer, Sheffield College of Art, January 8, 2025. (Sheffield Libraries entry stating only Mrs E. Harwood. Artist formally Sheffield School of Art Staff, October 29, 1947.)

230. Spencer, John. "Journal." John Spencer Goldsmith, 2022. https://www.johnspencer.uk/journal.

231. Cartwright, Julyan H. "Sheffield Junior Art Department and How the Junior Art Department Shaped the Arts, Crafts and Design Careers of Its Pupils and of Its Teachers in Mid-Twentieth-Century Britain." *Interdisciplinary Science Reviews* 49, no. 5 (July 26, 2024): 550–565. https://doi.org/10.1177/03080188241236669.

232. "Disabled Persons (Employment) Bill." Hansard, December 10, 1943. Accessed December 19, 2024. https://api.parliament.uk/historic-hansard/commons/1943/dec/10/disabled-persons-employment-bill.

233. "Employment (Disabled Persons)." Hansard, July 21, 1959. Accessed December 19, 2024. https://api.parliament.uk/historic-hansard/commons/1959/jul/21/employment-disabled-persons.

234. Professor Sir Frank Wild Holdsworth FRCS (1904–1969) was a British orthopaedic surgeon remembered for pioneering work on rehabilitation of spinal injury patients.

235. Galton, Francis. "Eugenics: Its Definition, Scope and Aims." Accessed December 19, 2024. https://galton.org/essays/1900-1911/galton-1904-am-journ-soc-eugenics-scope-aims.htm.

236. "UK Disability History Month: Laws, Relationships and Sex." Accessed December 19, 2024. https://archives.blog.parliament.uk/2021/11/15/uk-disability-history-month-laws-relationships-and-sex/.

237. "Eugenics in Britain." English Heritage. Accessed December 19, 2024. https://www.english-heritage.org.uk/visit/blue-plaques/blue-plaque-stories/eugenics/.

238. Sheffield City Archives, King Edward VII Hospital collection (Ref. NHS11/4/1/4). Admission register, 1 Jan 1954–30 Dec 1958. Admission number 318 confirmed his admission on February 26, 1955.

239. Sheffield City Archives, King Edward VII Hospital collection (Ref. NHS11/4/1/4). Admission register, 1 Jan 1954–30 Dec 1958. Discharged under admission number 318 on June 27, 1955.

240. "Situations." *Yorkshire Post and Leeds Intelligencer*, November 26, 1942, 4, column 5.

241. The author has published the early life of Walter Parker in *A Victorian's Inheritance*. Available from https://geni.us/6SNCT5 or http://helenparkerdrabble.com/.

242. "Situations Vacant." *Sheffield Daily Telegraph*, April 4, 1950, 4, column 7; (03/11/2007), Newport, Doreen. "Student Nurses Prospectus in the 1950s." My Brighton and Hove. Accessed December 20, 2024. https://www.mybrightonandhove.org.uk/places/placecivic/brighton-general-hospital/brighton-general-hospital-6.

243. "Order Clerk." *Star Green 'un*, October 7, 1961, 8, column 3.

244. Harry always understood that Victorian Walter had his daughter's best interests at heart. Read more about Walter in *A Victorian's Inheritance*.

245. O'Dowd, Adrian. "A History of Nursing in Britain: The 1950s." *Nursing Times*, August 26, 2021. https://www.nursingtimes.net/history-of-nursing/a-history-of-nursing-in-britain-the-1950s-26-08-2021/.

246. "Student Nurses Prospectus in the 1950s." My Brighton and Hove. Accessed December 20, 2024. https://www.mybrightonandhove.org.uk/places/placecivic/brighton-general-hospital/brighton-general-hospital-6.

247. "Tuberculosis: A Fashionable Disease?" Science Museum Blog, September 9, 2024. https://blog.sciencemuseum.org.uk/tuberculosis-a-fashionable-disease/.

248. Good, Margaret, and Duignan, Anthony. "Perspectives on the History of Bovine TB and the Role of Tuberculin in Bovine TB Eradication." *Veterinary Medicine International* 2011 (2011): 1–11 [4]. https://doi.org/10.4061/2011/410470; Tobin, Ellis H.

249. Whitman, Royal. *A Treatise on Orthopaedic Surgery*. 2nd ed. Henry Kimpton, 1904, 334.

250. Mohideen, M.A.F., and Rasool, M.N. "Tuberculosis of the Hip Joint Region in Children." *SA Orthopaedic Journal*. Accessed December 20, 2024. http://www.scielo.org.za/scielo.php?script=sci_arttext&pid=S1681-150X2013000100008.

251. Whitman, Royal. *A Treatise on Orthopaedic Surgery*. 2nd ed. Henry Kimpton, 1904, 304.

252 Forrester-Brown, M. "The Splinting of Cases of Tuberculosis of the Hip." *Journal of British Surgery* 18, no. 69 (July 1, 1930): 54–77 [77]. https://doi.org/10.1002/bjs.1800186909.

253. Wilson, G.S. "The Pasteurization of Milk." *BMJ* 1, no. 4286 (February 27, 1943): 261–262. https://doi.org/10.1136/bmj.1.4286.261.

254. H.M. Stationery Office. *A Memorandum on Bovine Tuberculosis in Man: With Special Reference to Infection by Milk*. 1931, 7.

255. Atkins, Peter J. "The Long Genealogy of Quality in the British Drinking-Milk Sector." *Historia Agraria. Revista de agricultura e historia rural* 73 (November 15, 2017): 35–58. https://doi.org/10.26882/histagrar.073e01a.

256. Atkins, Peter. "Bovine Tuberculosis: The Human Impact." 19 Academia.edu, April 9, 2017. https://www.academia.edu/32351764/Chapter_3_Bovine_tuberculosis_the_human_impact.

257. Atkins, Peter. "Bovine Tuberculosis: The Human Impact." 18 Academia.edu, April 9, 2017. https://www.academia.edu/32351764/Chapter_3_Bovine_tuberculosis_the_human_impact.

258. "National Baby Week: Advice and Warnings." *Sheffield Independent*, June 30, 1933, 11, columns 2–3.

259. Doyle, Barry. "Voluntary Organizations and the Provision of Health Services in England and France, 1917–29." *European Review of History: Revue européenne d'histoire* 30, no. 5 (September 3, 2023): 791–811. https://doi.org/10.1080/13507486.2023.2247424.

260. McIntosh, Tania. *A Social History of Maternity and Childbirth*, June 19, 2013. https://doi.org/10.4324/9780203124222; Sheffield Survey Report, TNA MH66/1076, Maternity Section, n.d.

261. McIntosh, Tania. *"A Price Must Be Paid for Motherhood": The Experience of Maternity in Sheffield, 1879–1939*. Thesis, University of Sheffield, 1997, 58.

262. "Milk: A Nourishing Food." *Sheffield Independent*, November 24, 1934, 9, column 4.

263. "Dairy." Dairy | Food Standards Scotland. Accessed December 20, 2024. https://www.foodstandards.gov.scot/business-and-industry/industry-specific-advice/dairy.

264. Arrell Food Institute. "How We Came to Drink Pasteurized Milk." Arrell Food Institute, 2021. https://arrellfoodinstitute.ca/how-we-came-to-drink-pasteurized-milk/.

265. "Model Dairy." *Sheffield Daily Telegraph*, January 7, 1939, 12, column 3.

266. "James Herriot and Burnout – Hektoen International." *Hektoen International – An Online Medical Humanities Journal*, October 25, 2024. https://hekint.org/2021/08/17/james-herriot-and-burnout/.

267. "Permanent Harm." *Blyth News*, August 13, 1934, 3, column 4.

268. "Weekly Notes: Cleaner Milk." *Todmorden [West Yorkshire] & District News*, May 18, 1934, 3, column 7.

269. McNeil, Paul. "Joel Dommett's Great Great Grandfather: The Yeovil Dairyman Who Saved Cockney Children's Lives." Travelling Through Time to Trace Your Ancestors, August 22, 2024. https://timedetectives.blog/2022/10/27/joel-dommetts-great-great-grandfather-the-yeovil-dairyman-who-saved-cockney-childrens-lives/.

270. "Freeing Milk from Disease-Committee's Plan for Better Supply." *Sheffield Independent*, May 29, 1934, 5, column 5.

271. "Call to Boycott Milk Scheme: County Councils Not Consulted: Derby Objects." *Sheffield Independent*, September 27, 1934, 4 column 1.

272. "Doctors Differ over Tuberculosis: Challenge to Present Method of Diagnosis: Dormant Ministry." *Sheffield Independent*, July 18, 1936, columns 5–6.

273. Palmer, Mitchell V. and Waters, W. Ray. "Bovine Tuberculosis and the Establishment of an Eradication Program in the United States: Role of Veterinarians." *Veterinary Medicine International* (2011): 1–12. https://doi.org/10.4061/2011/816345. 477.

274. Teague née Drabble, Margaret. Letter to Helen Parker-Drabble, December 12, 2023.

275. "Milk and Dairies (Amendment) Act 1922." vLex. Accessed December 20, 2024. https://vlex.co.uk/vid/milk-and-dairies-amendment-808325801.

276. Bowden, Mary Ellen, Crow, Amy Beth, and Sullivan, Tracy. *Pharmaceutical Achievers: The Human Face of Pharmaceutical Research*. Chemical Heritage Press, 2003, 6.

277. Atkins, P.J. *A History of Uncertainty: Bovine Tuberculosis in Britain, 1850 to the Present*. Winchester University Press, 2016, 55. The Final Report of the Royal Commission for Bovine Tuberculosis in 1911 asserted that "a considerable amount of the tuberculosis of childhood is to be ascribed to infection with bacilli of the bovine type transmitted to children in meals consisting largely of the milk of the cow."

278. Waddington, Keir. "To Stamp out 'So Terrible a Malady': Bovine Tuberculosis and Tuberculin Testing in Britain, 1890–1939." *Medical History*. Accessed December 20, 2024. https://www.ncbi.nlm.nih.gov/pmc/articles/PMC546294/#fn59.9.

279. *"Your Enemy the Cow": The Construction of Early Medical and Veterinary Knowledge About Bovine Tuberculosis*, 18. Accessed December 20, 2024. https://www.researchgate.net/publication/315825299_'Your_enemy_the_cow'_the_construction_of_early_medical_and_veterinary_knowledge_about_bovine_tuberculosis.

280. *"Your Enemy the Cow": The Construction of Early Medical and Veterinary Knowledge About Bovine Tuberculosis*, 19. Accessed December 20, 2024. https://www.researchgate.net/.

publication/315825299_'Your_enemy_the_cow'_the_construction_of_early_medical_and_veterinary_knowledge_about_bovine_tuberculosis.

281. *"Your Enemy the Cow": The Construction of Early Medical and Veterinary Knowledge About Bovine Tuberculosis*, 20. Accessed December 20, 2024. https://www.researchgate.net/publication/315825299_'Your_enemy_the_cow'_the_construction_of_early_medical_and_veterinary_knowledge_about_bovine_tuberculosis.

282. "Milk and Dairies (Amendment) Bill [Lords]." Hansard, July 19, 1922. Accessed February 22, 2025. https://api.parliament.uk/historic-hansard/commons/1922/jul/19/milk-and-dairies-amendment-bill-lords.

283. Atkins, P.J. *A History of Uncertainty: Bovine Tuberculosis in Britain, 1850 to the Present*. Winchester University Press, 2016, 528; Davis, J.G. *A Dictionary of Dairying*. Leonard Hill, 1950.

284. House of Lords [HL] Deb 10 February 1931, vol 79 cc882–912.

285. "Boil Milk: Lord Moynihan's Advice." *Gloucester Citizen*, March 25, 1931, 6, column 1.

286. "School Milk Supplies: Holiday Period Surplus Snag: Tests Urged." *Sheffield Independent*, 30 January, 1935, 4, column 3.

287. "A History of Bovine TB; Cattle and Badgers." Accessed December 20, 2024. http://www.bovinetb.co.uk/article.php?article_id=144.

288. Rennie, John. *Report of the Medical Officer of Health, Sheffield City*. City Council, 1937, 198.

289. "Tuberculosis Danger." *Yorkshire Post and Leeds Intelligencer*, July 12, 1932, 12, column 5.

290. Waddington, Keir. "To Stamp out 'So Terrible a Malady': Bovine Tuberculosis and Tuberculin Testing in Britain, 1890–1939." *Medical History* 48, no. 1 (January 1, 2004): 29–48. https://doi.org/10.1017/s0025727300007043.

291. Atkins, P.J. *A History of Uncertainty: Bovine Tuberculosis in Britain, 1850 to the Present*. Winchester University Press, 2016, 26. https://www.academia.edu/

292. *"Your Enemy the Cow": The Construction of Early Medical and Veterinary Knowledge About Bovine Tuberculosis*, 20. Accessed December 20, 2024. https://www.researchgate.net/publication/315825299_'Your_enemy_the_cow'_the_construction_of_early_medical_and_veterinary_knowledge_about_bovine_tuberculosis.

293. Austin, R.S. "Bovine Tuberculosis in Children." *Archives of Pediatrics & Adolescent Medicine* 17, no. 4 (April 1, 1919): 264. https://doi.org/10.1001/archpedi.1919.04110280045004.

294. Atkins, P.J. *A History of Uncertainty: Bovine Tuberculosis in Britain, 1850 to the Present*. Winchester University Press, 2016, 4.

295. Borsay, Anne. *Disability and Social Policy in Britain since 1750: A History of Exclusion*. Palgrave Macmillan, 2005, 49.

296. Kellett, Arnold. *On Ilkla Mooar Baht 'at: The Story of the Song*. Smith Settle, 1998, 55.

297. "The Dead Body of a Child Found in Frog Walk." *Sheffield Evening Telegraph*, December 21, 1887, 5, column 2.

298. "The Child Found Dead in Frog Walk." *Sheffield Evening Telegraph*, December 23, 1887, 3, column 2.

INDEX

(*Italic* indicates an illustration of, or relating to, the subject matter)

A levels 3
Abbeydale (Sheffield) 112
Abbeydale Cinema / Picture House (Sheffield) 173, 210
abscess/es 31–2
accents 162, 171 *see also* Sheffield accent *and* Yorkshire accent
Advanced Intermediate violin exam 189
Aesop's Fables 142
Africa 207
Agriculture and Food, Ministry of *see* Ministry of Agriculture and Food
Aldis lights 158
Alice in Wonderland (Carroll) 142
All Creatures Great and Small (Herriot) 239
Allies (Second World War) 80
Amazon (company) 5
American forces (Wortley) 128
An A.B.C. of Guiding (Maynard) *210*
Anderson shelter 78, 85, 86, 114 *see also* Morrison shelter
Anderson, Sir John, MP 72
Angel Street (Sheffield) 112
Angels with Dirty Faces (film) *164*
Archer Road (Sheffield) 239

Armstrong, Louis 172
Army & Navy Stores 146
Arthur Lee company (Sheffield) 112
Arundel Street (Sheffield) 149
Aryan 'master race' 104
Atkins, Professor Peter 237
Attercliffe (Sheffield) 112, 119
Attested Herds Scheme (1935) 245–6
Auxiliary Fire Service (AFS) 72–3, *74–5*, 86, 112

Bachelors Foods / Peas 137, 227
Band of Hope pledge card *174*
Barber's House (Sheffield) *159*
Barbirolli, Sir John 171
Bardney (Lincolnshire) 16, 98
Barge, G. W. *156*
Barnsley Road (Sheffield) 163
Basie, Count 172
Battle of Britain 105
BBC *see* British Broadcasting Corporation
Beatles, the 172
Beck, Jack *192*
Beck Road (Sheffield) 161
Beck Road Council School (Sheffield) 69, 93, *94*, 118–19

Index

Beck Road Men's Choir 162
Beck Road Methodist Chapel 161, 193
Beck Road Quartet 136, 191, 192, 218
Beckwith, Jack 204–6, *205*, *206*
Beeley, David 171, 220, *231*, 232
Beethoven House (Sheffield) 159
Belfield, Reginald *15*
Belgium 102, 159
Bennet, P. J. *156*
Bennett, William E. 195–6, *196*
Bermuda 106
Betws-y-Coed (Wales) 7, 21
Bible 128–9, 140, 214 see also King James Bible
Bingham, Edith D. 196
Blacka Moor 98
Blackburn Brook (Sheffield) 12, 140
Blackpool 168, 170
Blitz *see* Sheffield Blitz
Bluebell Road (Sheffield) 135
Blythe News 239–40
Board of Education 45, *120*, 142
Borax 190
Boules, Jackie 140
bovine tuberculosis (bTB) 3–4, 17, 25–6, 29, 30–1, 236–47 *see also Mycobacterium tuberculosis (M. Tuberculosis)* and non-pulmonary tuberculosis (non-pulmonary TB)
Bowlby, Dr John 41, 118
Bradley, Tom ('Old Tom') 60–2, 132
Bramhall Lane (Sheffield) *229*, 230
Brighton *73*

Brightside Foundry and Engineering Co. 137, 198–9
Brincliffe Edge (Sheffield) 112
Britain / British 28, 30, 202, 222, 228
 children in 4
 in Second World War 69, 71–2, 76, 79–80, 83, 104, 105, 108, 130–1, 220
 and bovine tuberculosis 237, 240, 241, 244, 247
Britannia metal 189
British Broadcasting Corporation (BBC) 138, 183
British government 141–2
British Isles map *20*
British Medical Association 30
British Orthopaedic Association 30
Brixham 202
The Broad Highway (Farnol) 157, 158
Brodie, F.J. 196
Brodie helmet 74
Brontë, Emily 49
Broomhill (Sheffield) 112
Brown Bayley's steelworks (Sheffield) 112
Brownies 209
Brownly, Brian *192*
Bruce, Jean *28*, *35*, *187*
BSA (Birmingham Small Arms Company) *219*
bTB *see* bovine tuberculosis
Building Department, Central Technical School (Sheffield) 135, 145
Building Diploma, 2nd Class 177

Bunting, Elizabeth 6, *17*

Bunting, Isaac 6

Burbage Moor 98

Burngreave (Sheffield) 112

Butterthwaite Farm 12, *13*, 241

Butterthwaite Road (Sheffield) 7, *12*, 14, *21*, 69, 70, 76, 78–9, 138, *139*, *225*, 241

Cambridge Street (Sheffield) *166*

Canada 239

Capitol Cinema (Sheffield) 163

Cartwright, A. Edward *196*

Caruso, Enrico 162

Castle Hill Market 88

Catholic religion 65

Centenary of the Royal Hospital Sheffield, 1932 23

Central Library, Sheffield 149

Central Technical School (CTS), Sheffield 135, 144–5, 146, *147*, 148, 149, *150*, *155*, *156*, 157, *177*, *178*, 180, *252–60*

Certificate of General Nursing *221*

Chadwick, Eliza 6, *17*

Chamberlain, Neville 71–2

Channel Islands 106

Chapeltown 136, 191

Chard hair clippers *64*

Chartered Institute of Management Accountants 183

Chatsworth 221

Chester Castle 21

Children's Hour (radio programme) 100, 107

Christmas 101, 195, *225*, 250

Churchill tanks 83

Churchill, Winston 80

cinemas / cinema-going 72, 162–3, *164*, 165–6, *165*, *166*, 173

City General Hospital, Sheffield 108, *163*, *220*, *221*

City Watch Committee (Sheffield) 26

Civil Nursing Reserve *106*, 108, *110*

Clarence Road (Sheffield) 214

Clyde Steelworks site 84

Cole, Nat King 172

Colwyn Bay *224*

Commonwealth Fund of New York 44

consumption 238 *see also* pulmonary tuberculosis a*nd Mycobacterium tuberculosis (M. tuberculosis)*

Continent (of Europe) 247 *see also* Europe

Conwy Falls 21

Cookson Road (Sheffield) 97

Coppice Wood *61*

Coronation, Queen's 136, 201

COVID-19 3

Cowper Crescent (Sheffield) 112

Crookesmoore (Sheffield) 112

Daily Independent 17

Dambusters raid 158

Dankworth, Johnny 172

Davis, Dr J. G. 244

297

Index

Dee, River 21

Defence, Ministry of *see* Ministry of Defence

Derbyshire 170, 191, 221, 232

Devon 168

A Dictionary of Dairying 244

Dinky cars 76

Disabled Persons (Employment) Act 198

Don, River 98

Dove, Mr 147, 157, 171, 180

Drabble, née Parker, Doreen 6, 137

   early life and relationship with parents 208–11, *210*, *211*,

   honeymoon 232–3, *232*

   meeting and courtship with Harry Drabble 203–4, *206*, 206–7, *211*, 212–15, 216–18, *216*, *217*, 220, 221–2, 223, 224–7,

   nursing career 205, 208, *208*, 211–12, *214*, 220, *221*, 222–3, *222*, 228, 233

   wedding 228–9, *229–31*

Drabble, née Fox, Emily 6, 110–11, 117

Drabble, George 6, 63–4, 140

Drabble, Harry, Snr 6, 29, 99, 110, 124, 138, 160

   acquiring new council house 11–12, *12*, *13*, 14

   and brass band music 173

   cycling 20–1

   early married life 9–10

   employment 17–18, 79, 84, 86, 87, 92, 183, 202

   and family holidays *167*, 168, *169*, 170

   and Harry Jnr's education 144, 145, 146, 168

   and Harry Jnr's illness 22, 25, 29, 39, 40–1, 63, 121, 128, 139

   hiking with family 98–9

   and parental home 14

   and Second World War 71, 78, 79, 85, 86, 113, 114

      and Auxiliary Fire Service (AFS) and National Fire Service (NFS) 72, 86

   and steam engines 16

   and Yorkshire accent 49

Drabble, Harry, Jnr 6, 7, 111, 141, 166–7

   as a baby 10–11, 16–17, 20–1, *21*

   baby competition winner 18, *18*, *19*, 20

   and Beck Road Men's Choir 162

   and Beck Road Quartet 136, 191–3, *192*

   and Beckwith, Jack 204–5, *205*

   and Beeley, David 220, 232

   and Bible 128–9, 140

   birth of 9–10

   and Boules, Jackie 140

   and Bradley, Tom ('Old Tom') 132

   and broken leg 137, 220, 221

   and Central Technical School (CTS) 135, 145–52, *147*, 155, 156–8, 161, 176–7, 180

      awarded 2nd Class Building Diploma 177, *177*, *178*, *179*, 260 musical performance at Speech and Graduation Day 180, *181-2*

term reports from *252-9*

and cinema-going 162-3, 165-6, *165*, *166*

and dating girls 202

diagnosis of bovine TB 24-5

and Drabble, née Parker, Doreen (wife) 137, 203-4, 206-7, 211, 212-15, 216, 217-18, 220, 221, 223, *224-7*, 228-9, 233-4

honeymoon 232-3, *232*

wedding 229, *229-31*

and Drabble, George (cousin) 140

and Drabble, George (uncle) 63-4

and Drabble, Margaret (sister) 124, 125, 138, 169, 170

and Drabble, Urban and Emily (paternal grandparents) 117-18

and Drabble, Walter (uncle) 140

and drink/drinking 173, 192

and embroidery 126-7

employment with Bachelors Foods/Peas 137, 227-8

employment with Brightside Foundry & Engineering Company 137, 198-9

employment with Firth Vickers & Samuel Fox 137, 215, *215*

employment with H. Parkin & Son Ltd 184-5, 189-91

and evangelists 128

examination at Royal Hospital 22-3, *23*, *24*

experience of Second World War 78, 84-5, 86, 99, 102, 103, 104-5, 111-12, 128

and family camping holiday 135, *167*, 168, 169-71, *169*, *171*

and father 29, 30, 40-1, 43, 63, 86, 87, 88-9, 91-2, 103, 118, 121, 128, 136, 139, 170, 173

and *The Good Old Days* (TV programme) 163

and *The Goon Show* (radio programme) 170

and Gough, Sheila 121, 203, 204

and Gough, Sybil 204

and Grimesthorpe Brass Band 173

and Harrison, John A. (music teacher) 135, 175

and Hartley Brook Secondary (Modern) School 135, 142-5, *144*

and Hartley Brook School Junior Department 70, 120-2, *120*

hiking with family 98-9

and hip operation in Royal Infirmary 136, 137, 185-6, 199-201, 213

and 'Home for Idiots and Imbeciles' 69, 119

and illness linked to milk from Butterthwaite Farm 241

interest in mail-order catalogues 116

and Jones, Sister/Matron Elsie 52, 128-9, 186-7, *187*, 213-14

member of City Hall's Jazz Club 172

member of Listeners Club 171-2

Index

and Middleton, Maureen 202–3

and Moore, Beatrice (cousin) 93

and mother 30, 40–1, 43, 63, 78, 83, 86, 87, 92–3, 99, 103, 116, 118, 119, 122–3, 126, 127, 138–9, 147–9

as music teacher 2

and Parker, Hilda (mother-in-law) 216

and Parker, Walter (father-in-law) 216, 217, 228

and Parker-Drabble, Helen (daughter) 1–2, 2–5

and radio programmes 99, 100

and reading and use of libraries 140–1, 168

and rehabilitation scheme 194–5, *196*, *197*, 198

return to home from hospital in August 1941 114, 116, 119–20

return to home from hospital in September 1939 75–8, 83, 87, 101

and Salvation Army band 173

and Sheffield Cripples Aid Association 94–7

shooting at Vickers Shepcote Rolling Mills 191

and silversmithing course at Sheffield College of Art 183

and singing 99–100, 162

and smoking 62, 139, 173, 188–9, 200

and snooker 172–3

and social prejudice against people with disabilities 202

treatment for bovine TB at King Edward VII Memorial Hospital 25–6, *27*, *28*, 28–30, 31–2, *33–4*, 34–9, *35*, *37*, *38*, *39*, 40–1, 43, 44, 46, 49–67, *57*, *61*, 69, 70, 103–4, 105, 107–8, 114, 122, 125–7, 129–32, 136, 137, 186–9, 203–7, *204*

and Turner, Leonard and Lizzie (maternal grandparents) 97–8

violin-playing and exams 135, 136, 159–60, *161*, 186, 189, 193

watching Hallé Orchestra 152, 171

Drabble, Margaret 124, 125, 132, 138, *167*, 169, *169*, 170, *231*

Drabble, née Turner, May 6, 14, 15, 93, 100, 110–11, 117, 119, 125, 146

and Boules, Jack 140

cycling 20–1, *20*, 98

in domestic service 16, 99

early life 16, *17*

early married life 9, *9*

early motherhood 16–17, 18

and Harry Jnr's education 118–19, 120, 142, 147–9

and Harry Jnr's illness 22–3, 24–6, 30–1, 39, 40–1, 43, 44, 63, 83, 86–7, 97, 238, 241, 246–7

and holidays 167–8, *167*, *168*, *169*

meeting Harry Snr 16

and Parker, Doreen 223

pregnancy and birth of Harry Jnr 10–11

and Second World War 71, 72, 78, 79, 83, 85, 105, 116, 122, 124–5

and Civil Nursing Reserve 108–9, 118

300

and VE Day 138
Drabble, Urban 6, 110–11, 117
Drabble, Walter 140
Duchess Road (Sheffield) 103

East Helca Works (steel) 112
Ecclesall Woods (Sheffield) 207
Ecclesfield 139
Edmund Road (Sheffield) 211
Educated (Westover) 4
Education Act (1944) 141
Education Committee (Sheffield City Council) 119, 145
Education, Board of *see* Board of Education
Elizabeth I, Queen 65
Endcliffe Park (Sheffield) 207
England 20, 25, 30, 76, 104, 172, 236, 237, 239, 241, 242, 245, 247
English Steel Corporation 83
Eugenics Society 202
Europe 104, 105 *see also* Continent
Euthanasia Program (Nazi) 105

Fargate (Sheffield) *215, 216*
Farnham (Surrey) *219*
Farnol, Jeffery 157
First World War 32, 151
Firth College (Sheffield) 147, *147*
Firth Park (Sheffield) 93, 140–1, 162, 175
Firth Viaduct *171*

Firth Vickers & Samuel Fox 137, 215, *215*
Fitzgerald, Ella 172
Fitzwilliam, Earl of 97
Flamborough *226*
Food Guide (Ministry of Food) 117
Food, Ministry of *see* Ministry of Food
food consumption / importation / preparation 16, 79–80, 89, 89–91, 91, 111, *117*, *122*, 123, *123*, 131, 221, 222–3, 238–9
   in King Edward VII Memorial Hospital / Rivelin 45, 50, 52, 105
food rationing *see* rationing
Forces Favourites (radio programme) 99
Forge Dam (Sheffield) 98, 222
Forrester-Brown, Maud 30
Forum Cinema (Sheffield) 165–6, *165*
Fox, Emily *see* Drabble, née Fox, Emily
France 76, 102, 106, 159
Freemans catalogue 116
Frog Walk (Sheffield) 250, *251*
Fulwood (Sheffield) 16, 99

Galen, Bishop Clemens August Graf von 105
Galton, Sir Francis 202
Gell Street (Sheffield) 9
General Cemetery (Sheffield) 250
General Nursing Council 211
Germany 69, 76, 80, 84, 104–5, 112, 114, 130, 138, 158

Index

Gilbert and Sullivan music 193

Gill, Councillor J. 94

Girl Guides 209–10, *210*

Gleadless (Sheffield) 112

Gleadless Road (Sheffield) 11, 233

Glossop Road (Sheffield) 112

Godbehere, Derek 35, 161

The Good Old Days (TV programme) 163

The Goon Show (radio programme) 170

Gough, Sheila 121, 203, 204, 214

Gough, Sybil 204, *205*

Gower Street (Sheffield) *215*

Grade A milk 240–1

Graham, Billy 128

Graves, Billy 126

Grayson, Patricia 220

The Great Caruso (film) 162

Great Ormond Street, Hospital for Sick Children *see* Hospital for Sick Children, Great Ormond Street

Greek language 248

'Greensleeves' (folk song) 180

Gregory, Mr 153, *155*

Greystones Secondary School (Sheffield) 209

Grimesthorpe (Sheffield) 112

Grimesthorpe Brass Band 173

Guernsey 69, 104

Guide Law 209–10

Guinness (stout) 192

Gulliver's Travels (Swift) 142

H. Parkin & Son Ltd 135, 184

H. L. Brown & Sons *215*, *216*

Hadfields Steelworks (Sheffield) 83, 112

Hallé Orchestra 147, 152, 171, 217

Harold's (Harry's) Tin Shop 149

Harrison, John A. 135, 175

Harrogate Opera House 185

Hartcliffe Hill Road (Penistone) *127*

Hartley Brook Dike (Sheffield) 12, 120–2, *120*

Hartley Brook Road (Sheffield) 135

Hartley Brook School Junior Department (Sheffield) 70

Hartley Brook Secondary (Modern) School (Sheffield) 135, 142–5, *142*, *144*, 203

Hatter, Mr 160

Health Committee 240

Helca (Sheffield) 112

Heeley (Sheffield) 9, 11, 233

Heeley Bottom (Sheffield) 173

Heeley Parish Church (Sheffield) 7, 11, *11*

Heeley Parish Church Baby Competition 7, 18, *18*, *19*

Henry VIII, King 65

Herries Road (Sheffield) 165–6, *165*

Herriot, James 239

Herzog, Dr E. G. 46–7, 62, 186

High Greave (Sheffield) 128

High Storrs (Sheffield) 151

High Street (Sheffield) *115*

Highfield police station 250

Hill, née Wardley, Ann 210

Hippodrome cinema (Sheffield) 163, 166, *166*

A History of King Edward VII Orthopaedic Hospital Sheffield (Herzog) 34

Hitler, Adolf 69, 104, 105

Holdsworth, Frank 199–200

Holly Street (Sheffield) 149, 155

Holocaust Encyclopaedia (online) 105

'Home for Idiots and Imbeciles' 69, 119

Hospital Council (Sheffield) 26

Hospital for Sick Children, Great Ormond Street 40

House of Lords 244, 245

How Green Was My Valley (Llewellyn) 157

Hoyland, J. Erwin *196*

Hulley ice cream factory (Sheffield) 128

Hunter, John 156

Hurricane aircraft 83

Infant Welfare Centres 237–8

Information, Ministry of *see* Ministry of Information

Intermediate Violin Playing qualification 136, 186

International Committee of the Red Cross 130–1

IQ reasoning tests 145

Italian prisoners 130

It's That Man Again (radio programme) 100

Jersey 69, 104

Jessop Hospital for Women 7, 9, 10

Jones double hip-abduction frame 32, *33, 34*, 61

Jones, Sister/Matron Elsie 52, 128–9, *186*–7, *187*, *213*–14

Junior Technical School Minute Book *179*

Kellett, Arnold 249

Kierkegaard, Soren Aabye 4

King Edward VII Memorial Hospital for Crippled Children / King Edward VII Orthopaedic Hospital 7, 24, 29, 75, *130*, *133*, 135, *187*, *205*, *206*, *207*, *208*, 211, 248

    Drabble, Harry Jnr's treatment in 25–6, 27, 28–30, *28*, *34*, 35, *35*, 37, 39, 46, 56, *57*, *61*, 69–70, 114, 125, 136, 137, 186–7, 203–7, *204*

    See also Rivelin

King James Bible 129 *see also* Bible

King Street (Sheffield) 112

Koch, Robert 25

Labour, Ministry of *see* Ministry of Labour

Lancaster bomber 83

Lancet Commission on Nursing 48

Langtons hall (Sheffield) 173

Index

Lanza, Mario 162
Lathkill Dale (Derbyshire) 232, *232*
Leavygreave Road (Sheffield) 9
Leeds 163
Leopold Hotel (Sheffield) *155*
Leopold Street (Sheffield) 148, *159*
Lincolnshire 98
Listeners Club 171–2, 180
Little Doubting Farm *127*
Little Hill (Sheffield) *154*, 155
Littlewoods catalogue 116
Llewellyn, Richard 157
Locarno Ballroom (Sheffield) 210
Lodge Moor Camp (POWs) 130–1, *130*
London 41, 44
London College of Music 135–6, 137, 160
Longley Housing Estate (Sheffield) 165–6
Lords, House of *see* House of Lords
Luftwaffe 84, 104, 105
Luxembourg 159
Lyceum Theatre (Sheffield) 149
Lyttleton, Humphrey 172

MacDonald, Betty 63
Malin Bridge (Sheffield) 207
Manchester Road (Sheffield) 47–8
Manor Cinema (Sheffield) 173
Marsh, K. *156*
Matilda tanks 83
Matthew, Gospel of 214

Meccano set 76
Meersbrook (Sheffield) 112
Mellanby, Mrs May 32
Melton Tunic *73*
Methodists 161–2
Metro-Goldwyn-Mayer 162
Middleton, Maureen 202–3
Middleton, Mr 203
milk 50, 83, 87, 116
    and bovine tuberculosis (bTB) 17, 236, 238–44
    condensed 16, 92
    legislation relating to 241, 244–7
    and National Milk Scheme 124–5
    pasteurisation of 238–40, 242–5, 246–7
    and Royal Hospital, Sheffield *24*
    skimmed 82
Milk and Dairies Amendment Act (1922) 241, 244–5
Milk and Dairies Order (1926) 245
Milk Marketing Board 246
Millhouses (Sheffield) 112, 239
Mills, Kathleen *196*
Mills, Tony *192*
Minister of Health 244
Ministry of Agriculture and Food 241
Ministry of Defence 98
Ministry of Food 82, 89, *90*, *107*, 116, *117*, *122*, *123*
Ministry of Health 246
Ministry of Labour 193–4, 198
Moffat, Stanley 148

Mond, Sir Alfred 244

Monsal Dale (Derbyshire) 170–1, *171*

Moonshine Lane (Sheffield) 114

Moore, née Lycett, Beatrice 93

Moorhead (Sheffield) 112

Morrell, Jean *196*

Morrison shelter 78–9, *79*, 114 *see also* Anderson shelter

The Motherhood Book 17, 26

Mother's Union 93

Moynihan, Lord 245

Mycobacterium bovis (M. Bovis) 25, 241 *see also* bovine tuberculosis (bTB) *and* non-pulmonary tuberculosis (non-pulmonary TB)

Mycobacterium tuberculosis (M. Tuberculosis) 236 *see also* consumption *and* pulmonary tuberculosis

National Fire Service (NFS) 72–3, *73, 74, 75*

National Health Service 22, 135

National Health Service Act 193–4

National Milk Scheme 124

National Service 71–2

National Service Guide 72–3, 108

National Veterinary Medical Association 242

Nazis 104–5, 130

Neepsend (Sheffield) 14, 111, 112

Nether Edge hospital (Sheffield) 125

New Capitol cinema (Sheffield) *164*

non-pulmonary tuberculosis (non pulmonary TB) 25, 237, 240 *see also* bovine tuberculosis (bTB)

Norfolk Street (Sheffield) 135, 180, 193

Norfolk, Duchess of 97

Norfolk, Duke of 97

Northern Ireland 239

Norton Lees (Sheffield) 112

Norwood Avenue (Sheffield) *139*

Nursing Auxiliaries 109

Nursing Mirror 35

Nursing Times 189

Old Boys' Association (Central Technical School) 155

'Old Tom' *see* Bradley, Tom

'On Ilkla Moor Baht'at' (song) 100, 249

Onion Distribution Scheme 106–7

Operation Crucible 113

Operation Sealion 105

Orwell, George 14

Osborn Steelworks (Sheffield) 11, 17–18, 84, 113, 202

'Our Food Today' (Ministry of Food) *82, 107, 123*

Over Haddon (Derbyshire) 232, *232*

Owlerton (Sheffield) 112

Padley Gorge (Sheffield) 98

Paignton (Devon) 168, *168, 227*

Park Hill (Sheffield) 112

Parker family 209, 210

Parker, née Emblow, Hilda 6, 208, 210, 216

Index

Parker, Walter 6, 208, 209, 210, 217, *217*, 228, 229

Parkin, Harold 151

Pasteur, Louis 242

Pattison, Dr Creswell Lee 22, 24–5, 30, 31–2, 34, 66, 103

Pearce, Charles W. *160*

Penistone (Sheffield) *127*, 128

Pennine Way 222

'Penny in the Pound' scheme 28–9, 103

Perthes' disease 30

Peterborough 214

Piling, Stanley 151

Pilley (Sheffield) 136, 191

Pinstone Street (Sheffield) 159, *159*

Platt Report (1959) 46

Player's cigarettes 188

Playhouse Theatre (Sheffield) *154*, 155

Pocock, Mrs 233

Portland Duchess of 97

Portland, Duke of 97

Powell, Sandy 100

prisoners of war (POWs) 129–31, *130*

Protestant religion 65

Pugh's method 34

pulmonary tuberculosis 26, 31, 236, 237, 241 *see also* consumption *and Mycobacterium tuberculosis (M. Tuberculosis)*

Queen's Coronation *see* Coronation, Queen's

Queen's Road (Sheffield) 103

Queen Street (Sheffield) 149

RAF 158

rationing (Second World War) 80–3, *81*, *82*, 89–*91*, 105–8, 107, 116, 117, *117*, 122–3, *123*, 124–5

RE *see* Religious Education

Reader's Digest 141

Red Cross 130–1

Redmires Reservoir (Sheffield) 130

Religious Education (RE) 151, 152

Remploy group 142

Rhos-on-Sea (Wales) 225

Richard, Cliff and The Shadows 172

Ringinglow (Sheffield) 98

Ripon Cathedral 185

Rivelin 7, 75, 77, 78, 93, 94, 100–1, 102, 111–12, 118, 121, 128, *133*, 212, 213, 220, 222

    Drabble, Harry Jnr's treatment in *27*, 28, 30, 32, 38, 39, 43, 49, 103, 105, 108, 114, 122, 125, 186, 204, 234

    See also King Edward VII Memorial Hospital for Crippled Children / King Edward VII Orthopaedic Hospital

Rivelin Valley (Sheffield) 28, 28, 98, 102, 211

Rivelin Valley Road (Sheffield) 47–8

The Road to Wigan Pier (Orwell) 14

Robertson, James 41–2, 43–4, 45–6, 48, 77

Rolls-Royce Merlin engines (Spitfires) 83

Romans 6:23 (Bible) 214

Royal Air Force *see* RAF

Royal Hospital, Sheffield 7, 22–3, *23–4*, 27

Royal Infirmary 136–7, 185–6, *186*, 200, 213

Ruhr Valley 158

Rural Life Living Museum 219

Ryalls, R. *156*

Salvation Army 173

Samuel Osborn & Co. 84, 202

Savage, (Sir) William 242–3

Scholars Christian Unit (Central Technical School) 151–2

School Song (CTS) 157

Schweizer, H. *156*

Scotland 239, 245

Scotland Street (Sheffield) 135, 184

Scout Dike (Sheffield) 128

Second World War 69, 71–2, 75, 76, 79–80, *79*, 83, 102, 104, 105, 108–9, *109*, 130–1, 209, 220, 244 *see also* Anderson shelter, Auxiliary Fire Service (AFS), Morrison shelter, National Fire Service (NFS), rationing, Sheffield Blitz *and* U-boats

Seymour, Philip 153, *155*, *156*, 176

Shakespeare, language of 129, 157, 192

Shannon, Kathleen 30

Sharrow (Sheffield) 112

Sheaf Market (Sheffield) 88–9

Sheffield 10, 14, 18, 22, 26, 30, 32, 35, 49, 71, 72, 76, *84*, 85, 140, 163, *164*, 166, *166*, 173, 191, 208, 210, 238, 239, 246

   in Second World War 78, 83–4 *see also* Sheffield Blitz

Sheffield accent 158, 210

Sheffield Blitz 69, 108, 111–13, 114, *115*

Sheffield Central Technical School *see* Central Technical School (CTS), Sheffield

Sheffield child guidance clinic 44–5

Sheffield city centre 9, 103, *115*

Sheffield City General Hospital *see* City General Hospital, Sheffield

Sheffield City Library 141

Sheffield City Memorial Hall 171

Sheffield College of Art 183, *183*, 195–6, *196*

Sheffield Corporation 11, 248

Sheffield Corporation Bill 248

Sheffield Cripples Aid Association 94–5

Sheffield Evening Telegraph 164, 251

Sheffield Forum (website) 152

Sheffield Independent 25, 237–8, 238–9, 241

Sheffield Ministry of Health 246

Sheffield School of Art 135

Sheffield Town/City Hall 11, *155*

Shepcote Lane Rolling Mill (Sheffield) 137, 191, 215

Shiregreen Estate (Sheffield) 7, 12, *13*, 69, 94, *120*, *139*, *193*

Shiregreen Lane (Sheffield) 140

307

Index

Skegness 135, 168, *169*, 170

Slack, H. 179

snooker 172–3

Snowdon (Wales) 21

Southey Hill (Sheffield) 114

South-West England 30

Spain 106

Spencer, Jack *196*

Spencer, John 195–6

Spitfire aircraft 83, 98

St John's first-aid volunteers 26

St Mary's Church (Sheffield) 137, 228–9, *229*, *230*

Stanley, Rt. Hon. Oliver F.G. *120*, *142*

Stanton, Mr 158

Steel, Peech and Tozer company 171

Stork Margarine Cookery Service 89, *89–91*

Stryker, Homer Hartman 59

Suez Crisis 218

'Sunbeam Club' 94 *see also* Sheffield Cripples Aid Association

Swallow Falls (Wales) 21

Switzerland 159

'T-4' Program (Nazis) 105

Tavistock Clinic (London) 41

Terramycin antibiotic 203

Theory of Music, Intermediate exam 137

Theory of Music, Junior Honours exam 136

Thomas splint (medical application) *38*, *39*, 137

Todmorden & District News (West Yorkshire) 240

'Together' (song) 100

Tommy helmet *74*

Torquay 202

Townhead Street (Sheffield) 149, *154*, *155*

A Treatise on Orthopaedic Surgery (Whitman) 38

tuberculosis (TB) 4, 22, 26, 30–1, 32, 33, 38, 53, 62, 63, 69, 118, 125, 135, 187, 189, 199–200, 202, 236, 237, 245, 248 *see also* bovine tuberculosis, consumption, *Mycobacterium tuberculosis (M. Tuberculosis)*, non-pulmonary tuberculosis (non-pulmonary TB) *and* pulmonary tuberculosis

Tuberculosis Dispensary (Sheffield) 103

Tudor Way (Sheffield) 149

Turner, Harold 6, 114, *115*, 166

Turner, Leonard 6, 15–16, 22, 97–8, 183, 186, 250

Turner, née Bunting, Elizabeth/Lizzie 97–8

Tweed, W. 246

U-boats 80, 82

Ukrainian POWs 130

Unitarian Church 193

Upper Chapel, Norfolk Street (Sheffield) 193

USA 44, 69, 247

VE Day see Victory in Europe Day
viaduct, Monsal Dale *171*
'The Vicar of Bray' (song) 65–6
Vickers corporation 83, 191, 215, *215*
Victoria Hall (Sheffield) 135–6, 137, 180, *181*, *182*
Victorian/Edwardian music hall 163
Victory in Europe Day (VE Day) 70, 138, *139*
vitamins 32, 83, 125, 240
voluntary organisations (Sheffield) 238

Wadge, Herbert 152, *155*, 156
Wadsley Bridge (Sheffield) 137, 227
Wales 7, 20, 21, 25, 223, *224–5*, 236, 237, 239, 241
Walkley (Sheffield) 112
Walkley Community Centre (Sheffield) *172*
Wallace Road (Sheffield) 14, 110–11, 113
Wardley, Ann 210, *211*, 231
Washington Road (Sheffield) 250
West Street (Sheffield) *147*
West Yorkshire 240
Westfield Terrace (Sheffield) 7, *23*
Westminster Infants Hospital 40
Westover, Tara 4
Wharncliffe, Countess of 97
Wharncliffe, Earl of 97
Whatstandwell (Derbyshire) 140
'Where the Shells Came From' (Belfield) 15

Whit Monday and Hymn Singing Festival of Joy 162
Whitman, Royal *38*
Wicker, the (Sheffield) 84
Wight, James 239 *see also* Herriot, James
Wilton carpet 166
Winter Gardens (Blackpool and Skegness) 170
Wortley Air Ammunition Depot (Sheffield) 128
Wortley, Lady Mary 97
Wuthering Heights (Emily Brontë) 49
Wybourn (Sheffield) 112

X-rays 30, 32, 38, 151, 220

Yorkshire 100, 108, 158, 226, 239–40
Yorkshire accent 49
Yorkshire Post and Leeds Intelligencer 207
Yorkshire pudding 83, *90*
Youth for Christ group 151

Also from the author

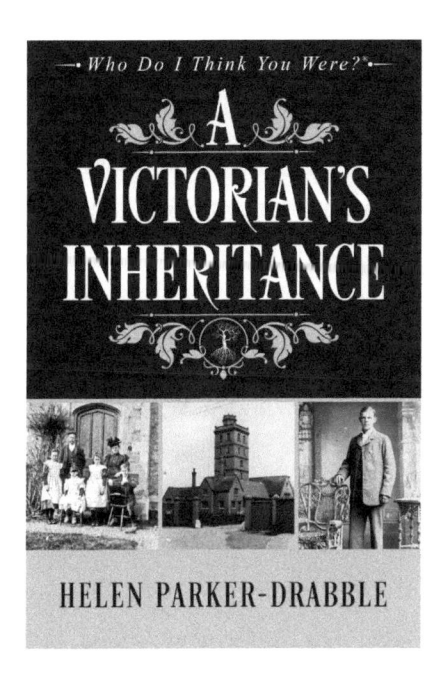

A window into Victorian lives—and what it means for ours

What psychological inheritance have you received from your ancestors?

We inherit more than heirlooms. The struggles, triumphs, and even traumas of our forebears can be handed down through generations, shaping who we are.

In *A Victorian's Inheritance*, family historian and former counsellor Helen Parker-Drabble brings to life the working-class world of her Victorian grandfather, uncovering how his mother's hardships, bereavements and alcoholism in 19th-century England left their indelible mark on him. Through a unique blend of family history, social analysis, and groundbreaking research, she reveals how addiction, grief, and mental health challenges can influence future generations.

This deeply personal, yet relatable, book invites you to reflect on your own family's untold stories. Whether you're an avid genealogist, a lover of Victorian history, or simply curious about how your ancestors' lives have shaped your own, *A Victorian's Inheritance* will inspire you to discover the hidden legacies of your family—and better understand yourself and your relations.

Available to buy here: https://geni.us/6SNCT5

Visit my website at https://helenparkerdrabble.com for articles and more. You can also sign up for news, offers, publication dates and giveaways.

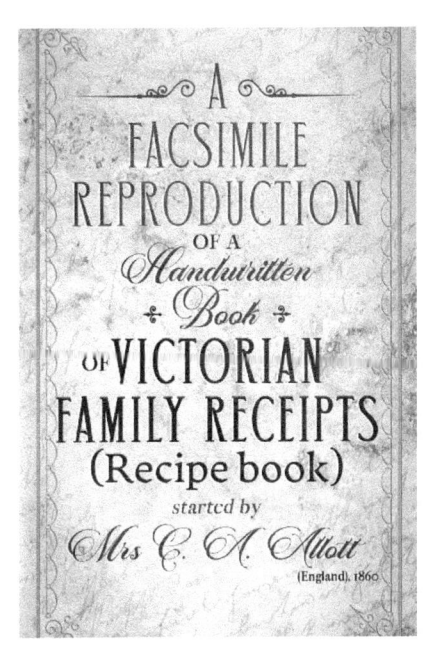

A FACSIMILE REPRODUCTION OF A Handwritten Book of VICTORIAN FAMILY RECEIPTS (Recipe book)

started by

Mrs C. A. Allott

(England), 1860

What did Victorians eat? Taste the past with these handwritten family recipes

This faithful reproduction of an original manuscript provides a fascinating glimpse into mid-19th century culinary traditions.

In 1860, Mary Allott (née Hopkinson) began compiling her personal recipe book, a cherished collection that embodied the heart of middle-class domestic life. For Victorian women, exchanging recipes wasn't just about cooking, it was a way to connect, share, and refine their domestic expertise. Successful recipes were gifts, strengthening the bonds between friends, families, and communities.

This facsimile edition preserves Mary's 115 pages of recipes, or "receipts" as she called them, offering a rare treasure for family historians, food enthusiasts, and those curious about the lives of Victorian middle-class women.

Through them, you can relive the richness of one Victorian woman's household by savouring the morsels of her past.

Coming soon

At the time of publication, Mary's biography is a work in progress.

Please visit my website at www.helenparkerdrabble.com and sign up to the waitlist for news, offers, publication dates and giveaways.